Christian Evidence Society

Strivings for the Faith

Christian Evidence Society
Strivings for the Faith
ISBN/EAN: 9783337417451
Printed in Europe, USA, Canada, Australia, Japan
Cover: Foto ©Lupo / pixelio.de

More available books at **www.hansebooks.com**

PREFACE.

THE following Lectures were delivered in the same Hall where the lectures contained in the volume entitled "Popular Objections to Revealed Truth" were delivered last year. They are intended similarly to combat some of the objections, or to meet some of the difficulties that are raised at the present day in reference to Christianity, dealing more particularly with some of the points insisted upon by the "Secularists."

The Committee trust that these "Strivings for the Faith" may prove useful both to many who may themselves be feeling the force of the objections referred to, and to many who may be seeking for further confirmation of that faith which already they hold.

Whilst these lectures were delivered at the request and under the auspices of the Christian Evidence Society, the Committee wish it to be understood that each author is responsible for the statements and arguments of his own lecture; no revision of the lectures having been in any way made by the Committee.

2, DUKE STREET, ADELPHI, LONDON, W.C.
August, 1874.

CONTENTS.

LECTURE I.

DIFFICULTIES ON THE SIDE OF UNBELIEF IN ACCOUNTING FOR HISTORICAL CHRISTIANITY.

BY THE

REV. G. F. MACLEAR, D.D.,

Head Master of King's College School, and late Assistant Preacher at the Temple Church.

I. Limitation of subject.
II. Remarkable cessation of the old universal custom of sacrifice.
III. The sense of sin, the basis of the idea of sacrifice, still remains, and has become intensified.
IV. Although sacrifices have ceased, sacrificial terms are associated with the remarkable rite of the Lord's Supper, which professes to commemorate the death of its Institutor.
V. Sketch of the Life of Christ, and of the Institution of the Lord's Supper.
VI. The universal adoption of this rite; the simplicity of the narrative of its origin; the difficulty of accounting for its continued observance, if nothing were implied, beyond the death of its Founder.
VII. The historical fact of the Resurrection alone an adequate ground for celebrating this rite.

VIII. Difficulties to be met, supposing the Resurrection not to be true. 1

LECTURE II.

THE VARIATIONS OF THE GOSPELS IN THEIR RELATION TO THE EVIDENCES AND TRUTH OF CHRISTIANITY.

BY THE
REV. T. R. BIRKS, M.A., Camb.,
Professor of Moral Philosophy in the University of Cambridge, and Honorary Canon of Ely Cathedral.

I. Common characteristics of the Gospels, and marks of their unity in respect of their brevity—their silence—their simplicity—their proportion—their selection of minor incidents—their common object in regard of proving the Messiahship of Jesus.

II. Consideration of five possible modes of variation in the testimony of witnesses, Under which are we to class the variations of the Gospels?—Are the alleged contradictions contained in them apparent or real?

III. Examination of some of the variations in the four Gospels: (i.) Their mutual relation as to sameness and diversity; (ii.) The historical unity and special adaptation of each Gospel; (iii.) The moral and spiritual character of the Gospels; (iv.) The genealogies; (v.) The accounts of our Lord's infancy; (vi.) The main scene and locality of our Lord's public ministry.

IV. Conclusion.—The seeming divergences in the Gospels conceal below their surface deep evidence of real consistency and truth. Importance of patient and prayerful thought and labour in order to ascertain the true harmony of the revelation contained in God's Word . 37

LECTURE III.

THE APOCRYPHAL GOSPELS.

BY

B. HARRIS COWPER, Esq.

I. Unfair treatment of Apocryphal Gospels by attempting i.) to exalt them to the level of the Canonical Gospels; (ii.) to lower the true Gospels to the level of the Apocryphal.

II. An explanation of the origin and intention of the Apocryphal Gospels. Some of the characteristics of them—distinguished from the genuine Gospels.

III. The Apocryphal Gospels not supported by ecclesiastical authority. Examination of traditions referring to the formation of the canon, and of unreliable statements on the subject made by some infidel writers.

IV. Testimonies of ancient writers as to the existence of certain apocryphal books, and a brief account of the six false Gospels now extant.

V. Conclusion.—The Apocryphal Gospels (i.) not so ancient as the four canonical Gospels; (ii.) not received as of equal authority with them (except by certain sects); (iii.) not genuine productions of the apostolic age or of apostolic men. The Apocryphal Gospels distinguished from the canonical in regard of their general character and literary style 73

APPENDIX.—An outline of the Apocryphal Gospels of Matthew and of Nicodemus 102

LECTURE IV.

THE EVIDENTIAL VALUE OF THE EARLY EPISTLES OF ST. PAUL VIEWED AS HISTORICAL DOCUMENTS.

BY THE

REV. PETER LORIMER, D.D.,

Professor of Theology in the English Presbyterian College, London.

The Epistles of St. Paul to the Thessalonians, Corinthians, Galatians, and Romans, allowed by all eminent scholars to be genuine. To be examined now simply as historical documents (as we might examine the letters of Cicero, etc).

Their evidential value (i.) as to the outlines of the life of Christ;

(ii.) As to the personal history of St. Paul, especially with reference (*a*) to the independent origin of his preaching—*not* derived from Greek and Oriental sources; (*b*) to the relation between himself and St. Peter and the other Apostles; (*c*) to his alleged mythological development of the teaching of Christ.

(iii.) As to the supernatural element in the earliest propagation of Christianity. Important to observe that these Epistles give the testimony both of St. Paul and of those to whom he writes as to facts of which both he and they were witnesses.

1. Testimony to the new character and life which had sprung up under St. Paul's teaching.
2. Testimony to the supernatural origin of the Gospel, as proved by its moral and religious influence.
3. Testimony to the Divine presence and power which accompanied St. Paul's preaching of the Gospel, as manifested by his miracles, the "signs of an Apostle."
4. Testimony to the same, as manifested by the "spiritual gifts" of the Church.

Contents.

Concluding remarks:

(i.) The Church of Christ was planted before any part of the New Testament was written:—and hence the existence of the Church is not really endangered by any attacks made upon the writings of the New Testament.

(ii.) These early Epistles of St. Paul are genuine historical documents, and worthy of credit, quite apart from the question of their inspiration.

(iii.) Facts, such as those concerning the early Church, mentioned in the Lecture, are evidence of the existence of God, and of His providential government; they cannot be explained or accounted for satisfactorily by any naturalistic solution. 109

LECTURE V.

LORD LYTTLETON ON THE CONVERSION OF ST. PAUL.

BY THE

REV. JOHN GRITTON.

Variety of evidence required for the conviction of various classes of minds,—illustrated by variety of effect produced by scientific or historical difficulties, etc., on those who may have been induced by the evidence of prophecy, or of miracles, or of the character of Christ, to accept the Bible as containing a Divine Revelation.

Testimony to the Divine origin of Christianity derived from the life and writings of Lord Lyttleton, particularly from his treatise on St. Paul's conversion.

The facts which Lord Lyttleton postulates acknowledged to be true, even by unbelieving critics.

The testimony to St. Paul's miraculous call to the Apostleship, as contained in his own speeches before Festus and King Agrippa, and before the Jews in Jerusalem; in St. Luke's record in the Acts; and in the confessedly genuine writings of St. Paul.

Three suppositions may possibly be made to account for the facts of the case, without allowing the miraculous element:

  I. That St. Paul said what he knew to be false, with an intent to deceive. Difficulties of this supposition: (i.) What *motive* could St. Paul have for thus acting? Possible motives, as the desire of wealth, fame, or power, or the desire to gratify some passion, examined, and shown to be baseless. (ii.) He could have had no reasonable prospect of success in carrying out his imposture (*a*) in relation to the other Apostles; (*b*) in preaching among the Gentiles, and contending (1) with the policy of the magistrates; (2) with the interests of the priests; (3) with the prejudices of the people; (4) with the wisdom of the philosophers.

  II. That he was an enthusiast, imposed upon by the force of an overheated imagination. But he exhibits none of the marks of an enthusiast, and it is even more difficult on this supposition than on the previous one to account for his life and works.

  III. That he was deceived by the fraud of others. This supposition shown to be impossible and absurd. Hence we must fall back on the supposition that St. Paul does give an authentic account of his conversion, and we must conclude, therefore, that Christianity is a Divine Revelation 145

LECTURE VI.

ALLEGED DIFFICULTIES IN THE MORAL TEACHING OF THE NEW TESTAMENT.

BY THE
REV. C. A. ROW, M.A.,

Prebendary of St. Paul's,
Author of "The Nature and Extent of Divine Inspiration," "The Jesus of the Evangelists," "The Moral Teaching of the New Testament," etc.

Subject limited to examination of certain objections made by Mr. F. W. Newman and Mr. J. S. Mill. Opposition between Mr. Newman and Mr. Mill, as to whether principles contrary to truth and right preponderate in the teaching of the New Testament. Both agree that its teaching is *defective*.

A "system of moral teaching" must set forth general *principles*, but cannot contain specific *precepts* applicable to every detail of duty. Superiority of the New Testament in this point over other professed systems of morals.

Leading principles of Christian morality,—love to God, love to our neighbour, self-sacrifice (this last entirely overlooked both by Mr. Newman and Mr. Mill); also the principles of truth, honour, justice, and the morally beautiful, etc., are appealed to.

Some special objections made by Mr. Newman, stated and examined: (i.) That their sense of the nearness of the future world, as insisted upon by the writers of the New Testament, must have rendered them inadequate moral teachers; (ii.) That the New Testament is deficient in its teaching as to our political relations; (iii.) That it contains no precept regulating the practice of war; (iv.) Nor any precept directly commanding the abolition of slavery; (v.) That it is deficient in not enunciating the rights of man.

Objections made by Mr. Mill considered: (i.) That in

Christian ethics the duty of patriotism is not sufficiently esteemed or set forth; (ii.) That all recognition of the idea of public duty in modern times is derived from Greek and Roman sources, not from Christian ones; (iii.) That in the morality of private life all sense of personal dignity, honour, etc., is derived from the human and not from the religious part of our education.

Objections considered in reference to the alleged contradiction between the New Testament and the teachings of Political Economy:—

  (i.) The principles of Political Economy inadequate to grapple with many difficulties which can only be dealt with by the energy that is supplied by the principles of Christian morality.

  (ii.) The precepts of Christ *not* all intended to be understood literally.

  (iii.) Christian teaching in relation to the principle of prudent saving and to the accumulation of capital.

  (iv.) Mr. Newman's objections considered against St. Paul's teaching as to the relations between masters and servants, parents and children, husbands and wives.

Conclusion.—The personal influence of Christ as a moral and spiritual power—Quotation from Lecky's History of Morals. 181

LECTURE VII.

THE COMBINATION OF UNITY WITH PROGRESSIVENESS OF THOUGHT IN THE BOOKS OF THE BIBLE,

AN ARGUMENT IN FAVOUR OF DIVINE REVELATION.

BY THE

REV. J. H. TITCOMB, M.A.,

Vicar of St. Stephen's, South Lambeth, and Rural Dean of Clapham.

The extent of time covered by the enquiry. The Old Testament Scriptures represent the religious faith and hope of the Hebrews, from at least the time of Abraham to Christ.

I. Inquiry whether there is not a unity combined with progressiveness of thought in the Scriptures, running over a prodigious lapse of time, yet making up one harmonious and perfect whole.
  (i.) The *historical* development of the traditional hope respecting a coming Deliverer.
  (ii.) The *doctrinal* development, with reference (*a*) to the Prophetic or Teaching Office of the Redeemer, (*b*) to His Kingly Office.

II. Contrast, in respect of this "unity with progressiveness," between the religion of the Hebrews, and the religions of Egypt and China, and the systems of Buddhism and Brahminism.

III. The only explanation of this characteristic of the Hebrew Religion to be found in the belief that it is a result of Divine Revelation.
  (i.) Consideration of the fact itself:
    (1) It is set forth in the books of the Old Testament, which were certainly in existence about 200 B.C.
    (2) These books contain the remains of an actual faith and hope never extinguished in Israel.
    (3) This faith and hope confirmed by a succession of religious teachers, and set forth in a variety of methods.
  (ii.) Consideration of the circumstances attending this fact:
    (1) The vicissitudes in fortune of the Israelites.
    (2) The writers who developed this hope were men of various positions, modes of thought, etc.
    (3) Many of the facts, predicted of the coming Redeemer, of such a kind as to be at once capable of refutation, if not actually fulfilled.
    (4) Harmony between the statements respecting Jesus of Nazareth contained in the confessedly genuine Epistles of St. Paul, and the anticipations regarding the Messiah set forth by the Old Testament writers.

  (*a*) The promised Redeemer was rejected and slain by His own people.
  (*b*) The result of His teaching was to introduce a new dispensation, open to Gentiles as well as to Jews.
  (*c*) This new dispensation was in the course of actually breaking up the whole Jewish nationality.
 (iii.) Three possible explanations of this fact on natural grounds considered, and their unsatisfactoriness exhibited.
  (1) That the sayings of the Old Testament had no proper application to a coming Redeemer.
  (2) That these sayings were only the surmisings of genius, strangely and unexpectedly fulfilled.
  (3) That Christ and His Apostles purposely moulded events so as to bring about the fulfilment of the guesses and speculations contained in the Old Testament.
 (iv.) Christianity supplies the only key which unlocks with reasonableness the full meaning of the books of the Old Testament 221

LECTURE VIII.

THE AUTOBIOGRAPHY OF JOHN STUART MILL.

BY

W. R. BROWNE, M.A.,

Fellow of Trinity College, Cambridge.

Value of an Autobiography, especially of such a man and thinker as J. S. Mill.
Examination of the book with respect to Mill's religious opinions.

He accepted and continued throughout life to hold the religious opinions impressed upon him by his father, rejecting on *à priori* grounds everything supernatural.

Reasons why no weight is to be attached to his Scepticism. (1) He seems never to have thoroughly investigated the evidences of Christianity. (2) The result of his early training was to look upon Christianity exactly as upon any of the ancient religions, as something which in no way concerned him. (3) Disbelief in the freedom of the will at the bottom both of his own and of his father's scepticism.

Consideration of the doctrine of necessity. The freedom of the will shown to be necessary for the development of virtue and of all morality. The existence of evil shown to be at once possible, when the freedom of the will is admitted. Evil essential for the discipline and growth of virtue. The dignity of suffering as exhibited in the Christian religion.

James and John Mill, whilst rejecting free-will, and *therefore* rejecting Christianity, still retained those conceptions of right and of duty, which *imply* free-will—hence an argument *in favour* of Christianity.

The philosophy of the Secularist powerless as to any moral influence;—thus contrasted with Christianity . . 259

DIFFICULTIES ON THE SIDE OF UNBELIEF IN ACCOUNTING FOR HISTORICAL CHRISTIANITY.

BY THE
REV. G. F. MACLEAR, D.D.,

Head Master of King's College School, and late Assistant Preacher at the Temple Church.

Difficulties on the side of Unbelief in accounting for Historical Christianity.

I.

1. THE subject on which I have to speak this evening relates to the "Difficulties on the side of Unbelief in accounting for Historical Christianity."

2. I think it will be best, in treating such a subject, to confine myself to one or two points, instead of surveying a large number, which could not be satisfactorily dealt with in the compass of a single lecture.

3. I propose, therefore, to ask you to review certain facts of history, which, as it seems to me, remain and must remain absolutely inexplicable and unintelligible without the solution Christianity supplies, and I wish to inquire whether the difficulties these facts present do not, except on the supposition that Christianity is true, involve conclusions more miraculous and unaccountable than anything that has ever occurred in the world.

II

1. In a famous letter, written between A.D. 104 and 110, by the pro-prætor Pliny to the Emperor Trajan, he mentions that in his province of Pontus and Bithynia certain strange tenets had for some years been spread abroad, in consequence of which the temples of the gods were forsaken, the sacred solemnities intermitted, and *the sacrificial victims found very few purchasers.*

2. It has been remarked by Paley* that no evidence remains, by which it can be proved that the description he gives is to be confined to these provinces, and was unknown in other parts of the Roman Empire. The evidence, indeed, rather points to the contrary, and the words of the pro-prætor are brought forward here because they refer to the commencement within historic times, and not at a period so remote as to be lost in a fabulous antiquity, of one of the most striking religious revolutions which the annals of the past record.

3. How singular this revolution is we can, perhaps, estimate most effectively by supposing a Jew of the days of Solomon or Herod, or a Gentile of the days of Pericles or Augustus, to visit one of the churches of modern Christendom. Amongst many other things which would strike him, none, it may be believed, would do so with greater force than the absence of that ancient sacrificial ritual, with which he had been familiar from earliest

---

* *Evidences*, Part II. chap. ix. It is to be remembered that his province included several important towns—Neocæsareia, Chalcedon, Nicomedeia, Amisus, Trapezus, and the colonies of Heracleia and Sinope. See Merivale's *History of the Romans under the Emperors*, viii. 144.

childhood, and without which he could not conceive the possibility of any religious worship at all.

4. To us the phenomenon presents nothing either difficult or singular. Our difficulty rather is even to realise the celebration of those sacrifices, which once obtained almost universally throughout the world, and which were once regarded as the true modes of approaching the Supreme Being, under whatever form He was conceived, and with whatever attributes He was clothed.

5. The traveller, it is true, in lands still heathen, will discern traces of this once universal ritual, but in all countries calling themselves Christian, that is to say amongst the most enlightened and cultivated nations of the present day, it has not only ceased, but, in spite of all the violent reactions of nearly two thousand years, has never, as a form of national worship, been permanently restored.

6. But it will be well perhaps to endeavour to realise more clearly what we say has disappeared.

7. A form, then, of religious worship has passed away, which the oldest Book in the world represents as prevailing at the very infancy of the human race,* and which once gave employment to thousands and tens of thousands of a particular caste in the Mosaic Tabernacle, in the costlier and more enduring structures of Solomon and Herod, in the temples of classic Greece and imperial Rome.

8. A form of religious worship has passed away, which was once equally accepted by the "Father of the

---

* Gen. iv. 4; viii. 20; xii. 7, 8: Job i. 5; xlii. 8.

faithful," by the sweet Psalmist of Israel, by the Grecian statesman, and the Roman magistrate; which was once inextricably entwined with all the more solemn epochs of man's domestic life—birth, and marriage, and death; with all the most momentous epochs in his national and political life—the foundation of cities, the ratification of treaties, the declaration of war, the celebration of solemn triumphs; with all the most powerful emotions of his personal and religious life—his hopes and fears, his joys and sorrows, his hours of despondency, his consciousness of guilt, his yearning for restoration to the Divine favour.

9. A form of religious worship has passed away, to which men once resorted almost instinctively, whether they desired to acknowledge the power and supremacy of the Deity they adored, to present him with some pledge of homage and subjection, to return thanks for gifts received or protection afforded, to deprecate anger, or to implore reconciliation, and without the intervention of which, in some form or other, it is hardly too much to say that once no morning dawned, no evening closed, no public entertainment was celebrated, no private meal was eaten, no harvest was housed, no vintage was gathered in, no sin was expiated, and no ceremonial impurity was removed.

10. In other matters, nations and tribes have differed as widely as it is possible to conceive. In this habit of sacrifice they have been as one. And yet, universal as it once was, it is now unknown to the civilised world. This is a fact, brought home to us by our daily experience. The solemn procession of sacrificial victims, the slaughtering of them before the altar, the sprinkling of

their blood upon the offerer, the sacrificial feast that followed—these things are with us entirely matters of the past, and whether we read of them in Jewish history, or the poems of Homer, or the narrative of Livy, we experience the utmost difficulty in realizing to ourselves that they ever obtained amongst men.

11. Now it does not require a very extended acquaintance with human nature to know that of all habits, ideas, and associations, none retain their ascendancy more pertinaciously over man than those which concern him as a religious being.*

12. And yet, in reference to one religious custom, though the most ancient and the most universal of all, for the sake of which, indeed, priests, altars, and temples originally came into being,† we have only to look around us to be confronted with a spectacle of a change so complete and overmastering that it would fill us with astonishment if we were not accustomed to it from day to day.

III.

1. I have already observed that this remarkable revolution of thought and feeling may be traced back to a period not lost in a hazy antiquity, but to one strictly within the domain of history, to a period which had its records, its archives, and its monuments. Important as this fact will be found to be hereafter, I propose first to notice another feature of this religious revolution, which is no less striking and no less deserving of attention.

---

* This is fully acknowledged by Renan, *Les Apôtres*, chap. xvii.
† Döllinger's *Gentile and Jew*, i. 225.

2. Without entering upon the question of the origin of the ancient sacrifices, it may be asserted without fear of contradiction that they were to a considerable extent based upon a sense, more or less real, of personal shortcoming; that they were gifts, whereby man sought to make good his imperfect consecration of himself to his Maker; that they represented the conviction that something over and above mere repentance was needed to expiate the consequences of guilt.*

3. Now to the practice of sacrifice the great exception is found, as is well known, in the system of Buddhism. But along with sacrifice Buddhism rejects the notion that lay at the root of it, namely, that past sin presents any objective obstacle to man's reconciliation with God.† If, then, among the nations of Christendom, together with the cessation of sacrifice there had passed away also man's conviction of personal shortcoming, there would be a *consistency in the revolution, and the disappearance of the conviction would account in a great measure for the disappearance of the sacrifical observance.*

4. But is this the case? Has the conviction of personal shortcoming vanished from the midst of Christendom like the phantom of a troubled dream? So far is this from being the fact, that it may be safely said there has never been a time when the conviction of sin has been more and more intensified amongst the most cultivated nations than during the last eighteen hundred years.

---

* Butler's *Analogy*, Part II. chap. v.

† Kreuger, *Symbolik*, i. 2, 5; Hardwick's *Christ and other Masters*, ii. 60; Macdonnell's *Donnellan Lectures*, p. 90.

5. In saying this I do not seek to depreciate for a moment the feeling upon this momentous subject which undoubtedly existed in the ancient world. .I would acknowledge freely the sense of inward contradiction, and of the awful power of conscience expressed by many of the wisest of the heathen. I would give their full force to all those proverbs in ancient writers which represent sin as disharmony, as spiritual bondage, as the transgression of limits prescribed by Virtue, as inflicting wounds upon the soul, as entailing terrible consequences in the world to come.

6. But no one will deny that all this has been infinitely deepened and intensified. The very word "Sin" has acquired a meaning such as it never bore in the mouth of the greatest of the moral teachers of Greece and Rome. A mournful catalogue of terms based on a great variety of images has been employed in writings of inspired authority to set forth its heinousness and disastrous effects. A code of morality has been promulgated, which is stricter than the strictest requirements of the Mosaic Law, and brings out, as was never done before, the infinite distance between the guilt-laden sinner and the infinitely holy Creator. Words have been reverberating through the last eighteen centuries—passing into laws, into proverbs, into doctrines, but *never passing away*—demanding the obedience of the heart and soul, as well as of the hand and tongue.

7. These words have found a lodgement in the breasts of men like no other words before or since. They have exercised and are exercising still a momentous influence. Moreover, on the authority of the voice that uttered

them, life has been invested with a more real and mysterious import than ever was associated with it in the ancient world. Not only is it the portal of another life, but beyond it lies an awful tribunal before which all must stand. It is the Judgment Seat of no shadowy Æacus or Rhadamanthus, but of One who *trieth the very hearts and reins*,* and who will judge every man *according to the deeds done in the body*.†

8. I do not here assume that these convictions have exercised anything like an adequate effect on the lives and actions of men, but I say they have exerted an effect such as never was known before the modern era, and they have gone far to foster a national conscience, and to deepen the sense of individual responsibility. There may be much in modern society to startle and alarm any who will look below the surface. There may be times when the philanthropist is tempted to doubt the reality of any progress at all, and the moralist to sigh almost in despair over the grossest violations of justice and honesty. But, taken as a whole, there never was a period when sin was less generally regarded with indifference, or the consciousness of it less deemed an infirmity and an illusion.

9. It will not be disputed that man is now mainly what he has been from the beginning. He is still a being subject to all the vicissitudes of earthly existence; he still " cometh up and is cut down like a flower;" he still " has but a short time to live and is full of misery;"‡

---

* Ps. vii. 9.   † 1 Cor. iv. 5; 2 Cor. v. 10.
‡ " We live in a world which is full of misery and ignorance, and the plain duty of each and all of us is to try and make the

he still acknowledges the inability of the things of time and sense entirely to satisfy his longings; he still confesses by the voice of his greatest poets the nothingness of his highest glory,* and he has often testified by the terrible earnestness of his penances and self-tortures that the side of his life most full of suffering is the religious side,† and that, great as he may be, he yet contains within him some profound source of misery.‡

10. And yet, though the conviction of personal shortcoming has been thus deepened and intensified, the ancient sacrificial ritual has never succeeded in regaining its hold. Though man has never constructed for himself a religion of despair, yet during the last eighteen hundred years he has never sought relief in a system which was once almost universally recognised as the proper means for seeking reconciliation with God. Though he still is conscious that he is not as he ought to be, yet this sense of demerit has not restored the sin and trespass-

---

little corner he can influence somewhat less miserable, and somewhat less ignorant, than it was before he entered it."—Prof. Huxley.

* "Read Johnson's *Vanity of Human Wishes;* all the examples and mode of giving them sublime. 'Tis a grand poem, and so true."—Byron's *Diary,* 1821. "If all that the old poets have sung, in isolated passages, of the miseries of existence; if all those sad songs of a truly terrible view of the world which the notion of a blind fate has scattered amidst the legends and histories of various nations in deeply significant tragedies were collected into one picture, and the transitory and poetic fancy exchanged for true and lasting earnestness, the peculiarity of the Indian view of life would be best comprehended."—Fr. Schlegel, *Ueber der Sprache und Weisheit der Inder,* quoted in Luthardt, 338 n.

† Ackermann's *Christian Element in Plato,* pp. 203—207.

‡ Pascal, *Pensées,* ii. 88, 104.

offerings of the Jew, or brought back those propitiatory sacrifices of the Gentile, which were once, especially in seasons of national or domestic calamity, multiplied with such frightful prodigality, and prompted man to surrender even *the fruit of his body for the sin of his soul.*

11. Here, then, we are confronted with another and very singular feature of the religious revolution we are considering. Sacrifices, we know, formed a part universally of ancient worship. The sense of Sin was then confessedly weak. How is it, now that it has been so strengthened and developed, that the old ritual has passed away? It will scarcely be pretended that it concerned the mere surface of man's life. If there be any emotions, deep, serious, and permanent, in the human breast, they are those which prompted these modes of bridging over the gulf between the creature and his Creator. What has caused this surprising change of thought and feeling? To say that the sentiment of mankind was gradually alienated from and that imperial decrees* forbade the ancient rites only removes the difficulty a single step backwards. The question still remains, *whence came the feeling that inspired the legislation,* and how comes it to pass that legislation, in religious matters notoriously weak and incompetent, has succeeded in thus effectually eradicating a system once so universal?

IV.

1. May we conclude, then, that with the ancient sacrificial ritual the ancient sacrificial phraseology has

---

* Like those of Theodosius, A.D. 381; Gibbon, iii. 413, and notes.

disappeared also? Are such expressions as "victim" and "offering," "oblation" and "satisfaction," "propitiation" and "atonement" utterly unknown? Do we trace them only as relics of a vanished world of thought in the pages of the Pentateuch or the writings of Livy?

2. What we might naturally have expected, what on every ground of probability we had almost a right to expect, *has not taken place.* Sacrifices have passed away, sacrificial terms remain, and they not only remain, but they have found a centre, round which they group themselves; they have found a fact of history, to which they have been transferred.

3. There exists at this day in every part of Europe, and in various parts of Asia, Africa, and America, one single Rite, that of the Lord's Supper, which alone approximates to the complex system that has passed away.

4. It has been celebrated for eighteen hundred years. However it may have come, whencesoever it may have come, here it is. "It has lasted through a great many storms and revolutions. The Roman Empire has passed away; modern European society has risen out of its ruins. Political systems have been established and overthrown. Even the physical world has undergone mighty alterations, and our conception of its laws is altogether changed."* But this Rite still survives. Manners, habits, modes of thought, theories, opinions, philosophies, have changed. This Rite has outlived them all.

5. But does this mode, in which the Rite is celebrated, recall also the old sacrificial habit? Would it in any

---

* Maurice's *Kingdom of Christ*, ii. 5.

degree remind a Greek of the days of Pericles, or a Roman of the time of Augustus, of the ancient ritual? The ceremonial to which they had been accustomed from their earliest years was extremely complex. The victim, adorned with garlands, was led up to the altar; meal and salt were mixed and crumbled over its head; a libation of wine was poured out; the victim was slain; its blood was poured on and about the altar; certain portions were burnt with wine, meal, and incense, and the rest of the flesh was distributed to the people.

6. Of all this how much survives in this Rite? What are the outward and visible signs presented during its celebration to the eyes of the worshippers? Suppose the pro-prætor of Bithynia had been present at one of those meetings of the early Christians which he describes in his letter to the Emperor Trajan, and about which he was so anxious, what tokens of any sacrificial ritual would he have beheld? In some upper room, perhaps, lit up with the light of many torches, or the first rays of the rising sun,* he would have seen couches laid and the walls hung, after the manner of the East,† for a harmless banquet.‡ To this meal the rich would have contributed of their abundance and the poor of their poverty, and all would be joining in it with singleness of heart. Then, after the offering of prayer and the reading of holy writings and exhortation to a godly life, he would have seen Bread brought in§ and placed before some elder amongst the company, and likewise a cup of Wine. He would

---

* "Ante lucem," Plin. *Ep.* xcvi. † Stanley on 1 Cor. xi. vol. 1. p. 249.

‡ Plin. *Ep.* xcvi. § Comp. Justin. *Apol.* cap. lxv.

have seen the Bread solemnly blessed, broken, and eaten. He would have seen the Wine solemnly blessed, poured out, and drunk by those assembled.

7. Now, it is true that in ancient times, though the victim itself was the efficacious element of sacrifice, it was offered with and by means of bread and wine, and that mealtime and sacrifice were so essentially connected together that "even the modes of expressing the two acts were frequently interchanged."*

8. But what thoughts would have instantly risen in the mind of the pro-prætor? What question would he most certainly have put? Would he not have asked, "If this is a solemn meal, a religious feast, when and where was the sacrificial victim offered? The victims for our sacrifices find few purchasers, the temples are abandoned, the sacred rites are neglected; where is He whom ye worship,† and what is the sacrifice ye are celebrating?"

9. To such a question, what would have been the reply of any Christian in his province? Would he not have said, "This Meal, whereof we partake, is a sacred Feast, instituted by Him, from whom we are called Christians. He commanded Bread to be eaten, and Wine to be drunk by us in memory of His Death, which He underwent upon the Cross"?

10. A Christian of Bithynia would undoubtedly have

---

* For the religious importance attached by Jews to the actions of breaking bread and pouring out wine, even at a common meal, see Lightfoot's *Temple Service;* Godwyn's *Moses and Aaron,* pp. 89, 90; *The Book of Jewish Ceremonies,* by Gamaliel Ben Pedahzur, pp. 51—56; Cudworth's *True Notion,* chap. i.

† "Carmenque Christo quasi Deo dicere," Plin. *Ep.* xcvi.

gone on to say more upon the subject to his inquirer.* But the answer, even as far as it goes, brings out a very remarkable feature in reference to this Rite. It claims to rest not upon any conception or theory, but upon *an objective, historical fact*, and this fact is *the death of its Institutor*.

11. Now this is deserving of note. The disappearance of an ancient, time-hallowed mode of religious worship is a fact of history. The celebration of this Rite is a fact of history, the rise and origin of which can be traced back *to a certain, definite period, of which we know a great deal*.

12. We are relegated, then, for an explanation of the origin of this unprecedented Rite, not to a land of hazy theories or shadowy mythology, but to one where we can plant our footsteps on solid ground.

13. This Rite claims to rest within historic times on the death of a Person. Either this death took place, or it did not. If it did, there must have been circumstances connected with it utterly unlike any other that has taken place in history, if we are to account for its commemoration ever since by means of the reception of Bread and Wine, to which Jew and Gentile alike attached a solemn and even a religious importance.

V.

1. Who, then, instituted this Rite? When did He institute it, and under what circumstances? The answer to these enquiries is not a matter of dispute. All the Churches that have received the Symbol, Latin or Greek,

---

* The question of a higher or lower view of the Eucharist is not material to the argument. The question is, *What is the meaning of the Rite at all?*

Catholic or Protestant, whatever other view they may take of it, agree in referring it to one and the same Person, and to one and the same time.

2. The Institutor—such is the testimony of Christian writers, and it is strengthened by every incidental notice of the facts which occurs in profane authors—appeared about eighteen centuries and a half ago, during the reigns of the Emperors Augustus and Tiberius, in Palestine, an obscure corner of the ancient Roman Empire.

3. Apparently He was of the humblest origin. His reputed father was a carpenter of Nazareth, a town hidden away amidst the Galilean hills, unknown and unnamed in the pages of the Old Testament Scriptures. His mother was a Jewish maiden of Bethlehem in Judæa, who lived at Nazareth. Here for thirty years the Institutor of this mysterious Rite grew up, sharing with the town its seclusion and obscurity, far removed alike from the stir and bustle of the great capitals of the Empire, and the disputes of the theological schools of His native land.

4. When the thirty years of seclusion were over, He left His humble home and came forth as a Teacher of His countrymen, and after a while gathered round Him a small body of disciples of equally humble origin as Himself—peasants, publicans, fishermen of Galilee.

5. To these His followers He endeared Himself by a life of self-sacrificing devotion to their highest interests. With them He went about amongst His countrymen. He visited their capital, their towns, their villages, and addressed Himself as a teacher to all classes, rich and poor, learned and unlearned.*

* For the sake of the argument, the supernatural element involved in the Saviour's miracles is not here pressed.

6. His teaching, it has been already* noticed, has exercised a very remarkable influence in the world. It combined terrible severity against sin with infinite tenderness towards sinners; it united a marvellous simplicity with a claim unhesitatingly and unfalteringly urged to an absolutely boundless authority† over the minds and souls of men. But it provoked determined opposition. Its denunciations of hypocrisy, pretence, and formalism, its assertion, never retracted or modified, of the Speaker's natural title to universal royalty and coequality with God,‡ arrayed against Him the most powerful classes of His countrymen, and they resolved to compass His death.

7. The extant biographies§ of the Institutor of this Rite tell us that He was well aware of the deepening intensity of this opposition. He saw the tide setting in steadily against Him, and He never disguised from His followers

---

* See above, p. 4, and Milman's *History of Christianity*, i. 189.

† "Jesus makes everything depend upon His person; in fact, His person is His matter. When He would most emphatically assure or confirm, His words are, *Verily, verily, I say unto you*. We are to believe His words, not because of the truth of their matter, but because of the dignity of His person—and yet He was the meekest of men!"—Luthardt's *Fundamental Truths*, p. 284; Liddon's *Bampton Lectures*, 166—179; see also the comparison in this respect between Christ and Socrates in *Ecce Homo*, pp. 94, 95.

‡ John v. 17, 18.

§ "Into the question of their authenticity and genuineness it is not necessary to enter here. That the three earliest Gospels at any rate existed before the siege of Jerusalem, and that they had before the middle of the second century acquired a sacred authority, may be regarded as a conclusion which has been wrung from the inevitable candour of reluctant adversaries."—Farrar's *Witness of History to Christ*, pp. 52, 53.

its inevitable issue. It formed the subject of frequent and earnest conversation with them.* Without the slightest trace of misgiving, and with an unearthly calmness, He never faltered in His declaration that on His death depended the most momentous issues alike to His disciples and to the world at large.

8. At length the hatred and opposition of the ruling powers reached its climax, and they were enabled, owing to the treachery of one of His own disciples, to ensure His delivery into their hands. The evening before their designs were carried out was the Eve of the Passover, the great historic Festival of His countrymen. Jerusalem was crowded with strangers and pilgrims from every quarter of the world. The hills around were whitened with countless flocks of sheep and lambs ready for the morrow's Festival. The Institutor of the Rite we are examining had made careful preparation† for celebrating this Feast with twelve of His more immediate followers, and on the evening in question He celebrated it with them according to the custom of the nation.

9. The end, which He had foreseen, and of which He had so often spoken, was now close at hand. But He was neither perturbed, nor alarmed, nor anxious to retract or modify any of His boundless claims. Calmly and quietly, He took, as the Festal Meal proceeded, one of the unleavened cakes that had been placed before Him as Master of the Feast, and giving thanks, He brake it, and gave it to them, saying—" *Take, eat, This is My body,*

---

* (1) Matt. xvi. 21 ; Mark viii. 31 ; Luke ix. 21, 22 ; (2) Matt. xvii. 9 ; Mark ix. 9 ; Luke ix. 44 ; (3) Matt. x. 33, 34.

† Matt. xxvi. 17—19 ; Mark xiv. 12—16 ; Luke xxii. 7—13.

which is given for you; do this in remembrance of Me." Afterwards He took a cup of wine, and having given thanks in like manner, He gave it unto them, saying—"*Drink ye all of this; for this Cup is My Blood of the New Covenant, which is shed for you and for many for the remission of sins; this do as oft as ye shall drink it, in remembrance of Me.*"

10. Such was the institution of the Eucharist. The evening on which it was instituted deepened into night, but before the following morning dawned He who instituted it was apprehended by His enemies. Their malice did its worst; He was dragged from one tribunal to another; He was beaten, buffeted, spit upon, and at last He was led out to crucifixion, and He died the death of the malefactor and the slave.

11. The fact of His death is recorded in each of the four biographies of Christ. However condensed they may be in other portions, they "expand into the minute particularity of a diary," as they approach the foot of the Cross. The historical fact of His decease is mentioned by later authors as a matter of common notoriety, and it gave point to the opprobrious epithets applied to the first disciples. In an historical age, which had its archives, its registers, and its monuments, the fact was always accepted, *and never disproved.*

12. Now, in the annals of the world, is there anything really parallel to this? " Other founders of systems or societies have thanked a kindly Providence for shrouding from their gaze the vicissitudes of coming time." But the Institutor of this Rite, though to all outward appearance He stood literally alone in the world, though

amongst the little band of his attached followers He had none on whom He could lean, or from whom He could receive the slightest real sympathy or support, though in the immediate foreground of His future was an awful and humiliating death, yet was so far from deeming this any hindrance to His plan of establishing a Universal Kingdom, that He actually made provision for its commemoration to all future time! About to disappoint every hope and every anticipation of His followers, He established the commemoration of that disappointment in a mysterious Ordinance, and directed that it should be universally celebrated!*

VI.

1. Marvellous and unparalleled as this is, the fact remains that this Rite has been uninterruptedly observed. The anticipations of the Institutor have been fulfilled.

2. Now it will be allowed without hesitation that there is nothing so rare as to find any religious system which is capable of transcending the limits of race, clime, and the scene of its historic origin; a religious system which, if transplanted, will not quickly vanish away, which by any

---

* Even Schenkel admits that "never before had Jesus stood at so lofty a height as at the moment of instituting the Lord's Supper. With a violent death before Him, expecting from His disciples, in their weakness of character, neither help nor comfort, without prospect for the victory of His cause from man, thrown with His hopes and expectations only upon His heavenly Father, and upon the truth and power inherent in His life and works, and uniting with all this such elevated repose, such still submission, and also such perfect patience with him who at this very moment was meditating the basest treachery!" Schenkel, p. 278,, E. Tr.

real permanence can prove itself anything better than a mere local or national outgrowth of superstition.

3. But this Rite, though it is utterly unlike anything ever thought of, invented, or taught before, though it commemorates a cruel and ignominious Death, though that Death was the disappointment of every hope and every anticipation of the first disciples, has been found capable of universal transplantation, has transcended alike the scene of its historic origin and the limits of race and clime, and wherever it has been received and celebrated the multiplied sacrifices of antiquity have retired before it into the darkness of oblivion.

4. Now we can trace back this revolution to its source. We can tell when the old system gave signs of "vanishing away," and the new Symbol, so unique and unprecedented, began to take its place. It is not a point so distant that we strain our minds in vain to realize it amidst the mists of a hoary antiquity. It is not a period of which we have no certain records or memorials. It produced historians of good repute, whose narratives of the events of their own time are universally accepted as authentic and trustworthy. It was a period in which the "transactions of every province within the limits of the late Macedonian and then Roman Empire—the barbarian, so termed, as well as the Grecian, and the acts of Herod among the number—were the objects of research and careful narration, by natives of the soil as well as by strangers."*

---

* Mill's *Pantheism*, II. ii. sect. 11; *Eclipse of Faith*, p. 210; *Aids to Faith*, p. 71; *Restoration of Belief*, pp. 40, 41; Sherlock's *Trial of the Witnesses*, Discourse iv. 360.

5. To represent, therefore, that this Rite can be regarded as embodying a gradually developed Mythology, is to ascribe it to causes utterly inadequate to meet the facts of the case. There is no known instance of a mythical history growing up in such an age,* under such circumstances, and with the rapidity we know it spread amongst Christian societies of many different nations and languages. A Rite of such marked peculiarity presupposes an act of institution. Its universal spread presupposes a general acquaintance with the history of the institution. The first Christians were neither mystic philosophers, enthusiastic dreamers, nor weak and credulous men. They were not likely to accept the history on mere hearsay, nor to celebrate a Rite so strange and unique without some adequate explanation. Men do not lightly take up a creed which hits their fancy, or vaguely embodies their aspirations, at the cost of their lives, and with the certainty of being exposed to danger, suffering, and persecution.

6. But when we look at the history of the institution of this Rite as it has come down to us,—and it is to be remembered that there is no other account of it,—we cannot but be struck with its remarkable brevity and conciseness. Considering all it was designed to import, considering its utterly unprecedented character as a

---

* "The idea of men writing mythic histories between the time of Livy and Tacitus, and St. Paul mistaking such for realities!" Arnold's *Life*, ii. 58. " In the whole sphere of criticism there is no absurdity more uncritical than the idea that a rite which universally prevailed should have grown up accidentally and gradually, especially a rite of such marked peculiarity." Ebrard, *Gospel History*. p. 409.

Jewish institution, considering the shock which the idea of commemorating the death of a Crucified Messiah must necessarily have involved to the mind of every Jew, it is brief to a degree perfectly astonishing. We find nowhere any long, laboured, and specific justification of its institution. We find nowhere any minute and circumstantial directions as to the method of its celebration, such as we find in the Apostolic constitutions.* In the Evangelic narrative the account is brief, simple, and artless. In those documents the particularity of direction is like that of a " modern rubric."

7. Paley has noticed these features of the narrative as strong proofs of its genuineness. If the account "had been feigned," he remarks, "it would have been more full: it would have come nearer to the actual mode of celebrating the Rite, as that mode obtained very early in Christian Churches; and it would have been more formal than it is."† To this we may add, that it is too brief, simple, and concise for a scheme resting either on imposture or on an eclectic Mythology. The superstructure is too solid and weighty to rest on such foundations as these. The simplicity of the account is too grand for the impostor or the enthusiast, and we will now present our conclusion from the facts we have reviewed.

10. The early Christians must have been able to *give some adequate account of the historical facts of the case,*‡ before they could either have celebrated themselves or taught others in different lands to adopt a Rite so novel

---

* See Paley's *Evidences*, I. vii. 3.   † Ibid. Part II. chap. iii.

‡ More substantial than the *teinte de suave mysticité*, which Renan ascribes to their imagination, *Vie de Jésus*, chap. xxiii.

and unprecedented as this. The historical fact this Rite proclaims was their Master's cruel and ignominious death; and He ordained it to proclaim His death. Now, if after it took place—and this we know has never been disproved—He passed away and was no more seen; if between His death and the celebration of the Rite by the first disciples there was no intervening event to link the one thing with the other—the celebration of this Rite, at such an age of the world's history, and by those who celebrated it, is, on natural principles, more miraculous and more inexplicable than anything that ever occurred in the world.

VII.

1. Was there any event, then, intervening between the death of the Institutor and its celebration by the first disciples? Was there anything which transfigured the shame of their Master's Death, and presented the whole action in a new light?

2. Their own conduct when that Death took place has been described minutely with the most artless simplicity. When He died, the Evangelic narratives admit that one alone of the Apostles was standing by His Cross,* that one had denied with an oath he had even known Him,† that all had forsaken Him and fled.‡ This is their own account of the matter. They neither hide nor disguise, they neither palliate nor excuse it. With singular open-

---

* John xxi. 25, 26.
† Matt. xxvi. 69—75; Mark xiv. 66—72; Luke xxii. 54—62; John xviii. 15—27.   ‡ Matt. xxvi. 56.

ness, with surprising particularity, they dwell upon the story of their own cowardice and faithlessness.

3. What interest they had in describing themselves as worse than they really were it is difficult to see. But if then they were cowards, stupefied with sorrow and overwhelmed with despair, what made them bold afterwards? If before they never could bear the idea of their Master's Death, and when it took place were crushed to the earth with disappointment, with what conceivable object could they have joined within a very short period in this Eucharistic Feast, and that in the very city where He died?* Why did they ever rally together again to commemorate His Death, and to proclaim by a symbolical action the sad fate of One, whom they had given up everything to follow, but in whose grave every hope was now buried?

4. An adequate and consistent explanation of these extraordinary facts is needed. Is there one such producible?

5. There is one, which, in spite of obloquy, contempt, and cruel persecution, the first disciples made it the business of their lives to proclaim, which every extant letter of every Apostle, and every author contemporaneous with the Apostles, of the age immediately succeeding them, and every Christian writer from that age to the present, concur in representing as a fact no less historical than that of the death of the Institutor of the Eucharistic Feast.

6. The Evangelists inform us that when He died, His

---

* Acts ii. 46; xx. 7, 11. Why also did they continue to attach to this Meal even the "mystic sense" which Renan admits, *Les Apôtres*, chap. v.?

Body was taken down from the Cross and laid in a new tomb.* They are careful to impress upon us—with what object it is difficult to see, unless it was true—that even this act of kindness and consideration was due not to any of the Apostolic body, but to secret disciples and comparative strangers. In that tomb the Holy Body lay during the Friday night, Saturday, and Saturday night which followed the sad scene on Calvary. A sealed stone and a guard of Roman soldiers,† we are told, protected the spot and defended it from the intrusion alike of friends and enemies. But early in the morning of the third day, a day which ever since has been observed,‡ that stone was found to have been rolled away, and the sepulchre was discovered empty.§

7. A fact more momentous in its significance it is impossible to conceive, but as a fact it was placed beyond all doubt, and it is related with the same simplicity, calmness, and absence of strain and effort as any other incident in the life of the Lord. Indeed, so simple and artless is the narrative at this point, so blended is it with confessions of fear, doubt, misgiving, and incredulity, that as we read the record we almost forget the marvellous features of the occurrence, and can with difficulty realize its exceptional character.‖

---

* Matt. xxvii. 57—61; Mark xv. 42—47; Luke xxiii. 50—56; John xix. 38—42. † Matt. xxvii. 62—66.

‡ Barnab. *Ep.* xv. Διὸ καὶ ἄγομεν τὴν ἡμέραν τὴν ὀγδόην εἰς εὐφροσύνην, ἐν ᾗ ὁ Ἰησοῦς ἀνέστη ἐκ νεκρῶν.

§ Thus much Renan, *Les Apôtres*, chap i., and Schenkel, p. 311, admit.

‖ Westcott's *Gospel of the Resurrection*, p. 157.

8. But if the sepulchre was empty, where was **He who** had been laid therein? He was no longer there,* He had risen, and by many infallible proofs He gave token of the reality of the fact. On the world's first Easter Day He show Himself to Mary Magdalene,† to the other ministering women,‡ to St. Peter,§ to two disciples journeying towards Emmaus,|| to ten of the Apostles in the upper room at Jerusalem, when St. Thomas was absent.¶ Eight days afterwards He manifested Himself to them when that Apostle was present.** Subsequently He was seen by seven of their number on the lake of Gennesaret,†† then by St. James,‡‡ then by more than five hundred brethren at once on a mountain in Galilee,§§ and lastly by all the Apostles once more on one of the hills near Bethany, where He was parted from them, and ascended into heaven.|| ||

9. Simple as the narrative is, it is circumstantial in the details it records. Every avenue of misconception was closed up, every ground for delusion was removed. "It was not one person but many who saw the Risen Saviour. They saw Him not only separately, but together; not by night only, but by day; not at a distance, but near; they not only saw Him, but touched Him, conversed with Him, ate with Him, examined His Person to satisfy their

---

* Luke xxiv. 3. † John xx. 11—18 [Mark xvi. 9—11].
‡ Matt. xxviii. 9, 10; Mark xvi. 5—7; Luke xxiv. 4—8.
§ Luke xxiv. 34; 1 Cor. xv. 5. || Luke xxiv. 13—35.
¶ Luke xxiv. 36—43; John xx. 19—25 [Mark xvi. 14].
** John xx. 26—29. †† John xxi. 1—24. ‡‡ 1 Cor. xv. 7.
§§ Matt. xxviii. 16—18; 1 Cor. xv. 6.
|| || Luke xxiv. 50—53; Acts i. 3—12.

doubts."* It is conceivable that the enthusiasm of a single member of the Apostolic company could have given an imaginary shape to individual hopes. But it is impossible to conceive how a number of witnesses, all incredulous,† and one pre-eminently so, could have been simultaneously affected in the same manner.

10. The Institutor of this Rite rose from the dead. This is the historical fact, to which the Apostles declared that they were raised up to bear witness. Upon it they staked everything, their life, their credit, their veracity,‡ and their hopes. In order to proclaim it they confronted danger, suffering, and death itself in some of its most appalling forms. As believers in it they were obliged to become separate from other men, to sever the ties of home and family and common intercourse, to exchange all that life holds dear for sacrifices which made life little better than a daily martyrdom. It is important ever to bear in mind what joining the Christian Society meant in early times; for even if we allow that the majority of men were at this period uncritical and credulous, aud that they were unacquainted with the rigorous demands of "exact science," yet it cannot be said that they were

---

* Paley's *Evidences*, II. viii.

† "It is most instructive to notice that the *report* of the Lord's Resurrection was in each case disbelieved. Nothing less than *sight* convinced those who had the deepest desire to believe the tidings: and even sight was not in every case immediately convincing."—Westcott's *Gospel of the Resurrection*, p. 111.

‡ 1 Cor. xv. 15. "There is something to him very touching in the manner in which the Apostle writes this monstrous supposition. That *he* should be a false witness! a thing incredible and monstrous."—Robertson's *Lectures on First Corinthians*, p. 253.

more credulous than men in any age have been found to be when worldly interests are in jeopardy and an entire change of conduct is demanded, when old habits have to be broken up, and insult, contempt, danger, and a death of torment, to be confronted.*

11. A hope of a life beyond the grave, a prospect of his own resurrection, was all that the early Christian had to support him in hours which try men to the uttermost, and show of what stuff they are made. If his hopes were bounded by this life only, if they were rounded off by this "bank and shoal of time," then indeed he was *of all men most miserable.*† His life was a blunder, a gratuitous folly, and it is impossible but to believe that the early converts weighed carefully the evidence upon which they were called to exchange ease for toil, comfort for discomfort, quiet for perpetual danger.

12. The more the subject is considered, the more hopeless it will be found to reconcile with what went before the vast and overmastering change which came over the entire thoughts and feelings of the Apostles after the death of their Master, *without some intervening fact as certain and as historically real as that event itself.* The more the subject is considered, the more hopeless it will be also found to reconcile the celebration of the Eucharist, considering all that it imported, and the age in which its celebration began, with the gradual cessation of the ancient sacrificial *cultus*, except on the supposition that something occurred between the Passion and the

---

* See Butler's *Analogy*, part II. chap. vii.
† Ἐλεεινότεροι πάντων θρώπων ἐσμέν, 1 Cor. xv. 19.

observance of this Rite, powerful enough to remove once and for ever the torturing doubts which must ever have attended the celebration of the Eucharist, and glorious enough to transfigure the desolation and despair of the Story of the Cross.*

13. A "splendid guess," a "vague but loving hope," a doctrine founded on subjective ideas, the dream of an enthusiast,—these will not account for facts so hard, objective, stubborn, and indubitable. They will not bear the weight of the superstructure they have to support, they crumble to dust before the vastness of the revolution for which they have to account. The Resurrection—and the Resurrection alone—supplies an adequate cause, an historical event sufficient to account for historical facts. "As a fact with which the disciples were familiarised by repeated proofs, it was capable of removing each lingering doubt: as a Revelation of which the meaning was finally made known by the withdrawal of Christ from the earth, it opened a new region and form of life, the apprehension of which would necessarily influence all their interpretations of the Divine promises. If the crucified Lord did rise again, we can point to effects which answer completely to what we may suppose to have been the working of the stupendous miracle on those who were the first witnesses of it: if He did not, to what must we look

---

* "We shall not say too much if we designate the Supper the climax of the ancient Christian worship, in which the congregation celebrated its reconciliation with God in Christ, the Mediator between God and man; and find in its uninterrupted celebration the first proof of the steadfast faith of the Church in the Divine nature of Christ."—Dorner's *Person of Christ.* i. 186, E. Tr.

for an explanation of phenomena for which the Resurrection is no more than an adequate cause?"*

VIII.

1. Before I close, let me finally review the difficulties with which we are confronted, supposing that the Resurrection was not a fact and the Gospel History is not true. Let us survey them calmly, and see if they do not involve conclusions more miraculous and unaccountable than anything that has ever occurred.

2. If the Resurrection is not an historical fact, we are called upon to believe that plain, simple, unsophisticated men like the Apostles, who had been trained from their youth up in sacrificial habits, who from early associations would naturally have been disposed to exalt the ancient ritual, and did adhere to many of their ancient customs, yet could bring themselves to assert that the entire system of sacrifice was "done away" and "fulfilled" in and through the death of One, who by that death only disappointed every hope and dashed to the ground every anticipation they had ever cherished.

3. We are called upon to believe that they could detach themselves from and persuade many others also to forsake a religion which even at the final siege of Jeru-

---

* Westcott's *Gospel of the Resurrection*, pp. 118, 119. "The fact of a Christian Church *being formed at all* notwithstanding the shock which the idea of a crucified Messiah must necessarily have given to the mind of every Israelite of that day, can only be explained on the assumption of the Divinity of Christ and the historical reality of His Resurrection."—Ebrard's *Gospel History*, p. 447.

salem still exercised an irresistible spell over the minds of thousands and tens of thousands in Palestine; which with all its far-back memories and associations could kindle a fire of enthusiasm in the heart even of the renegade Josephus :* which could rally to the banner of the boasting impostor Barcochab multitudes of the nation burning with zeal and filled with the enthusiasm resulting from the consciousness of past greatness and former triumphs;† that they could forsake all this and persuade others to join a Society which could offer as a compensation for the loss of recollections so august, and of institutions so hallowed by time, *literally nothing.*

4. We are called upon to believe that men who till the last moment could not bring themselves to realise the possibility of their Master's death, who whenever He spoke to them on the subject could not understand His words or comprehend His meaning, who on the day He died were scattered as sheep without a shepherd, every hope buried in His grave, could within fifty days after the event be transformed into new men, with new hopes, new conceptions, new impulses, could confront danger, face persecution, and ascribe to a Crucified Man divine, predicates, which stood in direct contradiction to Jewish monotheism—though for such an ascription they could adduce no reason or justification higher at best than a " vague impression " or an " enthusiastic fancy."

* Joseph, *Bell. Jud.* chap. i, ; Stanley's *Sermons on the Apostolical Age,* p. 354.

† " Even after the destruction of Jerusalem many Jews clung to the hope of the renewal of the Temple, and the restoration of the services in their full splendour." Döllinger, ii. 416.

5. We are called upon to believe that in an age when neither civilisation nor philosophy had eradicated or simplified the ancient sacrificial ritual, when men were rather exhausting themselves in their efforts to invent some fresh ceremony of superstition, and were seeking in cruel and revolting rites purification from guilt and ease of mind, yet there emerged at this period, from the centre of Judaism, a Society of men to embody in a mysterious Rite the idea that all sacrificial observances had found their consummation and fulfilment in the degrading death of an obscure Galilean, who expiated the charge of blasphemy on the Cross.

6. Finally, we are called upon to believe that though the Rite only commemorated another of the innumerable triumphs of the great conqueror Death, though it only embodied a Disappointment, and enshrined Despair, yet, in spite of the proverbial difficulty of discovering any religion which can transcend the limits of its original home, it has secured an undisputed acceptance among the most cultured nations, and has succeeded in banishing into the darkness of oblivion one of the most deeply rooted forms of religious worship which has ever appeared in the world.

7. It is only necessary to review these difficulties, to see that they remain, and for ever must remain, absolutely unintelligible without the fact of the Resurrection. But if we accept the Resurrection as a fact as truly historical as the Passion, then we are in a position to interpret events which are notorious, which took place not in a fabulous age, but one of which we know a great deal, and which had its records, its monu-

ments, and its archives. We can understand whence came the flood of light which irradiated the minds of the first disciples, and which revealed to them once for all the true meaning of a Death they had not before dared to contemplate or even make the subject of enquiry.

8. If we accept the Resurrection as a fact, we can look back and see how it came to pass that, in spite of the shame of the Cross, the Christian Society could gather and concentrate itself around the Person and Work of Him who died thereon, and how the associations connected with a grand historical Deliverance of a single nation, commemorated in a Paschal Feast, could be absorbed in the commemoration of a grander, wider, more universal Victory.

9. This solution places us on sure and solid ground. We can look back and trace out the efficient cause of the greatest religious revolution the world has seen. In the Passion and Resurrection of our Lord, the Past and the Present find a common meeting point,* and shed each on the other a mutual light. That which was *Perfect* had come, that which was in *Part* was *done away*.

10. But if the Resurrection is nothing higher than a "vague impression" or a "glorious guess," what hope have we in this mysterious world? We must believe that its religious history was for upwards of four thousand years a long, purposeless parenthesis of useless rites and idle ceremonies. We must believe that Judaism pointed on to nothing, which was to be the reality and substance

---

* See Schlegel's *Philosophy of History*, p. 278; and Professor Westcott's remarks on the *Resurrection and History*, pp. 53—134.

of its mysterious ordinances.* We must believe that there was no Perfect Sacrifice, for which the ten thousand sacrifices of heathenism were a confused outcry. We must believe that " Death still remains the great Conqueror," of whose defeat no pledge event† has been given to mankind.

10 " Nature," says Goethe,‡ " tosses her creatures out of nothingness, and tells them not whence they come or whither they go : she wraps man in darkness, and makes him for ever long for light." Is abject prostration before her terrible forces and inexorable laws still to remain the only attitude for man ? What else is left for him, if the deepest yearning of his heart has never been satisfied, if He, who died upon the Cross, still lies near a Syrian town, and His Resurrection is a dream ?

---

* See Archer Butler's Sermons, i. 262. "Judaism with a typified atonement may be a miracle, or a chain of miracles ; but Judaism without it is a greater miracle still."

† On the death and resurrection of Jesus Christ as the *pledge* of our redemption, see Canon Swainson's *Hulsean Lectures*, p. 213; Archbp. Trench *On the Miracles*, p. 35.

‡ Goethe's *Aphorisms on Nature*, quoted in Farrar's *Hulsean Lectures*, p. 43 n.

THE VARIATIONS OF THE GOSPELS IN THEIR RELATION TO THE EVIDENCES AND TRUTH OF CHRISTIANITY.

BY THE

REV. T. R. BIRKS, M.A., CAMB.,

Professor of Moral Philosophy in the University of Cambridge, and Honorary Canon of Ely Cathedral.

The Variations of the Gospels in their Relation to the Evidences and Truth of Christianity.

"THE variations in the Gospels, in the midst of substantial unity, are no argument against their historical truth." Such is the original title of this lecture. The assertion is very modest and cautious. But I cannot do justice to my own convictions, or to the line of thought I wish to unfold, without going much beyond this purely defensive and limited averment. The real thesis I shall seek to establish, so far as time will allow, may be stated in these words: "The unity of the four Gospels amidst their partial diversity, and their diversities amidst substantial unity, are a powerful argument for their veracity, and the truth of the main facts they record. They are also a proof that the writers were guided and controlled by a higher wisdom than their own, and thus confirm the claim of the Gospels to be viewed as a Divine message to mankind."

The four Gospels, even apart from their sacred character, have certain features in which they seem unique and without a parallel. The number of persons, of whom memoirs have been published, is very great; and that of the memoirs themselves, of course, is much greater still. They vary widely in size and extent, from a few pages to several volumes. In this vast multitude of writings, I doubt whether another instance can be found of four memoirs, and four only, of the same person, professedly written by eye-witnesses of his life, or their immediate companions, each complete in itself, so brief that six or seven would be needed to make a volume of ordinary size, so closely connected that three of them have often been supposed to have made use of some common document, so distinct that friends as well as adversaries have often ascribed to them partial contradiction, and still oftener entire independence, and yet producing, when compared together, an almost irresistible impression of reality, honesty, and truth. In the whole range of known biographical literature, this fact seems to stand alone. No writings of the kind have left on plain and simple readers a stronger impression of reality. None have occasioned more difficulty to those who look below the surface, compare them with each other, and seek to explain in a reasonable way at once their differences and their agreement. The instrument is most simple. The effect produced is constant, long-lasting, and profound. These four simple, unadorned narratives, amounting to less than three hundred octavo pages, have determined and upheld the faith of millions of readers, have inspired the great, the noble, and the wise, with thoughts and hopes full of immortality, and have moulded the very history of the world through sixty generations down to the present day. Devout Christians see and own in this great fact the finger of God. The more closely they study it, the more will they find to confirm their faith. And sceptical doubters may well be invited to turn aside and see this strange sight, like that which Moses saw in the desert. The bush is so mean and humble in form and size, but it is lit up manifestly with a Divine glory. It has been beat upon with the fierce light of opposition and hatred, and surrounded by flames of persecution; and still it abides in its lowly beauty, unconsumed and imperishable, from age to age.

Let us first observe the remarkable unity of the four Gospels in the midst of their manifold diversity. We shall find here many clear marks of Divine wisdom, adapting them to their great object, and scarcely capable of being assigned to the purpose of the separate writers. I would single out these features, their fourfold character; their brevity, their silence, their simplicity, their proportion, their selection of minor incidents, their common aim and issue, rising through facts of history into a message of religious faith.

The first and simplest view of the Evangelists is that they are witnesses to the truth of certain facts, on which the whole fabric of Christianity depends. Now the rule of common sense and of the Jewish law is the same, that " in the mouth of two or three witnesses shall every word be established." A single Gospel, of the same length as the four we now have, and including all their details, would by no means answer the same end, and supply the historical basis which is needed, where the superstructure is of such immense importance. There would then be no concurrence of testimony. The building of our faith, instead of resting harmoniously on four pillars, would rest on one pillar alone. The principle laid down alike by Divine and human law would be set aside; and, however honest the solitary witness might be, his testimony would be wanting in the simplest, the most usual, and the most decisive mode of confirmation. And hence, while some histories of the Old Testament are confirmed only by fragmentary repetition in other books; and others occur in a double narrative, as in Samuel, Kings, and Chronicles; and some in a threefold account, as the Assyrian invasion and overthrow; a fourfold witness, exceeding the alternative of two or three witnesses prescribed in the law, is reserved for the Gospel record alone as the crowning and most vital part of the whole sacred history. This could be no plan of the earlier Evangelists. No sign of its contemplation, as a distinct purpose of the writer, appears even in the fourth Gospel, where there is no mention of the three which had already appeared. But a wisdom higher than their own has thus secured for all plain and simple readers an evidence of substantial truth, by the direct concurrence of two, three, and sometimes of four witnesses, which could not have been attained so fully and simply in any other way.

A second feature of the Gospels, closely allied to the list, is their brevity. When four narratives are given instead of one, each of them needs to be more brief, or else the total may become of inconvenient length. For one object in records of such events as these, which bear a sacred character and are intended to found a new faith, must be ready accessibility and ease of reproduction. A Gospel history, rivalling in size a folio volume, would have been greatly inferior in practical value. It would have been more rarely copied, more seldom studied and read, and even perhaps by a very few learned students alone. Christianity would thus have been in danger of becoming an esoteric creed, a kind of Eleusinian mystery, blindly received, with no roots in the general conscience, instead of a message appealing to mankind at large. Its moral worth must have been obscured and clouded, even if it did not wholly disappear. But the Gospels, from their brief size, are within the reach of the learned and unlearned alike, and may easily be read, or heard and remembered when read by others, by all who really care to become acquainted with the great truths and facts they reveal.

The Evangelists, if eye-witnesses, or intimates of eye-witnesses, must have had access to very large materials in those three years of our Lord's ministry, in which every day had its work and message of Divine love. Where the topic was of such absorbing interest, each of them would thus be naturally tempted to compose a very full account of the sayings and doings of One whom they loved and adored. Or, even if we assume for a moment the rival hypothesis that they were idealists and enthusiasts, who lived rather later, and whose actual materials were more scanty, still in such enthusiasts the same temptation would have appeared in another form. They would be prone to amplify their materials by comments, fancies, and rhetorical or poetical additions of their own; so that their work would gain in bulk, while it lost in solidity, and the rainbow hues of their own ardent fancy would have prolonged the narrative, and tinged it with a colouring due to that fancy alone.

Such a result seems probable on either view, had the Evangelists been common writers, and, in composing these sacred memoirs of the Lord, whom they so reverenced and honoured, had been left to their own human impulses and instincts alone. But now, on the contrary, a singular brevity marks all the four Gospels. Two of them correspond nearly in length to eighty pages of a modern octavo, the second to only fifty, and the fourth to sixty pages. And this in recording thirty years of a life, which they must have regarded with most profound interest, and three years of public labour, in which every day had actions or discourses worthy, in their view, of lasting honour and veneration.

Near akin to this brevity of the Evangelists is their remarkable silence. Two of them give an account of the birth and infancy of the Lord Jesus, and one records a solitary visit to Jerusalem at twelve years of age. But with this one exception, all of them pass over thirty years of His life in absolute silence. From the visit to Jerusalem with Joseph and Mary, when He stayed behind in the temple, to the opening of the Baptist's ministry, not one word is given on the life, the occupation, the friends, the companions or relatives, of the Master whom they loved and adored. Assuming the histories to be genuine, it is clear that their authors must have had access to a great variety of facts and incidents during those earlier years, of which no trace appears in the narrative. Indeed the later apocryphal

Gospels, the products of unrestrained and unscrupulous fancy, abound in supposed incidents of this very kind. The instinct of human curiosity, when freed from the secret control which guided the four sacred writers, indulged itself by filling up a void of which it was impatient. The common reverent silence of all the four Gospels on those earlier years of privacy and retirement is one out of many signs, that they were secretly guided in their work by a wisdom higher than their own.

Another feature of the four Gospels is their historical simplicity. The narrative they set before us is naked and unadorned. There is no independent preface or conclusion, no rhetorical amplification, but only narrative of the simplest, plainest, and most straightforward kind. They record events full of wonder, miracles of startling grandeur, words of surprising tenderness and dignity, which must have touched and stirred the deepest chords of believing and pious hearts. But the most superstitious devotee hardly abstains more rigorously from food on a fast day than the Evangelists refrain from commenting, in their own person, on the great events and sacred discourses they record. In the three first Gospels this abstinence seems to be complete. In the fourth, the writing of St. John in his old age, and intended plainly for those who had read one or more of the earlier Gospels, the rigour of this law is relaxed, and a few passing comments are interposed. But even when we include the sublime and reverent introduction, and the digression in chap. xii. on Jewish unbelief, they amount altogether, even here, to less than one-twentieth of the whole. This strict and severe historical simplicity, complete in the three earlier Gospels, and slightly relaxed, under special reasons for the change, in the fourth only, is wholly unlike the practice of mere enthusiasts. It implies a secret control exercised over the minds of the writers, restraining them from all utterance of their own deepest emotions, and confining them to the one office of providing a true and faithful record of the events themselves.

Another feature common to the four Gospels is their historical proportion. Two only give some account of the birth and infancy of our Lord. But the space occupied by this part of the narrative is only one-twelfth of the Gospels where it appears, or just one-twentieth of the whole record. Except one brief incident in St. Luke, the thirty years that follow are passed over, in each alike, in entire silence. The three years of the public ministry occupy two-thirds in St. Matthew and St. Mark, three-fourths in St. Luke, and three-fifths in St. John. The single week of conflict and suffering at the close, with the appearances after the resurrection, form one-third of St. Matthew and St. Mark, one-fourth in St. Luke, and two-fifths in St. John; or one-third of the four narratives, taken together. This one week then, with its sequel, fills as large a place in one Evangelist, and a larger in the rest, than each year, on the average, of the public ministry. Such a fulness in this part of the record may be explained in some measure by the deep interest it awakened in the minds of the writers, and of their readers, the first disciples. But this near approach to the same proportion in all the four, when combined further with their common silence as to all the earlier years, is a mark of Divine unity of plan in the fourfold narrative, hardly to be explained by human authorship alone, and which must impress every thoughtful and observant mind.

The large proportion of common incidents or repeated narratives is another prominent feature of the Gospels. Nearly every incident which is given by St. Mark appears also in St. Matthew, and also more than half, perhaps nearly two-thirds, of those which are recorded by St. Luke after the public ministry began. Now the facts and words recorded in all the Gospels must bear a small proportion to the events themselves. This contrast receives a passing notice from St. John at the close of the fourth Gospel. During the three years of our Lord's ministry each day would have had its work, or its sayings and discourses, public or private, worthy of record, and all would be of deep interest to the first believers in Jesus as the long promised Messiah, the Incarnate Son of God. Such words or actions, we may well suppose, filled up six or seven hours at least of every day throughout the thousand days of that public ministry. And how much, or rather how little, has been placed on record! All the sayings of our Lord in the four Gospels, even neglecting the plain fact that repeated records are given of the same address or conversation, might be read or spoken deliberately within six or seven hours only. Thus it appears that what is actually recorded is not one part in a hundred, but more nearly one in a thousand, of the whole amount of what the Lord Jesus did and spoke during His public ministry. Thus the words of St. John are a very lawful hyperbole, that if the whole were recorded, " the world would not be able to contain the books that should be written."

How is it that, while the materials in themselves were so ample, the writers traverse plainly so much common ground? The fresh facts in the third and fourth Gospels show clearly that means of enlargement and expansion were within their reach. Consciously or unconsciously, they thus fulfilled one main purpose of consenting witnesses of the events, by confirming each other's testimony to the main facts of their common narrative. If the later had seen the earlier, as must clearly have been the case with St. John, this does not affect the conclusion. One main object of a fourfold record is signally fulfilled, and, most of the selected incidents being the same, in the mouth of two or three witnesses the words are established.

There is another mark of unity, nowhere obtrusive, which underlies all the four narratives. Their common object is to prove the great doctrine that Jesus of Nazareth is the true Messiah of God. And hence, unlike the Epistles, or even the Book of Acts, the personal name, Jesus, is used simply throughout, almost to the exclusion of every other. This practice is uniform and constant in the two earlier Gospels, with one exception at the very close of the second. In St. Luke there are only about ten exceptions, and in St. John about six or seven in explanatory remarks, while the name Jesus is actually used more than two hundred times in either Gospel. Titles of honour and reverence, such as occur perpetually in all the Epistles, must have risen spontaneously to their lips. That they should uniformly have refrained from them is more than a mark of unity in the midst of diversity. It is a sign also of that secret wisdom by which these sacred memoir-writers were guided and controlled. The hand of God's Spirit was upon them, while they wrote, and, in spite of their strong instinct of deep reverence for their Divine Master, confined them to the use of that simpler title, Jesus, which suited best with the great purpose of their record. An advocate is unskilful, and damages his own cause, who assumes in the outset that guilt or innocence of his client which it is his business to prove. The Evangelists, then, were not allowed to obtrude prematurely their own deep convictions on their readers. The facts were to speak for themselves without a commentary. And this design, common to all the four writers, is simply and clearly stated at the close of the latest Gospel: "These things are written, that ye may believe that Jesus is the Christ, the Son of God, and that believing ye may have life through His name."

The variations of the Gospels, however, have often been held to counteract the evidence of their truth and inspiration, derived from these and other marks of striking unity in the four narratives, and their consent in all the main facts they reveal. I believe that they have really, when closely questioned, and seen aright, an opposite effect; and supply still stronger reasons, because more latent, and needing deeper thought for their detection, to prove them not only honest and veracious narratives, but inspired messages of sacred truth. The subject, however, is too wide and inexhaustible to be treated properly in a single lecture. I will strive to condense as much as possible under seven or eight heads, some of the main grounds which lead me, without any hesitation or doubt, to this important conclusion.

The mutual relation of differing witnesses to the same facts or events may be roughly classed under five varieties: dishonest and collusive agreement; honest agreement, but deceptive and illusive; honest discordance, so wide and deep as to render the consent nearly worthless; a like discordance so limited and partial, as to strengthen the remaining concurrence, and leave the weight of the testimony not seriously impaired; and, last of all, consistent and reconcilable diversity, which confirms in the first place the independence and plurality of the witness, and, when questioned more deeply, serves to establish its perfect truth.

The first case is that of a collusive and fraudulent concert to bear false witness. In this case the agreement, at first sight, may seem more perfect than with genuine evidence. But the seeming perfection of the harmony, unless the witnesses are of high character, and well-known, awakens strong suspicion, and the consent breaks down in a rigorous cross-examination on points overlooked and forgotten in the concerted story. The diversities of the Gospels, which have perplexed believers, and gratified hasty adversaries, have at least one clear gain. They exclude this first alternative altogether. No dishonest compact could have produced four Gospels with so much of seeming discordance hard to explain.

The second case is that of an agreement illusive, but not dishonest. In our courts of law important witnesses in a cause are not allowed to be present, while any one of them is giving evidence. It is not supposed that most of them would be dishonest, and consciously garble their own statements, so as to agree better with those which they have heard. But it is wisely judged that witnesses of imperfect memory and average clearness of thought and judgment would be biassed unconsciously by such previous knowledge. If they wished to confirm the general drift of the previous evidence, they would emphasize points of agreement, and insensibly pass by points of difference, or those of which their own first impressions were different and opposite. The evidence, if not rendered a mere repetition, would become more alike, or in the case of opposing witnesses more widely divergent, than if their depositions were made in perfect ignorance of those which had gone before. The divergences of the Gospels equally exclude this second hypothesis. There is no such agreement, either collusive or illusive, as would result from dishonest concert, or even from the unconscious moulding of independent testimony to avoid any appearance of discord and partial contradiction.

Many Christian writers have carried this view so far as to maintain that the Evangelists wrote in complete independence, and never saw each other's writings. But this is to assume an improbable fact, without evidence, in order to strengthen a conclusion which results directly from the certain facts alone. The divergences of the Gospels really prove the truth of one of two alternatives, and do not decide between them. The first is that the later had not seen the earlier, and were wholly independent. The second is that they were witnesses too honest, too vivid, and of too high an order, to garble their own testimony, or disguise divergences in their view of the life they record, in order to avoid the risk of being charged with contradiction, and thus to produce on superficial minds an impression of more complete agreement.

Three alternatives then alone remain. The first is that of the honest doubter or sceptic, who thinks that the Gospels contain proofs of partial contradiction, and these so extensive as really to damage and almost destroy their claims to credit, even where they agree. The second is that of many Christians, more candid and accommodating than thorough going and entire in their defence of the Gospel history. The third and last is that which has been the usual faith of the Church of Christ, and to which I myself fully and firmly adhere, that the contradictions of the Gospels are apparent, not real; that they change sides when closely and fairly examined, and are then transformed into more latent and decisive evidence of their common truth and Divine inspiration.

Now in comparing the two former views, truth requires an admission to be made on either side. If the facts recorded in the Gospels were common facts, and the case were the same as of an ordinary civil or criminal trial, or an historical inquiry of the usual kind, the preponderance in favour of the Christian advocate would be immense and overwhelming. The substantial agreement so far exceeds the partial disagreements, as, when every abatement is made for alleged inaccuracies or apparent contradictions, to leave the main evidence far stronger than that of any single testimony, however honest and trustworthy. But then, on the other hand, the case is not the same. The facts to be attested are special and extraordinary. They depart wholly from the usual character of human experience. They profess to be the groundwork of a Divine revelation, which claims the allegiance, and affects the present and future destiny, of countless millions of men. The foundation of a building needs to be strong, in proportion to the weight of the superstructure to be reared upon it. The Gospel history, from its very object and nature, needs a degree of strength in the evidence of its truth beyond the measure of a common suit at law, or any ordinary question in modern history. These writings claim indirectly to be sacred documents, records of a Divine message. As such they have been received and honoured by the Church in successive generations. An amount of inaccuracy and contradiction, which would scarcely have any sensible effect in lowering their character, and weakening the effect of their concurrence, if their contents were of a vulgar and ordinary kind, must here assume a very different importance. In the first place, it destroys at once their claims to special and Divine inspiration in the sense which Christians have usually attached to the phrase, for a God of perfect truth and holiness cannot prompt and inspire even partial falsehood. And it forms a moral objection, even to their substantial truth, of a very real kind. Such a message, involving results of immense and vital importance, according as it is neglected or received, must surely demand from the wisdom of its Author some answerable care in the mode of its delivery to mankind. It seems most unlikely, if truly Divine, that it would be obscured and placed in jeopardy, by entrusting it to ill-informed witnesses, who on many details disprove and contradict each other. So that these alternatives land us in a strange paradox. If the Gospel be viewed as a purely human message, the evidence is decisive and overwhelming to prove the truth of the main facts, and hence that the whole is Divine. If viewed as Divine, and the existence of partial and repeated contradictions be allowed, there arises at once a strong presumption against its supernatural claims, which must tend to lower it to the rank of an ill-attested and therefore human message.

But if, on the other hand, the seeming contradictions are apparent only, and the variations in the four Gospels are instances of reconcilable diversity, the body and form of the history and its moral essence are in harmony with each other. The apparent divergences are signs of the honesty of every separate witness, while their agreement; beneath the surface, when brought to light, becomes even a stronger proof than their direct and open correspondence for the truth of their common message, and the Divine inspiration under which it has been given. And if I can show, under many different heads, that the variations are of this character, that they are not signs of imperfect knowledge, or the chance-medley of uninformed and careless narrators, but are full of marks of design which become visible only after close research, and do not appear on the surface, the thesis of this lecture will have been abundantly, though not exhaustively proved.

The mutual relation of the four Gospels as to sameness and diversity is my first argument. Is this the result of chance and a fortuitous concourse of witnesses, if not dishonest, at least vague, enthusiastic, imperfectly-informed, or easily deceived? Or does it yield, when examined, all the signs of a hidden and mysterious wisdom? It may be urged, on a casual view, that St. Mark is so much like St. Matthew, and the incidents are so entirely common, that it hardly can be viewed as a separate testimony; and that the facts in St. John are so distinct as hardly to confirm the other Gospels, or to be confirmed by them, but rather to awaken the doubt how a miracle like the raising of Lazarus could have been silently omitted by three previous writers.

But now let us apply a key which the Bible and common sense both provide, and at once a secret and unsuspected harmony comes to light. "In the mouth of two or three witnesses every word shall be established.' In weighty questions of fact the concurrence of two witnesses is almost essential, that of three is desirable, to be the ground of a reasonable faith. A fourth is a kind of luxury or superfluity. Hence, if we have four successive memoirs on a subject of high importance, which hold the character of human or Divine witnesses, when they are taken in order, three results naturally follow. The second, compared with the first, will have for its main and almost sole object to confirm the earlier testimony. The third, compared with its two predecessors, will have the double object, in almost equal measure, to confirm facts already given, and to supplement them with fresh information. The fourth, again, being nearly superfluous for the end of confirmation, may be expected to be almost entirely a supplement and completion to the rest.

Now this, on close observation, will be found to be the exact relation between the four Gospels; assuming, as we may reasonably do, that the traditional order in which they now stand is also the true order of their first appearance. St. Mark differs doubly from St. Matthew, by a comparative absence of our Lord's discourses, and by the greater fulness with which the outward details of His miracles and journeyings are described. But the incidents recorded are almost wholly the same. The chief exceptions are only these—the presence of wild beasts in the hour of temptation; the healing of the deaf man in the coasts of Decapolis, and of the blind man at Bethsaida; the reply to St. John as to the man who was casting out devils in the name of Jesus; and the incident of the young man, who fled naked from the soldiers in the hour of temptation, treachery, and sorrow.

St. Luke, again, as compared with St. Matthew, holds exactly a middle place. He agrees with him, and differs from St. Mark, in recording the miraculous conception, the birth, and the infancy of the Lord Jesus. But the facts connected with them in detail are almost wholly different. Again, in the public ministry the facts recorded are either the same, or closely similar, through six chapters, or about one-fourth of the Gospel. The accounts then mainly diverge, though still with some common features, in Luke ix. 51—xviii. 14, or eight chapters and one-fourth of two others. The agreement is then substantial, though not complete and unbroken, through seven remaining chapters to the close. The confirmatory and supplemental characters thus coexist in nearly equal proportion.

In St. John the relation varies once more, but still conforms to the same secret law. Except the record of the miracle of the five thousand in the former half of chapter vi., and that of the eventful week of the Passion, all the incidents, without exception, are fresh and original, and such as had not been given by the three others. Even in the record of the last week, the new facts or new discourses greatly exceed those which are resumed, and had been already given before. Yet still there are so many allusions to facts already recorded, as familiar and notorious, that the Gospel takes its place as one harmonious and needful element in the structure of the conjoint and fourfold narrative.

This special relation of the four Gospels, inwrought into their whole texture, by which they are essentially diverse, with a distinct plan and method in their diversity, the second simply confirming the first, the third confirming and supplementing the first and second, the fourth and last restricted almost wholly to the office of supplementing those which had been published before, is a powerful argument that their variations, far from disproving their Divine origin, are really the direct consequence and effect of that Divine wisdom which presided at their birth.

2. The historical unity and adaptation of each Gospel is a second argument.

These four Gospels, however closely united and widely circulated in later times, must have had, each of them, its own immediate and special object, depending either on the date, or the special class of disciples or inquirers for whose use it was composed. The circle to which they all appealed was not homogeneous. In fact the history of the early growth of Christianity reveals four successive centres, and differing classes for whom such provision would naturally be made. The first centre was Jerusalem, or perhaps rather Galilee, the home and centre of the first disciples who were gained to the faith, and whose first thought would be the conversion of their Jewish brethren. The second centre was Cæsarea, where the first Gentile convert, Cornelius, the Roman centurion, was gathered in. The Roman soldiers and civilians resident in Palestine were the first class, beyond the Jews, to whom the Gospel was accessible, and Cæsarea, the scene of that conversion, was like the Syrian outpost of Imperial Rome. The third centre was Antioch, where the name Christian had its birth, and where extensive preaching to the Greeks first began. The fourth and last centre was Ephesus, where St. Paul resided two years, and St. John still later took up his residence, with the other Asian churches, which form the subject of address in the opening of that prophecy, which carries on the sacred history, and completes the record of the New Testament.

The four Gospels have features of marked correspondence with these four successive centres of the early church history. They seem adapted, in the first place, for Jewish or Galilean inquirers and disciples, for Roman military converts, for the Greeks of Antioch and Syria, and for believers established in the faith, like the churches of Asia, over which St. John presided in his latest years. St. Matthew begins with the promises to the Jews in Abraham and David, and a genealogy wich connects our Lord with the line of the kings of Judah. He introduces him at once under this special title, the King of the Jews. He presents Him to us as the Lawgiver, greater than Moses, and appeals throughout to the Jewish prophecies which He fulfilled. St. Mark, again, whose name is a Roman name, records chiefly the actions of Christ, and omits His discourses, in harmony with the practical and outward character of the Roman mind. He uses the Latin, not the Greek name, for the Roman centurion and the executioner. He expounds Jewish usages, as if writing directly for readers who were outside the Jewish synagogue. But he nowhere expounds or explains Jewish localities, which implies that he addressed readers familiar with the country, and the sites and towns of Palestine. St. Luke, by early tradition, was a native and resident of Antioch. His Gospel, and still more the Book of Acts, have the features of classic Greek histories. He professes to have inquired closely into the facts by a comparison of authorities, and to observe the order of time. He introduces features especially Syrian, the government of Cyrenius, the years of Tiberius, the four tetrarchies and their occupants, the rivalry of Herod and Pilate, and the name of Herod's steward, and speaks of Arimathea, "a city of the Jews," as if his readers were not familiar with Jewish localities. St. John, again, writes as for those who were established in the faith, and familiar with the names and character of the apostles, and he continually mentions the Jews in a way which implies that the separation of the Church from the Jewish people and synagogue was then complete. This unity, in character and tone of each Gospel, corresponding with four quickly successive stages of the Church's development, and of which the types may be seen in Jerusalem and the five hundred Galilean disciples; in Cæsarea, Cornelius, and the first Roman converts; in Antioch and the Hellenists who first received the title of Christians; and in Ephesus and the Asian churches, when Jerusalem had fallen, and the Church had received its full development, is one out of many proofs that the diversity of the Gospels far from being the result of chance, and involving imperfection and contradiction, arises from the reality of their adaptation to special classes of readers in the early times.

3. The moral and spiritual unity of each Gospel is a third argument that their diversity is no result of ignorance and imperfection, but fulfils a secret and important design of their Divine Revealer.

The Gospel is a message at once intensely real and sublimely ideal. In this it corresponds to the great doctrine on which it is based, the Incarnation. Each of the four has its distinctive unity on the real side, as adapted to a special class, for whose use it was first written. St. Matthew corresponds with the wants of the first Jewish inquirers, and St. John with those of the full-grown believers of the Asian churches. But there is a like distinction and contrast no less observable on the doctrinal and spiritual side. This has led to their association, from early times, with the sacred symbols of the cherubim. Space will not allow me to amplify and confirm this contrast. Stated briefly, it may be thus expressed. The first Gospel looks backward, and links the life of Christ with all the earlier messages of the Old Testament, and exhibits His claims as a Lawgiver and King. The second looks outward, and exhibits Him as the Great Husbandman, unwearied in patient labour. It omits His longer discourses, but gives the outward and visible details of His work far more largely than St. Matthew; and it retains this outward character to the last.

in the form of that parting charge, to preach the Gospel to every creature. St. Luke deals with the human and priestly or sacred elements of our Lord's person and work. His Gospel looks forward to the later triumphs of the faith, and the spread of the Church, and hence it finds its continuation in a later work of the same writer, the Acts of the Apostles. St. John's Gospel looks upward. It begins with a distinct revelation of the truth that Jesus is the Word of God, become incarnate for man's salvation. And it closes, not with a message concerning the earthly diffusion of the Gospel, but like the others, with a call to heavenward aspiration: "Jesus saith unto him, Follow Me!"

This double unity, which close observation reveals in each of the four Gospels, both on the historical and the ideal side, removes their diversity from the region of chance and imperfection into that of profound adaptation and Divine wisdom. As the slight diversities in the two pictures of a stereoscope are not accidental and trivial errors, but the very elements on which our full conception of solidity depends, so this fourfold presentation of the life of our Lord combines special adaptation to the wants of the Church in its first origin and growth, with an harmonious fourfold exhibition of His perfection, who is the King, the Shepherd, and the Sympathising High Priest, and more than all, the Second Adam, the Lord from Heaven.

Let us now examine rapidly a few of the main discrepancies in detail, and we shall see that they yield, when sifted, only deep and latent signs and proofs of unity and Divine wisdom.

4. The Genealogies.

The contrast of the two genealogies in St. Matthew and St. Luke meets us at the opening of the Gospels. It has given rise to a great variety of Christian comments and explanations; and to objections, often repeated and raised, on the part of opposers of the faith. The question to be answered is this. Does their contrast prove ignorance and error, or is it a reconcilable diversity, which gives the strongest evidence of special design, guiding and overruling this double record?

The true explanation, in spite of all sceptical cavils, and the frequent mistakes even of Christian commentators, seems to me clear, simple, and decisive, and amounts to a moral demonstration. St. Matthew and St. Luke both agree to affirm our Lord's " miraculous conception." He was, in popular estimation and in right of legal inheritance alone, the Son of Joseph. But He was really and substantially the Son of Mary, and had no earthly father. In common cases a man may have three genealogies. The first in precedence and dignity is the paternal, the line of his father. The second, which comes next, is the maternal, the line of his mother. The third, in some cases only, is the adoptive or purely legal, the line of an adopted father. By the first and second, natural qualities may be transmitted. The child inherits the likeness only of real parents; the third does not convey natural characters, but legal rights alone. The case of our Lord was peculiar and unique. He had a real mother, but no real human father. The paternal and the adoptive line were one and the same, and the maternal alone was the real line. One was the popular genealogy, and decided

His legal right of inheritance in the public eye; but the other alone was a true descent, and decided the form and true character of the great mystery of the incarnation. Thus the genealogy, which usually has the first place in dignity and importance, here becomes the second, and the second becomes the first. That Joseph should be of the seed of David was essential, if our Lord was to seem even to outward observers, ignorant of the mystery of His birth, to be the heir of the promises. That Mary should be of the seed of David was essential, that the promise of a Messiah of the seed of David might be really fulfilled, and not in deceptive appearance alone. The paternal genealogy would still be of high importance. It would serve to establish the claims of Jesus of Nazareth in the outward court of Jewish law and opinion, where the mystery of His birth was unknown. The other genealogy would be more important still, since on this would rest the fulfilment of many prophecies, and the real truth of His title as the Son of David.

This contrast, plain to a reflecting mind, explains the two sacred genealogies. Both in form belong to Joseph, but he could not have two fathers, two strictly paternal genealogies. If one is proper, one must be improper, that is maternal, conjugal, or adoptive. The proper line of Joseph could only give an improper, legal, and adoptive line of the Son of Mary. A maternal or other adoptive line of Joseph would be neither a proper nor an improper line of Jesus. But the conjugal line of Joseph, as the son-in-law of Mary's father, would be the true line of our Lord's actual descent. St. Matthew, coming first, gives the descent by which our Lord would be usually recognised by the Jews as the Son of Joseph. For he wrote for Jews, and his genealogy precedes his narrative of the incarnation. The term used is one which requires strict and real descent, and is never used of a father-in-law or a merely adoptive parent. In the last step, then, the imperfection of this genealogy comes to light. "And Jacob begat Joseph, the husband of Mary, of which Mary was born Jesus, who is called the Christ." In St. Luke the genealogy comes later, at the time of the baptism, after the mystery of the miraculous birth has been fully unfolded. The descent of Mary and Joseph alike is referred to the Davidic family. The name of her unborn Son, as the Son of David, is given Him in the same message which excludes an earthly father. And the connective term throughout the whole list would apply equally to a son, a son by adoption, or a son-in-law. In the Talmudical writings, also, Mary is called the daughter of Heli. The later Gospel, then, designed for Gentile converts, and tracing the line up to Adam, not down from Abraham, replaces the legal genealogy of our Lord's putative father by one still more important, that of His real mother, on which alone His Davidic descent and the mystery of His incarnation in human flesh really depend. The minor diversities would detain me too long. But I believe that they admit equally of a solution which shows the Divine harmony of the narratives and their common truth.

5. The accounts of our Lord's infancy in the two Gospels have been further charged by Strauss and others with direct contradiction. "It is impossible," he

states boldly, "that both can be true, and one must necessarily be false." St. Luke makes Nazareth the original residence. But Matthew ii. 22, it is said, "renders certain that Matthew did not suppose Nazareth, but Bethlehem, to have been the original dwelling-place." When he represents Joseph on his return as prevented from going to Judea solely by his fear of Archelaus, he ascribes to him an inclination to proceed to that province, unaccountable if the affair of the Census alone had taken him to Bethlehem, and which is only to be explained by the supposition he had formerly dwelt there.

This objection, made with a confidence truly amazing, will be found on examination, as is often the case, to change sides and become a strong evidence for the truth of the sacred history. It is here assumed that the good-will of a Jewish carpenter's business in a Galilean village, away from the traditional home of his family, would be an attraction of such extreme force, that no providential changes, however surprising, no angelic visions and messages, no hopes of honour and royalty for the new-born son, whose birth itself was a miracle unique and unexampled, could possibly break the spell, or ever induce Joseph to prefer the birthplace of Jewish royalty to the despised and ill-famed Galilean village. But what notion could be more unreasonable and preposterous? Are working carpenters so immovable from place to place in our own days? Once assume the reality of the main facts recorded, and their effect on the minds of Joseph and Mary might be foreseen with certainty, had the Gospel been silent, and the least knowledge of human nature might have made it plain,

even to the dull eyes of a dreaming speculator and
recluse. They had been brought to Bethlehem unexpectedly, at the very time when the promised child was
born. An angel had announced His royal honours. Wise
men from the east had laid royal gifts at His feet. Jerusalem had been stirred by the tidings, and Herod's fears
awakened by the tidings of a rival who was destined
to succeed to David's throne. The words in the
message to the Virgin had received repeated
pledges and signs of their truth. What place could
be so fit and natural as David's home for the
training and dwelling place of his heir and successor,
till the way should be open for His assuming His rightful
honours? All the indications of the present, the memories
of the past, and the hopes of a near future would conspire
to impress the parents with the thought that here surely,
in the city of David, to which the Roman decree had
brought them, where eastern sages had been guided to
come and worship, and where a prophecy, newly repeated
to Herod, had fixed Messiah's origin, was the right and
fitting place for the great work of educating for His
promised dignity the Son who had just been born.
The idea that Joseph would of course, on his return
from Egypt, have gone back to Nazareth to recover
his tools, or, to revive his suspended business as a
carpenter, and forsake his ancestral seat, the seat
of royal ancestors, and the birthplace of the coming
King, is worthy of a dreamy pedant, steeped in the
spirit of doubting and self-conceit, but unworthy of a
reasonable man. What is said to be a necessary proof
of falsehood is a clear sign of consistency and truth.
The Evangelist does not pause to explain what explains

itself, when all the facts are thoroughly considered. The seeming contrast of the two Gospels, when the transition in the minds of Joseph and Mary would follow so naturally and inevitably from the wonders recorded, and the hopes to which they must have led, is really a powerful indirect evidence of their common truth. The writers, it has been well said, "were too well aware of their agreement and consistency to be afraid of the effect of apparent collision. They neither apprehended it themselves, nor feared that it would be objected to them by others."

6. The main scene and locality of our Lord's public ministry is the next principal subject, on which seeming contrast and disagreement turns, on further search, into a remarkable harmony of statement. The three first Gospels agree to place our Lord's ministry in Galilee. They begin, after His baptism, by speaking of His removal from Nazareth to Capernaum. And after this all the local allusions are Galilean, down to the last week, when the passage through Judea and the entry into Jerusalem, were followed by the crucifixion. The places named in St. Matthew are successively, Capernaum, Galilee and Decapolis, Capernaum, the Sea of Galilee, the Gergesenes, Chorazin and Bethsaida, the sea side, Nazareth, a desert place near the sea, Gennesaret, the coasts of Tyre and Sidon, the sea of Galilee again, the coasts of Magdala, Cæsarea Philippi, Galilee once more, and the coasts of Judea beyond Jordan. In St. Mark nearly the same, with one added miracle in Decapolis, and one at Bethsaida, In St. Luke, we have Nazareth, Capernaum, Gennesaret, the wilderness, Capernaum, Nain, the land of the Gadarenes,

Bethsaida, Chorazin, the midst of Samaria and Galilee, and Jericho. The disciples are identified by their Galilean dialect. And in the Book of Acts the same feature is conspicuous on the question at the day of Pentecost, "Are not all these which speak Galileans."

But here an objection will arise. For our Lord is described as saying before His death—"O Jerusalem, Jerusalem! how often would I have gathered thy children, and ye would not!" The complaint is given, at different times, both by St. Matthew and St. Luke. Yet strange to say, in all the three first Gospels we have no single line to show that this complaint was true, or that such attempts had ever been made.

When we turn to St. John, in its almost entire diversity of materials, its wholly supplemental character, we have a key by which the perplexity is entirely removed. This Gospel speaks scarcely at all of the Galilean ministry. Its contents belong, with one exception, to the successive visits our Lord paid to Jerusalem. The first of these is recorded in ch. ii. at the first Passover, and was followed by a stay of some weeks in Judea, before the opening of the Galilean ministry. The second was the visit when the impotent man was healed, at a feast of the Jews, which was probably the second Passover. At the third Passover, from the malice of the Jews, which then endangered our Saviour's life, no visit was paid to the metropolis, because the time of His sacrifice was too remote. Here only one main event in Galilee is recorded, shortly before the Passover, and then we are told that He went on walking in Galilee, because of that murderous malice of the Jews. But then followed, in the latter part of that year, two successive visits, one at the Feast of Tabernacles, and another at the Feast of Dedication. And thus, by comparison, the enigma is solved, and the Divine complaint of the Saviour is verified. The ministry was mainly Galilean. But its course had been intersected by four visits to Jerusalem at the first and second Passovers, the third Feast of Tabernacles and of Dedication. And it was during a fifth and final visit that those sacred words were uttered, of complaint and sorrow at their persevering unbelief.

Other main topics, to which the same truth will fully apply, that seeming divergence conceals below its surface deep evidence of real consistency and truth, are these: the apparent dislocation of separate sayings or miracles, the real irregularity of one part of St. Matthew, the relation of the Sermon on the Mount to the same or a similar discourse in St. Luke, the visits to Nazareth, the call of the four apostles, the two miraculous draughts of fishes, the celebration of the Last Passover, and the narratives of the Resurrection. But each of these would almost require a separate lecture, and my time is nearly exhausted. I would close with a few remarks upon the first alone.

Whenever it is made an objection to the accuracy of the Evangelists that the same, or nearly the same, parable or saying or miracle is found in very different parts of the narrative, one plain fact seems to be forgotten, or at least the weight is not given to it which its importance deserves. All the sayings of our Lord, recorded in the four Gospels, including every repetition of those doubly or trebly recorded, might be spoken deliberately without undue haste, in much less than the working hours of a single day. But our Lord's public ministry lasted three full years, or more than a thousand days. None of these were spent in dull inaction or total silence. Each of them was filled with its own works and words of love. And thus the whole of His sacred words, if all alike had been given in their own time and place, must have formed a volume nearly a thousand fold larger than the collective amount of the four Gospels. But His life was one of ceaseless journeying from town to town, and from village to village. The same discourse in substance, even when of considerable length, may probably have been delivered to some thronging audience ten or twenty times, but varied by new insertions and additions, and the omission of some parts which were spoken before. In the case of shorter sayings, brief parables or maxims of Divine wisdom, there is no reason why several of them may not have been really uttered, in different places, even hundreds of times. There is no presumption, then, when such passages are found differently placed in different Gospels, for supposing that one or the other has erred wholly in their arrangement. On the contrary, there may often be traced a remarkable suitableness and beauty in some change, which occurs in the later repetition, under fresh circumstances, of a saying already uttered. Thus we read in St. Matthew at the Mission of the Twelve, "Are not two sparrows sold for a farthing? and one of them shall not fall on the ground without your Father. But the very hairs of your head are all numbered." In St. Luke, apparently much later, after the Mission of the Seventy and their return, "Are not five sparrows sold for two farthings? and not one of them is forgotten before God. But even the very hairs of your head are all numbered." How strangely does the general truth, the care of Divine Providence even over events the most minute and seemingly insignificant, receive a fresh illustration, when our Lord can notice even so slight a change in the usual price, at one time or another, at one place or another, of the sparrows themselves!

I feel how impossible it is, within the limits of a lecture, to do justice to a subject so wide as the one on which I have offered these remarks. I would hope on some other occasion to complete the outline, and to throw some new light, which I believe to be possible, on the topics I have named, but am compelled for the present to pass by. I can only, in closing, express my own deep conviction, not lightly formed, but the result of careful examination, that the objections brought against the consistency and truth of the Gospel, even those which have sometimes been hastily accepted as real by Christians themselves, are due to imperfect, superficial study, or hasty and groundless inference alone, and that in the great majority of cases they serve only to disclose a secret harmony, too deep and full to be seen by careless eyes. For if hundreds of years are too short a time to trace out all the wonders of God in His works, and to discover and unfold those laws which order the course of the planets, and govern the currents and tides of the ocean, how can we wonder that difficulties should meet us at first sight, and only yield slowly to patient thought, prayerful inquiry, and intelligent comparison of Scripture with Scripture, in that Word of God which is more excellent in His sight than even all the works of Nature, and of which we read that stately description, "Thou hast magnified Thy Word above all Thy Name."

THE APOCRYPHAL GOSPELS.

BY
B. HARRIS COWPER.

The Apocryphal Gospels.

IT is worthy of notice that some writers who seek to disparage the four Canonical Gospels ingeniously endeavour to exalt the so-called Gospels which are Apocryphal. To raise these spurious and third rate productions to the level of the genuine Gospels is not all that is meant; if it were, the question would soon be decided. There is a sinister purpose behind, and that is, to pull down the true Gospels by means of the false. Now we believe the former are of inestimable value, while of the latter we say with Dr. Ellicott, the present Bishop of Gloucester: "Their real demerits, their mendacities, their coarseness, the barbarities of their style, and the inconsequence of their narratives, have never been excused or condoned. It would be hard to find any competent writer in any age of the Church, who has been beguiled into saying anything civil or commendatory."* Every word of this will be endorsed by the most accomplished of even sceptical critics, who will admit with M. Nicolas, who is not in the ranks of orthodoxy, that "in reality, they are all, without exception, infinitely beneath

* Cambridge Essays for 1856, p. 153.

the Canonical Gospels in all respects."* Such are the books we have to deal with now.

The course pursued by the more skilful opposers of the true Gospels is, to confess the want of authenticity, authority, veracity, and merit of the Apocryphal Gospels, and then to turn round upon us and say, " Your Gospels labour under similar defects, and yet the others are as ancient, and have been received with similar reverence by the Churches!" We, on the contrary, maintain that they are not as ancient, and were never of equal authority among orthodox Christians. We might demand of our adversaries the proof of what they say, but without waiting for that, we are ready to disprove it. The two classes of books have been carefully investigated, and the result is that only folly or fraud can place them on the same level. This is true, whether we regard them from a critical, an historical, a moral, or a religious point of view. Some of these matters I hope to make clear before I conclude; but I must proceed now to say what the Apocryphal Gospels are.

In the introduction to my translation of those which exist I have written as follows: " Several of these books are still extant in one language or another, but of the larger part we only possess fragments, or the mere titles. I would thus describe in a few words the character of the books in question: They are all spurious; they all relate to Christ and to those who were associated with Him in His earthly career, or to the Apostles and their associates; they all seek to supplement or develop

---

* Etudes sur les Evangiles Apocryphes. Pref. p. xxiii.

the writings of the New Testament; and all that we have are of more recent date than any of the Canonical books. The series commenced in the second century at latest, and continued for many centuries. The materials are drawn, partly from the New Testament, partly from traditions, and partly from the imagination of their authors. They are of no historical or doctrinal authority, and were never officially recognised in the Church." These remarks apply to all the New Testament Apocrypha, and therefore to the false Gospels, which alone at present concern us.

I will trouble you with another extract from my book, in which I give an explanation of the origin and intention of the Apocryphal Gospels, and similar books:—

"I. The Evangelical narratives were simple and meagre in their mode of describing what (1) preceded, (2) attended, and (3) followed, the facts with which they are mainly concerned. This applies to

"(1), The Family of Christ; (2), His Infancy; (3), His Inauguration; (4), His Trial and Crucifixion; (5), His visit to the Underworld; (6), His Resurrection and Ascension; (7), His Mother and the Apostles afterwards.

"II. The Evangelical narratives were almost or wholly silent on various points, *e.g.*

"(1), Doctrines to be believed, but requiring explanation; (2), Certain matters connected with the unseen and spiritual world; and (3), The organisation and discipline of the Church.

"III. Sundry sects, heresies, and parties wanted support from Apostolical and Divine authorities.

"IV. Men took pleasure in producing religious novels, fictions, Hagadoth (a Jewish form of religious fiction), or whatever we call them; and they knew such things were popular."

Let me repeat that "the materials are drawn, partly from the New Testament, partly from traditions, and partly from the imagination of their authors." This being the case, while we admit that they contain elements which are true, we are required to speak of them as fictions. They are not all wholly false, and they were not all meant to be taken as literal history. A similar principle holds good with other books and works of art. It is applicable to the "Paradise Lost" of Milton, the "Pilgrim's Progress" of Bunyan, and the "Robinson Crusoe" of Defoe, to the historical plays of Shakespeare, the historical novels of Scott, to Franklin's "Parable of Abraham," and to the "Ammergau Passion Play." It applies also to Godfrey Kneller's picture in Hampton Court Palace of "William III. Landing at Torbay," to David's painting in the Louvre of "Napoleon crossing the Alps," and to the "Shadow of Death" by Holman Hunt. These all rest upon a basis of truth, but not one of them represent events as they happened. As their merits are independent of historical accuracy, so are the merits or demerits of the Apocryphal Gospels.

In some respects certain of the false Gospels cannot be compared with the works I have enumerated; I mean those which were written in the interests of heresy or of superstition. That some were so written is matter of history, and that it is true even of a part of those which we have in a more or less complete state is apparent to every careful student,

Very few of the Apocryphal Gospels profess to be inspired, and none have been viewed as such by the Church of Christ. Occasionally they refer to our Gospels as of a more elevated rank, which is an acknowledgment of their own inferior pretensions. But when we come to look into them and subject them to criticism, we soon begin to see how far they are from any just claim to equality with our Gospels. Among the phenomena which present themselves to our notice are these :—1. The same book is often ascribed to different authors. 2. The same book appears with different titles. 3. Different books occur with the same title. 4. The same book may have different forms, one much longer than the others. 5. Two or three books are sometimes amalgamated into one. 6. The various readings are as divergent as they are numerous, immensely in excess of those which belong to the four Gospels, although the latter have been copied a hundred times more often to say the least. The negligence in copying, and the liberties taken in altering in every way, prove that these books were not looked upon with any veneration as sacred and Divine.

Now none of these things are true of the genuine Gospels, and therefore we may affirm that the eighteen centuries which have revered and testified to them have trifled with and borne witness against the others. I say that eighteen centuries have trifled with the Apocryphal Gospels, but I do not mean that we have any so ancient. I believe we have not, although I find things in some of them which Irenæus speaks of as in those of his day, seventeen centuries ago. You will, however, carefully observe that as these writers copied much from one another, similar statements occur in books written at most distant intervals. We cannot, therefore, decide the age of any one of these Apocrypha by a reference to Irenæus alone. With the genuine Gospels the case is widely different, and no one who reads them carefully can doubt whether they are the same as Irenæus mentions and uses so much. The one truth which we gather from Hippolytus, Origen, Clement of Alexandria, Tertullian, and Irenæus, is, that the series of spurious Gospels must have begun in the second century. Later authors, and the very books in our hands, make it plain that the series continued during several hundred years; perhaps it would not be too much to say they range over a thousand years or more. If I included the visions and revelations of monks and nuns and devout hypochondriacs, I should have to say that the long array of falsehoods extends from the second century to the nineteenth. As we must draw the line somewhere, I have decided now to consider only the anonymous Apocrypha of a few centuries.

Should I be asked why I call books anonymous which bear such well known names as Matthew, Peter, Thomas, James, and Nicodemus, I would answer, Because no one believes those writers were the authors, and, so far as we can tell, no one ever did believe it, unless incompetent. How different with our four Gospels! Every man who has recorded the writers' names has ascribed them to Matthew, Mark, Luke, and John!

With respect to the question of their first origin, I may be told that the Apocryphal Gospels must have begun before St. Luke wrote, because he says, "Many have taken in hand to set forth in order a declaration of those things which are most surely believed among us." The answer to this is that the Evangelist does not say one word of the fabulous character of the books he refers to; and from this I infer that they were honest, but unsatisfactory attempts to write the Gospel history. Whatever they were they passed at once into oblivion, and we have not a trace of a record of them afterwards. I am sure no one will believe in the ludicrous list of twenty-six Gospels referred to in the New Testament, as drawn up by Robert Taylor and printed at p. 75 of his "Syntagma." The utter untrustworthiness of this writer is now so well-known and admitted that no intelligent and candid unbeliever places any reliance upon him. Him, therefore, I dismiss without apology.

I may perhaps be reminded that some Christian writers have understood St. Luke as alluding to Apocryphal Gospels. I am quite aware of the fact, but have given my reason for a different opinion.

It may be said that several of the earliest Christian Fathers mention incidents and sayings not to be found in the four Gospels, but once existing in the Apocryphal. The inference is that in these cases Apocryphal Gospels were quoted. I am again of a different opinion, and after minute examination conclude that such incidents and sayings in all human probability belong to tradition. The compilers of false Gospels naturally embodied such facts and words in their books.

If it is alleged that several of the fathers, such as Clement of Alexandria, Origen, and Tertullian, avowedly quote from false Gospels, it need not be denied; but it must be observed that they do not appeal to them without reservation and explanation. These very quotations therefore supply historical proof that such Gospels were not accounted Canonical and genuine.

Leaving the question of antiquity for the present, let us look at that of authority. This is partly answered by a remark already made, on the way in which the early Fathers quote the Apocryphal Gospels. But it may be urged that at least one church, that of Rhossus in Cilicia, adopted a false Gospel, and that other examples might possibly be traced. It may be so, but the exception proves the rule, which is all I have need to establish. Even in the case of Rhossus an enquiry was at one instituted, and the true character of the spurious Gospel was made known.

The fact that the Apocryphal Gospels were drawn upon in after times, and their legends foisted into so-called histories and into liturgical works is no argument against my position, because the books which were borrowed from had already been declared Apocryphal by name in the decrees of councils or of Popes. The books themselves having been condemned, it is for those who plundered them to justify their thefts; I do not undertake to do so. If there are saints in the calendar and stories in the Breviary which come from the Apocryphal Gospels, it is a discredit to those who have adopted them without acknowledging, and even while condemning the parentage.

One curious fact connected with some of the Apocryphal Gospels must not be overlooked. Maurice, the author of "Indian Antiquities," wrote a book called "The Indian Sceptic Confuted, and Brahmin Frauds Exposed,"*

* London, 1812.

in which he directs attention to the existence of certain of these productions in India, among the ancient Christians established there. He undertakes to prove that these false Gospels were used by the Brahmins, who compiled the famous legends of Krishna. His arguments were highly commended by such men as Dean Vincent and Adam Clarke, and they are certainly every way worthy of attention. At an earlier date Sir William Jones, in his well known essay on the "Gods of Greece, Italy and India," expressed a similar opinion. He says, when speaking of the Krishna fables, "This motley story must induce an opinion that the spurious Gospels, which abounded in the first age of Christianity, had been brought to India, and the wildest parts of them repeated to the Hindus, who ingrafted them on the old fable of Cesava, the Apollo of Greece." Cesava is another name for Krishna, and hence we may infer, not only that the Krishna story as we have it is less ancient than our Gospels, but is indebted to those very Apocryphal Gospels which we have under our notice.

I will now mention the amusing shifts to which recourse has been had by some who have wished to make the unlearned believe that the Apocryphal Gospels were used in common with our own. According to one story the selection of Canonical books was made by the vote of a council of bishops; while another is that the selection was ascribed to some sort of miracle. The latter is an exceedingly silly fable, yet very often printed. It even appears in the second of the tracts bearing the title, "Christian Evidences Criticised: being the National Secular Society's Reply to the Bishop of London, and the

Christian Evidence Committee." The writer has got hold of the idea that the Canon of the New Testament was formed by the process of "selection," and after speaking of the uncertainty of the *time* when this supposed "selection" was made, he proceeds to say: "Equally uncertain is history as to the *mode* of selection. Some writers mention that when the bishops met to decide what should be the word of God, the books were put to the vote of the meeting, and those Gospels and Epistles which had the majority of votes, were regarded as 'Divine.' By other writers it is stated that the bishops put the whole of the books under the table, and besought those that were inspired to leap on the top, and it happened accordingly. To believe this, however, would require a leap of the imagination. What became of the rejected books we know not. The Apocryphal New Testament contains some of them, but there are many of which we have no trace."

Here we have the two untrue accounts—*first*, that the "selection" was made by a vote of bishops at some council, which is not named; and *secondly*, that the anonymous council obtained a decision by a miracle. We are told that "some writers" give one account, and "other writers" the other. The "some writers" in the one case are none of them named, and the "other writers" are equally nameless. Let me supply the deficiency by observing that Thomas Paine tells the first story, and that William Hone, who recanted his scepticism, tells the second, as you will find by referring to "The Age of Reason," and "The Apocryphal New Testament." Such are the allegations, and what are the facts?

1. That there is absolutely no genuine record or document, and no modern writer of note, to show that either the Council of Nice in 325 A.D., or that of Laodicea a few years later, and one of them must be meant, selected the Canonical books of the New Testament by a majority of votes against the Apocryphal ones. There is an ancient list of New Testament books which it is said was drawn up at Laodicea, but nothing about the false and spurious books. Besides, we have plenty of evidence that the New Testament in a collected form existed ages before this, and that it did not contain any Apocryphal Gospels.

2. The tale about the miraculous selection of the books which we receive seems to have been unknown for at least from five to six hundred years after its supposed occurrence. I am ashamed to feel called upon to give its history, but the obstinacy with which sceptics of a certain class continue to publish it on the platform and through the press renders it a duty. The pretended fact is taken from a book called "Libellus Synodicus," which was first published by a Strasburg professor named Pappus in the year 1601, and in Greek and Latin. It is said by the Abbé Bergier to have been written at the earliest in the ninth century, "by an unknown and visionary author." "It is," he adds, "a work full of errors, anachronisms and fables, and despised by all critics, not one of whom has ever made use of it."* M. Bergier mentions that by some sceptical writers of his time the fable by the unknown Greek had been produced with variations. The

---

* Traité de la Vraie Religion, Vol. VIII., p. 127. Paris, 1785.

author of the "Critical History of Jesus Christ," of which I have a copy in French without date, or name of place of publication,* says the inspired books got upon the altar. Another version is that the books were all placed upon the altar and that the Apocrypha fell off, while the inspired books remained. A third account is that the altar was artificially contrived to bring about the desired result.

This is the history of the matter. Until the time of Pappus the story was not even published, and it was not repeated until the French infidels got hold of it a century ago, or very little more. They did not believe it and nobody else believed it. Why then do our opponents make so much of it, as if it was any part of true and really ancient history? Is it because they are prejudiced men, who will not or cannot investigate the truth of what they say?

I will ask you diligently to note what I am about to say further in reference to the fable published by Pappus. The men who so often mention it without accepting its truth practically accept it as supplying a date when Apocryphal Gospels were finally excluded from all claim to authority by the adoption of our four. From this it follows, *first*, that the Canonical Gospels have held their place and stood supreme for fifteen centuries and a half. It follows, *secondly*, that no Apocryphal Gospel written since the Nicene or Laodicean Councils can have had any claim to a place in the Canon. Therefore all Apocryphal Gospels which have appeared since the Councils mentioned

---

* It appeared in French about 1770.

are confessedly excluded from all the honours which unbelieving writers have claimed for those written at an earlier date. This is a logical conclusion to which no reasonable man can object; and it suggests that we should find out the dates at which the Apocryphal Gospels first appear or were written. Every false Gospel which cannot be traced to an earlier date than the Nicene Council is rejected by the arguments of the Infidels themselves.

Another most important consequence follows, and it is that if at any earlier date than A.D. 325 we find our four Gospels only accepted as Canonical, all Apocryphal Gospels not older than that earlier date must be rejected. Whenever, no matter when, our Gospels were regarded as alone Canonical all other Gospels must have been uncanonical. Hence all we have to do is to find out who first mentions four Gospels as alone received, and then to discover what other so-called Gospels existed at an earlier date because they only can have claimed to be Canonical. To follow this course will very much simplify our enquiry, and its results will settle the question.

One hundred years before the Council of Nicea we find Origen writing in his Commentaries on Matthew: "I have learnt by tradition concerning the *four* Gospels which alone are uncontroverted in the Church of God spread under heaven, that that according to Matthew, who was once a publican but afterwards an Apostle of Jesus Christ, was written first; ...that according to Mark second; ...that according to Luke third: ...that according to John last of all."*

* As quoted by Westcott on the Canon, Part II., from Eusebius, Ecclesiastical History, 6, 25.

Tertullian, who was born about 130 years after the death of Christ, in his writing against Marcion* enumerates four Gospels only as genuine and ascribes them to Matthew, Mark, Luke, and John.

Clement of Alexandria, who belongs to the same period, speaks of "the four Gospels which have been delivered to us."†

Irenæus of Lyons, who wrote still earlier, reckons four Gospels as alone accepted by the universal Church of God.‡

For the purposes of this lecture I need not go further with the present branch of our enquiry. We have the evidence of four of the most eminent Christian writers of the second part of the second century, and of the first part of the third century, that only the four Gospels of Matthew, Mark, Luke, and John were then received by the Church. These four men represent Europe, Asia, and Africa, and had what may be called an immense acquaintance with Christian literature and opinions, orthodox and heretical. They all refer to Apocryphal Gospels, but it is manifest that such books were excluded by them from the sacred Canon.

There is still earlier testimony for the four Gospels and their place in the Church, but I pass it by, as not belonging to our actual business. It is enough for me that men, some of whom could look back to within a hundred and fifty years of the birth of our Saviour, and had conversed with other men much older than themselves, knew nothing

---

* Book 4, 2. † Stromata, Book 3.
‡ Heresies, Book 3, ch. 11, sec. 8.

of more than four Gospels as received by the Church, although they knew of other so called Gospels in use by certain heretical sects, as they carefully indicate.

Before proceeding to speak of the claims of the false Gospels now in existence to be older than the times of Tertullian, Clement, and Irenæus, and before saying anything of so-called Gospels which were earlier, but are now known only by name, by fragments and in other forms, I will ask you to compare with the facts already established a few statements made by writers with whom you are, most of you, familiar.

In his discussion with Mr. Woodman, Mr. Bradlaugh says (p. 32) : " I would ask him whether there are not many others of the Greek Gospels, some more ancient than these, which are abandoned and rejected? If our friend says not, I will read over a list of fourteen or fifteen Gospels, the names of which have been preserved, and some of which have been substantiated as being more worthy of credence than some that have been adopted." Hereupon I would say that we know of no Greek Gospels more ancient than those of the New Testament, and that no Apocryphal Gospel has been substantiated as more worthy of credence than some of the Canonical Gospels.

The same writer at p. 25 of his tract, " When were our Gospels written?" gives a list of what he describes as fabulous histories written not long after Christ's resurrection. Those in the list which are called Gospels are, "the Gospel of Peter ; the Gospel of Andrew ; the Gospel of John ; the Gospel of James ; the Gospel of the Egyptians." Why the Gospel of John, which is one of our four, is put down, I know not, and some information should have been given respecting the rest. This I know, that not one of the false Gospels named by Mr. Bradlaugh is mentioned within a hundred and fifty years of the Ascension of Christ. That of Peter first appears in notices of Serapion, Bishop of Antioch, whom Cave places at A.D. 190. That of Andrew first occurs in the decree of Gelasius, A.D. 492. That of James seems to be mentioned as one with that of Peter by Origen, though as a fact the Gospel of James does not occur under that title in any of the ancient Fathers. The Gospel of, or according to, the Egyptians is referred to by Clement of Alexandria, at the end of the second century.

A sceptic of a very different class, Dr. Perfitt, says the modern reader "hears of the *fact* that about the close of the second century various Gospels were known and highly esteemed, which are no longer accepted by the Churches; he finds that these rejected works were quoted in common with those received by the Fathers who are still praised alike by Catholic and Protestant believers," &c. This is an exaggerated statement, and consequently mischievous. We learn from Irenæus, that some of the extreme heretics had certain books which they had forged, and we get similar evidence from some later writers, but these books were not highly esteemed by the Churches, neither were they quoted in common with ours by Fathers in high repute. How, and how far they are quoted, will be duly stated as we proceed.

I cannot allude without a feeling of shame to p. 33 of "Our First Century,"—one of the tracts issued by Thomas Scott. The writer professes to gather together the principal incidents in the life of Jesus, according as they are related in the various extant New Testament writings. Under this designation he quotes most from the Apocryphal Gospels, an act which no upright and intelligent man can fail to condemn, because no explanation whatever is offered. True, he elsewhere says, (p. 18), "The extant Apocryphal New Testament literature is almost universally admitted to be a production of the second century," but even this is grossly inaccurate.

I must next mention Dr. Giles as one who has dealt unfairly with this matter in his "Christian Records." He gives six instances in which he says Justin Martyr "quoted sayings of Christ or events of Christ's life which do not occur in our Gospels, but were found in other uncanonical writings." For his first and second examples which are trivial, he offers no proof; and all he can say for his third is, that "Grotius and others *think* that it is taken from the Gospel according to the Egyptians." For his other three he does refer to Apocryphal books, but most of them do not appear till long after the time of Justin.

Among the boldest transgressors of accuracy I have met with is Mr. E. P. Meredith, who in his "Prophet of Nazareth" says, at p. 306, that the Gospels which are termed Apocryphal "are supported by quite as strong evidence of their genuineness, as can be adduced for that of the Canonical Gospels." He says "there is quite as much evidence of the genuineness of the Gospel of the Infancy, as there is of that of either of the Canonical Gospels. Indeed, we have evidence that it is of higher antiquity than either of them; for we have no proof that our present Gospels existed in the second century." Upon the respective items in this quotation, I simply say that, in the face of well known evidence, no more untrue series of allegations ever came under my notice. Not one of the details has the shadow of fact as its foundation.

If space permitted I would have set over against these too hasty utterances the calm and scholarlike views of the most eminent modern critics, who almost with one voice declare that the four Gospels were accepted as Canonical at a very early date, and do not regard the Apocryphal Gospels as having had any such position. If a party in Egypt had a peculiar Gospel; if another party in Judea had a peculiar Gospel; if the disciples of Basilides and of Marcion had their peculiar Gospels during the second century,—the Church as a whole had the Gospels of Matthew, Mark, Luke, and John, and no other. If we may judge by the specimens of false Gospels which have come down to us, the Church could never have entertained them. The intellectual, the moral, and the religious faculties of sober minded Christians would have revolted against them; for as the "Edinburgh Review" (July 1868) says: "What strikes every one, whatever be his opinion of the origin and merits of these writings, is their immeasurable inferiority to the Canonical Gospels. ......An impassable line separates the simple majesty, the lofty moral tone, the profound wisdom and significance of the Canonical Gospels from the qualities which we forbear further to particularise in the writings that claim to be their complement."

The most important of the few earliest non-canonical Gospels of which we find any trace, were more or less altered copies of those which we have. Thus the Gospel according to the Hebrews was a Hebrew or Aramaic copy, answering generally to that by Matthew. In like manner the Gospel of Marcion was only an altered copy of that by Luke. It is the opinion of Jeremiah Jones that six or seven of the early corrupted Gospels, styled Apocryphal, were simply modifications of Matthew. Under this head he places the so-styled Gospels of the Hebrews, of the Nazarenes, the Twelve Apostles, the Ebionites, and those of Cerinthus and Bartholomew. Others may perhaps come under the same description. We know very well that one or two fabulous Gospels about the Infancy of Christ have been multiplied by ingenious scribes into not less than half a dozen, but probably into a larger number. By doggedly pursuing the motley crowd of these Apocrypha, until we run them to earth, we secure two momentous results: *first*, that not a few of them are of far more modern date than has been asserted; and *secondly*, that the remainder become for the most part mere *aliases*, leaving a very small number of originals. Those which are proved to be too modern, are disposed of by the argument of our opponents themselves; such as are merely alterations of our Gospels have no logical place in the discussion; the Gospels of sects and parties have no right to compete with those of the Canon. If there be any others I do not know where to lay my hand upon them, nor do I know any one who does. What is the conclusion? Why evidently that four original Gospels and no more were received by the Church in its really early period. All others disappear, and, "like the baseless fabric of a vision, leave not a wrack behind."

Taking the sceptical ground, that the first to name a Gospel is the first witness for its existence, I turn to Jones on the Canon, where the authorities are ranged chronologically, with the following results :—

1. Hegesippus (A.D. 173.) contemporary with Irenæus is said to have used the Gospel according to the Hebrews. The authority for this is Eusebius, who wrote a hundred and fifty years later, and who does not say that Hegesippus gave the name of the Gospel in question. No matter whether he did or not, there is no doubt that the Gospel according to the Hebrews agreed in the main with our Matthew.

2. Irenæus, at the close of his first book against Heresies, says that the sect called the Cainites had a fictitious history, which they styled the Gospel of Judas; *i.e.*, Judas Iscariot the betrayer of Christ. The same author mentions, "The Gospel of Truth," which the Valentinians used. He also refers to false Gospels which he does not name.

3. Serapion, Bishop of Antioch, about the same time wrote against a book called "The Gospel of Peter," a forgery which had been received by some members of the Church of Rhosse, or Rhossus, in Cilicia.

4. Clement of Alexandria mentions the Gospel according to the Hebrews, and the Gospel according to the Egyptians.

5. Tertullian speaks of the Gospel of Valentinus, the Gospel of Marcion, and the Gospel of Peter.

6. Origen has references to the Gospel according to the Hebrews, the Gospel according to the Twelve Apostles, the Gospel of Basilides, that of Thomas, that of Matthias, and that of Peter or the Book of James.

7. Hippolytus, who lived at the same time with Origen, also refers to the Gospel of Thomas, but the extracts he gives do not appear in the Gospel with that name which has come down to our day.

8. Eusebius, a hundred years later, mentions several of the false Gospels above named, and adds the Gospel of Tatian, but that was only a Harmony formed out of our four Gospels, because he expressly says so, and calls it by the name of Diatessaron, which a similar work bears to this day.

These are all the false, falsified, or modified Gospels of which the writers of the Church speak down to the time of the Council of Nicea—three hundred years after the crucifixion of Christ. The total is thirteen, from which we must throw out several: the Gospel of the Hebrews, based on Matthew; the Gospel of Marcion, based on Luke; the Gospel of Tatian, a collection from our four; and the Book of James, which Origen speaks of as if the same with that of Peter. Of the nine which remain, the the Gospels of Judas and of Truth appear to have been mystical and not historical books, and that of Valentinus seems to have been like them. Six only have to be accounted for. (1) The Gospel of Peter, which is perhaps the same as a book styled the Preaching of Peter, but which we know to have been a forgery because Serapion declared it such in the time of Irenæus. (2) The Gospel according to the Egyptians, of which Clement of Alexandria speaks, but which he does not accept, and which seems to have been a really Apocryphal Gospel, part fable and part history. It has perished, which is very good proof that it was never Canonical. It was used only by some heretics. (3) The Gospel according to the Twelve Apostles, which Origen mentions as used by the heretics, and Jerome thinks was another form of our Matthew. There is little doubt that it corresponded with the Gospel according to the Hebrews. (4) The Gospel of Basilides, was written by an ancient heretic of that name, and as such, whatever its forms, it did not appeal to the Church at large. (5) The Gospel of Thomas, is mentioned by Origen as received by heretics, and is declared by Cyril to have been written by a Manichean of the name of Thomas. If Cyril is right it could not have been so ancient as the Apostolic age. There may, however, have been two or more books with that title, I think there were, and that the first was as early as the days of Irenæus. The original Gospel of Thomas is very likely the basis of those books which we now have under that name, but if so it was written to favour the Gnostics, and was opposed to the views of the orthodox, which shows that it could never have claimed to be Canonical. (6) The Gospel of Matthias, which we cannot identify with anything we now possess, which Origen says was used by the heretics, and which Eusebius condemns as impious and absurd, as well as heretical.

You will not forget that the first to really mention the false Gospels is that same Irenæus who first names all our four, and declares them alone genuine. If you wish to get beyond Irenæus you must adopt the methods we follow; you must rely on more modern authors, or upon alleged quotations. There is no third course open, and the sceptic is driven to uphold the claims of false Gospels by the very measures he condemns when used to uphold the true. There are other arguments in support of the four Gospels which cannot be employed for the Apocryphal books, but I have not time to enumerate them. They relate to the internal character of the books, the use made of them by sects, ancient translations, &c.

Such of the false Gospels as are now extant are contained in my translation of them,* with a careful account of them all. They are as follows:—

1. The Gospel of James, or Protevangelium, the latter title having been given to it by Postel in 1552. It exists in Greek and in Latin, and contains an account of the birth, education and marriage of Mary, of the birth of Jesus, and His being worshipped by the Magi. It probably received its actual form in about the fourth century, though some of its materials are older.

2. The Gospel of Pseudo-Matthew, otherwise called the Book of the Birth of the Blessed Mary and of the Infancy of our Saviour, and sometimes said to have been written in Hebrew by the Evangelist Matthew, and translated into Latin by Jerome. This book is a compilation not so ancient as the Gospel of James, but probably dating from the fifth century. The original seems to have been in Greek and an amplification of older documents.

3. The Gospel of the Nativity of Mary. This we have in Latin, and as the writer uses Jerome's translation, it is not older than the fifth century. It ends with the birth of Jesus.

4. The Gospel of Thomas, or Gospel of the Infancy of Jesus. We have this in several forms, very different from

* The Apocryphal Gospels, &c. London, 4th Edition, 1874.

each other, and it represents one of the oldest false Gospels of which we have any knowledge. It professes to record events in the life of Christ from his fifth year to his twelfth. There is no doubt that its origin was heretical, as it represents the infant Saviour in a very unorthodox light. We do not appear to have the primary form of the book, the nearest approach to it being in the Syriac text, which I have translated and printed at the end of my volume. Three others of different dates are given by me in the same work.

5. The Gospel of the Infancy, from the Arabic. This is by no means so ancient in its actual form as some of the others. I view it as a compilation from older books with large additions by the Arabic editor. It begins with the journey to Bethlehem and is continued down to the twelfth year of Christ's age, but ends with a summary mention of His life onward until His baptism.

6. The Gospel of Nicodemus, or the Acts of Pilate. This consists of two principal parts, which are often separated, the first giving an account of the trial, death, and burial of Jesus, and the second an account of His exploits among the dead. It has no right whatever to be called the Acts of Pilate, which is the title of a much older and quite different document. What we now have exists in several forms, but none of them can be older than the end of the fourth century or the commencement of the fifth.

From what has been said it will appear that five out of the six Apocryphal Gospels now extant relate solely to events which terminate with the infancy of Jesus. The sixth of them relates to the concluding scenes in the life of Christ and the time during which He lay in the grave. Hence it is evident that none of them are in any sense the rivals of our Gospels, but are lame attempts to supplement them by means of imaginary narratives. The logical conclusion is that none of them are so ancient as our Gospels, the existence and authority of which is implied by their avoidance of the period of the Saviour's public ministry, the history of which had been already written and was recognised as true.

The false Gospels which have perished were, so far as can be ascertained, of three kinds: 1. Such as were, like those now existing, endeavours to supplement the Canonical Gospels. 2. Such as were of a mystical and allegorical description, abounding in Gnostic speculations. 3. Such as were altered forms of one or another of our Gospels.

This brings us again to the conclusion that none of the Apocryphal Gospels were so ancient as Matthew, Mark, Luke, and John; that few of them ever pretended to rival these in authority, and when they did, that it was only within the limits of sects which departed widely from the common faith. Finally it follows, that no known Apocryphal Gospel, whether extant or not, can claim to be a genuine production of the Apostolic age, or of Apostolic men. Thus the only three questions of importance which can be raised are settled. The Apocryphal Gospels are not genuine, they are without authority, and they are too modern.

From a literary point of view the false and true Gospels are as different as books well can be. Most of them never were Gospels at all in the proper sense of the word; and those which were so, were paraphrases of our four. The language and internal features place them as far below ours as can well be imagined. The uncontrolled liberty taken with them by transcribers and editors is utterly inconsistent with the idea that they were regarded as inspired productions. They have been ridiculed and condemned from the first mention of them seventeen centuries ago down to our own day. Many of them have utterly perished. Their very titles and reputed authorship have not been respected, but have been changed according to the fancy of those who have copied and published them. No competent critic or scholar in any age or country has been able to give an honest verdict in their favour, although a few rationalistic or sceptical writers have been anxious to think well of two or three, of which we know next to nothing. I decline to accept as judges in such a case such avowed partisans of unbelief as have never studied either the Apocryphal Gospels or their history.

When men like Renan admit that by about the year 100 A.D. "all the books of the New Testament were almost fixed in the form in which we now read them,"* it ill becomes those of lesser note to advocate the opinion that the Apocryphal Gospels of later date were at any time in practice a part of the New Testament. We simply know they were not, and after an exile of so many ages, it is not possible for them to gain the title which they never had a right to.

I will conclude with three short extracts from the

---

* Vie de Jesus. 13th Edition, Introd. p. 34.

essay of Bishop Ellicott, one of the best ever written on the subject. Speaking of these Apocryphal Gospels, he says:—

"Our vital interest in Him of whom they pretend to tell us more than the Canonical Scriptures have recorded is the real, though it may be hidden, reason why these poor figments are read with interest, even while they are despised" (p. 156.) "We know before we read them that they are weak, silly, and profitless; that they are despicable monuments of religious fiction, yet still the secret conviction buoys us up, that perchance they may contain a few traces of time-honoured traditions—some faint, feeble glimpses of that blessed childhood, that pensive and secluded youth, over which in passive moments, we muse with such irrepressible longing to know more—such deep, deep desideration" (p. 157). "If they do not deserve to be known for their own sakes, they still involve several singular and interesting questions; they illustrate some curious phases of early Christian thought and feeling; they throw some light on ancient traditions, and certainly have not been without influence on ancient and mediæval art" (p. 158). The writer might have added that they have been very useful to the forgers of ecclesiastical fictions and superstitions, but have never promoted the true interests of the Gospel of our Lord and Saviour Jesus Christ.

APPENDIX.

I HAVE not in this Lecture dealt with every one of the documents which are included in my volume of Apocryphal Gospels. The reason for this is, that I have inserted in that volume, not only the extant false Gospels, but, as the title says, "other documents relating to the History of Christ." Those which are not mentioned in the Lecture are—

The History of Joseph the Carpenter; the Letters ascribed to Jesus, Abgar, and Lentulus; the Prayer of Jesus; the Story of Veronica; the Letters ascribed to Pilate and Herod; the Report of Pilate; the Trial and Condemnation of Pilate; the Death of Pilate; the Story of Joseph of Arimathea; and the Revenging of the Saviour.

Of the fictitious Gospels, it will be remembered that they fall into two classes:—(1) Those which end with the early years of our Saviour, and (2) those which begin with his trial and condemnation. We have no knowledge of any false Gospels, properly so called, which record the events of the ministry of Christ. The falsified Gospels which relate to his active ministry appear to have all been modifications, or corrupted forms of one or another of our four. Of purely mystical or allegorical Gospels we know little, and need say nothing.

It has been thought desirable to supplement the foregoing Lecture by an outline of some one of each of the two extant classes of Apocryphal Gospels. As those of each class contain so much in common, a sample of each will be sufficient to show what sort of materials they are made up of. For the first I select the false Gospel of Matthew, and for the second I take one form of the Gospel of Nicodemus.

Appendix.

The False Gospel of Matthew, or *Gospel of Pseudo-Matthew*, commences with an account of one Joachim, of the tribe of Judah and the city of Jerusalem, who was a shepherd, and married one Anna, with whom he lived twenty years without having a family. They were both very pious, and grieved over their childless lot, when a promise of offspring was given by an angel to Anna, and a like promise to Joachim, who was then absent from home. These promises were fulfilled in the birth of Mary, who at three years of age was consecrated to God, and was brought up in the temple till she was fifteen years old, when it was thought she should be married. The choice of a husband was decided by lot, and the lot fell upon Joseph, who was an old man, and had sons and grandchildren. Joseph was reluctant to take her, but consented to keep her till he knew which of his sons might have her to wife. Mary soon received messages from angels announcing the great honours in store for her, and after a time Joseph was distressed in finding her pregnant. The news spread, and Joseph was taken before the Chief Priest and subjected to an ordeal along with Mary, but both came out free from blame.

Soon after, the taxing was ordered by Augustus, and Joseph and Mary had to go to Bethlehem; but before they reached that place Mary was overtaken by the pains of childbirth, and entered a cave which was divinely illuminated. While Joseph went to seek assistance Jesus was born, and on Joseph's return with two women, Zelomi and Salome, the last had her hand wit heredas a punishment of unbelief, but was cured by touching the border of the infant's clothes. After a reference to the shepherds, and a star which shone over the cave, we read that on the third day Mary left the cave and went into a stable with the babe, where the ox and ass adored him. On the sixth day they entered Bethlehem, and on the eighth the child was circumcised, and Simeon and Anna worship Jesus in the temple. Two years later the Magi come from the East, Herod is enraged, and the flight into Egypt follows to escape from the death intended. The family enter a cave where dragons are seen, but they adore Jesus and leave him. Lions and leopards in the wilderness form a sort of reverential body guard and guide. After three days Mary longed for the fruit of a palm tree, and at the bidding of her infant it bowed down till all its fruit was gathered, a spring gushed from its roots, and an angel took one of the branches to plant in paradise. The journey being wearisome, Jesus miraculously shortened it, so that they found Egypt at once before their eyes. Entering Hermopolis they were refused hospitality, so entered a temple where three hundred and fifty-five idols were, and straightway these idols all fell to the ground and were broken. All the people of the city believed in the Lord God through Jesus Christ.

After returning from Egypt and being in Galilee, Jesus, now four years old, played by the Jordan, and collected water in pools with mud banks. A boy broke down the pools, and Jesus cursed him and he died, but on entreaty and with a kick restored him to life. Another day he made sparrows of mud, and when complaint was made that it was the Sabbath, he clapped his hands and bade the birds fly away, which they did. A second boy who broke down the pools was stricken with death. Joseph being afraid, took Jesus away to lead him home. As they went, a rude boy pushed against him and at once died. After entreaty, Jesus pulled this boy up by the ear and bade him live, which he did.

Some time after one Zaccheus wanted to teach Jesus, but the child quite confounded him with his speeches. However, a second application was made, and the pupil was intractable, so the master hit him with a stick, which brought from him another of his wonderful speeches. The family then removed to Nazareth, where, while playing on a house top with Jesus, a boy fell down and died, but was raised to life by Jesus. After this he was sent to the fountain for water, being now six years old, and on the way back a child thrust against him and broke the pitcher, so Jesus spread out his cloak and took home in it as much water as there was in the pitcher. Again, he sowed a little wheat, which multiplied immensely. At eight years of age, near Jericho, he entered a cavern where there was a lioness and her whelps. The old lion fawned on him and adored him, and the young ones fawned and played with him. He then crossed the Jordan with the lions, the river dividing to let him and them go over, and he dismissed them. Joseph being a carpenter received one day an order for a couch, and told Jesus to cut the wood, which he did, but cut one piece too short, which made Joseph angry. So Jesus made him take the two pieces, and they pulled the short one to the proper length. A second time he went to school, and the master struck him and died. A third time he went to school, and his sayings so amazed them that they worshipped him.

After these things the family removed to Capernaum, where he raised a dead man to life. Then they went to Bethlehem, where he cured the hand of James, which a viper had bitten. The whole concludes with a family sketch, indicating the reverence with which Jesus was regarded.

The Gospel of Nicodemus opens with a preface declaring that one Ananias had found the book in Hebrew, and translated it into Greek about A.D. 440. Then follows the accusation which the Jewish priests and others laid against Jesus before Pilate, who gave orders that Jesus should be brought. The officer who went to fetch him no sooner saw him than he worshipped him, and spread a scarf on the ground for him to walk on, but returned without him. Being sent again the officer did as before, and when Jesus entered, the tops of the imperial standards bowed to Jesus. This it was alleged was a trick of the men who held the standards, so others were chosen by the Jews themselves, with no better result. Pilate was troubled by this, and by a message from his wife who had had a strange dream. However, the trial proceeded, and charges were adduced, though witnesses proved them false. Eventually Pilate partly consents to his death, whereupon Nicodemus, followed by various others, bear testimony in his favour. Several details succeed, which are based upon the Gospel record, and Jesus is at last crucified and buried. Joseph of Arimathea is caught by the Jews and imprisoned. The report of the resurrection of Jesus is accompanied by the announcement that Joseph had been miraculously set at liberty. Sundry confirmations of these events, and discussions are introduced. Search is made for Joseph, who gives the story of his deliverance. Evidence is obtained of the resurrection of Jesus, and of his ascension. A wonderful impression in favour of Christ is produced, so that even Annas and Caiaphas seem to be convinced. Amid general demonstrations of joy, the first part of Nicodemus is brought to a close.

The second part begins with an intimation that of those whom Jesus had raised from the dead, the two sons of Simeon were living, and might perhaps be brought to narrate what they knew. The two men were accordingly sent for, and having made the sign of the cross and asked for pen, ink, and paper, sat down and wrote their story. They were in the underworld, or Hades, they said, among the departed, when there appeared a great light causing great commotion. Abraham, Isaiah, and John the Baptist point out the true reason, and Adam calls on his own son Seth to tell the story of the oil of mercy. Meanwhile Satan is in consternation, and holds an animated conversation with Hades, which is disturbed by the approach of Jesus, whom Hades is compelled, much against his will, to admit. Hades owns himself subdued, and the King of Glory orders Satan to be bound in irons and placed in charge of Hades. Jesus calls Adam and blesses him, and removes him from Hades with patriarchs, prophets, martyrs, and ancestors, who are taken to Paradise, where they meet Enoch and Elijah, and soon after the repentant thief. All this the two brothers saw and heard, and were appointed to make known. Having handed their papers to the chief priests, and to Joseph and Nicodemus, they vanished. With their disappearance the whole story ends.

It is evident that the so-called false Gospel of Matthew is little more than a series of idle and puerile stories, with only just enough allusion to the facts of our Gospels to show that the writer or writers knew them. The greater portion of the details are mythical and legendary, and therefore not at all founded on fact. Taken in connection with the malevolent character and capricious habits of Jesus, they stand in painful contrast with the representations of Him which we find in the four Gospels. As the string of fables which convey no moral resemble in no literary feature the Evangelical records, so the ideal Christ of the false Gospeller is quite a different Christ from that of the New Testament. Even in the narration of alleged matters of fact the false Gospel is often not only at variance with the true Gospels, but contradicts what we otherwise know to be true. The writer of Pseudo-Matthew used older similar books, and added to them or altered them as he chose. He never rises to the dignity of a historian, and indulges his fancy for the grotesque and marvellous. He has no critical faculty whatever, and seems to have written more to amuse children than to instruct men; unless, indeed, he wished to astonish the ignorant, and to propagate erroneous ideas of Christ. If his intentions were harmless, his views were incoherent and inconsistent, and he failed to produce even a plausible preliminary Gospel. What he wrote has probably been altered, but what we have is as near any approach to the mythical as can be imagined. He jumbles the impossible, the improbable, and the unnatural together in such a way that nobody can believe his tale. How different from the natural, truthful, and beautiful allusions and narrations of the Evangelists.

The Gospel of Nicodemus was written at different times and by different persons. Dr. Lipsius, an eminent German critic, believes that it comprises not fewer than five portions of various dates. The book he thinks was in substance written between A.D. 326 and 376, but it received additions and alterations at a much later date. The first great division makes free use of the Gospels, and introduces episodes and developments for the sake of effect. The second division is a simple fiction, the author of which allowed his imagination perfect liberty. Dr. Lipsius thinks this second part originated with the Gnostics in the third century, but its present form is not older than the latter part of the fourth century, after which it was adopted and moulded up with the other. It is needless to criticise it further, though it should be said that both divisions, with all their faults, are superior to the other Apocryphal Gospels. From the summary it will be seen that the object in view has been to produce a sort of supplement to the Gospels.

The attempts to concoct preliminary and supplementary Gospels are easily accounted for, one chief reason being the desire to be wise above what is written. The desire for such wisdom has led to the invention of these idle tales, as most of them truly are. The solemn simplicity and earnestness of purpose which the Canonical Gospels exemplify, will for ever as it heretofore has done, keep them at an immeasurable elevation above these poor rivals and helpers. The mythical spirit is a childish spirit, and its fruits are puerility. It cannot hope to win even literary respectability. But the spirit of the Gospel writers is pure and noble, and with literary honour, combines moral and spiritual power. Of moral and spiritual power the false Gospels are utterly destitute, because they fail to appreciate and exhibit the true and living Christ. Having neither intellectual, moral, nor spiritual vitality, none can wonder at the discredit under which they have existed. That they have existed, any of them at all until now, has been due partly to the curiosity which they have awakened, and perhaps a little to their vain promise to tell us a few facts about our Saviour and not in the four Canonical Gospels.

THE EVIDENTIAL VALUE OF THE EARLY EPISTLES OF ST. PAUL VIEWED AS HISTORICAL DOCUMENTS.

BY THE
REV. PROFESSOR LORIMER, D.D.,
Professor of Theology in the English Presbyterian College, London.

The Evidential Value of the Early Epistles of St. Paul viewed as Historical Documents.

THE early Epistles of St. Paul include two Epistles to the Thessalonians, two to the Corinthians, the Epistle to the Galatians, and the Epistle to the Romans. They are the oldest writings in the New Testament. They were all written between twenty-five and thirty years after the death of Christ, and have the remarkable distinction of being the earliest literary monuments of any kind, or from any source, or in any language, relating to Christianity and the Christian Church which have come down to us, without challenge from almost any quarter, from ancient times.

You will allow me to start with these statements without proof, for there is nobody now or hardly anybody who denies them. The genuineness of the last four of these Epistles is now conceded by all eminent scholars and critics, even by Strauss and Rénan themselves; and though Baur and a few of his disciples had something to say against the genuineness of the Epistles to the Thessalonians, we may take it as good proof that there was very little force in their objections when they are all set aside by such critics of our own as Prof. Jowett and Dr. Davidson, who are in no way characterised by a conservative or traditional style of criticism, but very much the reverse. The least conservative of the two is Dr. Davidson who, in the later and more rationalistic edition of his "Introduction to the New Testament," remarks that "the established authorship of these two Epistles will hold its place among critics notwithstanding the assaults it has encountered."

I propose to handle these early Epistles of St. Paul simply as historical documents—simply as I would make use of the Epistles of Cicero or Pliny, or the Letters and Despatches of Napoleon and the Duke of Wellington. I have nothing to say at present on the subject of their Inspiration or Divine Authority.

I am to treat of their *Evidential Value* as historical documents. By that I mean their value as attestations to the truth of Christianity—as vouchers especially for the authenticity and certainty of the earliest Christian history, at least in its chief outlines, as given in the four Gospels and the Acts of the Apostles. As attestations and vouchers of historical facts, no documents are more valuable than the original letters of the personages who were the chief actors in history. Hence the diligence and care with which the original correspondence of such persons is preserved, collected and edited, and published to the world. And if this is admitted by all as a general principle of historical criticism, how can it be denied in reference to Christian history? Was not St. Paul a chief actor in the earliest history of the Christian Church?

And why should not his original letters have the same primary authority in that field of inquiry as the original letters of any other historical personage in any other field?

There are three great subjects of Christian history on which the early Epistles of St. Paul can thus be brought evidentially to bear.

The first of these is the life and history of Jesus Christ Himself, the Author and Finisher of the Christian faith. Distinguish between the great historical outlines of that life and the minute details of word, deed and incident with which the four written Gospels fill up the outlines. It is not pretended that more than the outline-facts of the life are to be found in these Epistles; they contain or imply none of the details, or very few of them. But it is of great evidential importance that they clearly recite and everywhere imply the outline-facts, in which I include the advent of Christ, His public ministry in Judea, His crucifixion, His ascension, and His inauguration of the Pentecostal Church. This proves unanswerably that at least these chief Gospel facts were known and accepted throughout all the churches of the Gentiles, in Asia and Europe, before any of the Gospel histories were written. These facts were everywhere received as the ultimate historical ground of the Christian Church and the Christian life. Even, therefore, if you could destroy the credit of the written Gospels as genuine and credible writings of the Apostolic age, you should not thereby destroy the truth and reality of the outline facts which were everywhere received before them. These facts are to be distinguished from all the Gospel narratives, whether Canonical or not, that were afterwards written upon the basis of these facts. It was because these foundation-facts were from the first accepted as historical verities by all Christians that the full and detailed narratives of the life of Christ were afterwards composed. Nothing therefore of any real effect is done on the side of unbelief, if you merely try to destroy the authority of the written Gospels. What unbelievers need to achieve is to destroy the credit of the ground-facts which were received many years before these narratives were written. You do not attack the primary foundations in attacking the later histories. You do not shake the foundations by shaking the histories—even if I were to admit, which I do not, that you do shake them—and till the very foundations of the edifice are shaken and displaced the edifice will stand firm like an impregnable fortress upon a rock.

A second great subject to which these Epistles of St. Paul apply, in a very authoritative and decisive way, is the personal history of St. Paul himself—a point of early Christian history inferior only in fundamental importance to the history of Christ himself. What better or more authoritative evidence could we have on everything personally relating to St. Paul than the genuine Epistles of St. Paul himself? If Cicero's Epistles are of primary authority on everything relating to the life of Cicero—for instance, as to his home education, the schools in which he attained his knowledge of the Greek philosophy, and the foreign philosophers from whom he learned the most, and whom he valued most—why, I ask, should not Paul's Epistles be also of primary authority in everything relating personally to St. Paul? As to his education, for example, and the various sources or schools, whether in Tarsus or Jerusalem, from which he derived his culture and knowledge, who could inform us so well and with so much authority as Saul of Tarsus himself? And particularly as to the sources from which he drew his knowledge of Christianity itself; and how it came to pass that he who began his public career as a fanatical persecutor of the Christians very soon went over with his whole soul to the cause which he had persecuted, and became, to the equal astonishment of friends and foes, its foremost champion—surely St. Paul himself, on all ordinary principles of historical judgment, is better able to give us accurate information than any other man. Surely St. Paul himself is more worth listening to on all such points of his own biography, and better entitled to belief (if you simply allow that he was an honest man, and not a cheat and an impostor) than any critic of the nineteenth century can pretend to be. If I believe Cicero on such particulars of his personal history with entire reliance, why am I not to believe St. Paul on similar points? If Cicero is of *primary* authority on such personal particulars, why is St. Paul to be no authority at all? If you would not believe Rénan contradicting Cicero on such matters, known to none so well as to Cicero himself, why should you believe Rénan contradicting St. Paul on matters of which he and he only had and could have absolute knowledge? Why am I to believe Rénan assuring me that the Gospel which St. Paul began to preach was a mixed doctrine—partly Jewish, partly Greek, partly Oriental, put together skilfully by himself—

a Gospel which in this way was a mere natural product of all the world's best previous thinking, and having nothing supernatural in it at all either as to source or authority—Why, I say, am I to believe this teaching of his in the teeth of all that St. Paul says upon the subject himself? If I would be quite right to believe Cicero rather than Rénan on points of Cicero's mental history, am I not equally right to believe Paul rather than Rénan on points of Paul's mental history as a Christian disciple and convert? Of course I am speaking only of facts and incidents in the lives of either, not of Cicero's or Paul's deductions from the facts. They might be mistaken in their deductions, but they could not be mistaken as to the facts themselves. We may feel quite certain that St. Paul did not go to the sources of Greek and Oriental wisdom for the Gospel which he preached to the world, when he tells us himself as a point of his own biography that these were not his sources.

There are other important questions of St. Paul's life and the history of his work to which his early Epistles apply—as, for example, the relations in which he stood to St. Peter and the other Apostles, and the question whether Christianity in his hands grew as the development of a myth grows, or whether this new Straussian theory of the rise of the Christian system is without any real basis and historical foothold. On the first of these questions the Epistle to the Galatians is of primary authority; and as Paul knew best the whole history of his relations to the other Apostles, and the real state of his own mind and feeling with regard to them and their ministry and the churches which they had planted, and the forms of Christian and Church life which they favoured and propagated, no theory of these things—the theory of Baur, *e.g.*—can possibly be a true one which exaggerates or diminishes the statements of St. Paul himself, or makes him feel or act differently from what he tells us of his own feelings and acts in this Epistle. Nor is his great Epistle to the Romans less relevant and important in relation to that other grand question debated so keenly in our own time: Whether the theology of the Epistles of the New Testament is a mythological re-casting and re-clothing of a few natural elementary facts of the life of Christ? The evidence furnished by the Epistle to the Romans in negation of this theory appears to me to be final and decisive. Within less than thirty years after the death of Christ we have there a full, exhaustive and almost systematic exhibition of the whole body of Christian doctrine and morals. If Christianity be a mythology, as alleged by Strauss and others, in what a brief space of time has the myth been developed! And how extraordinary, how unexampled that all this should have been developed in a single mind, during the half of a single life! and this too (Saul's miraculous conversion being on the same theory denied) without any explanation being possible of the quarter from which the original stimulus to such a mythological process in this single mind was derived. The truth briefly is (for I cannot dwell upon the subject further at present), the existence of the Epistle to the Romans is, singly and alone, fatal to the credit of such a mythological theory of Christianity; its very early date, and its grand doctrinal fulness, and its thorough maturity of dogmatic statement, are all utterly irreconcilable with the theory. All the conditions are proved by this Epistle to have been absent, to have been reversed, which all experience has shown to be indispensable to the development of grand masses and systems of myth. It has taken eighteen centuries and more to develop the mythology of Mary in the Church of Rome, and the myth is not yet complete; but in less than three decades after the death of Jesus of Nazareth, the Son of David is already in the Epistle to the Romans "the Son of God with power," declared and set apart as such from all other sons of men by His resurrection from the dead. (Rom. i. 3, 4.) The Crucified One is already "Christ over all; Lord both of the dead and living; to whom every knee shall bow and every tongue confess." (Rom. xiv. 9, 11.) What a mighty difference in the two cases!—a difference which, more than any other of the Epistles, this Epistle helps us to estimate and to understand.

Such are two of the fundamental subjects of Christian history upon which the early Epistles of St. Paul can be brought to bear with much evidential force and effect. But I merely indicate them at present. I do not dwell upon them, for I wish to go more fully into a third subject of fundamental importance in the early history of Christianity and the Church, upon which these Epistles seem to me to have an interesting and effective bearing, and to which I purpose to devote the remainder of the present lecture.

The Christian Church maintains that there was a supernatural element not only in the life of Christ and in the conversion and mission of St. Paul (the two subjects to which I have hitherto referred), but no less also in the earliest propagation of Christianity throughout the world—in the earliest manifestations and church-organisations of the Christian life, both among Jews and Gentiles. As our Apostle expresses it—" Our Gospel came to men not in word only but also in power, and in the Holy Ghost, and in much assurance." He says, " *Our* Gospel "—meaning the Gospel which he himself preached and propagated throughout the world, and the working and effects of which upon men none knew so well as himself, or were so well able to speak about. Well, then, I propose that we should now listen to him speaking about these very points, and I could not have done better than to quote these few words of his just recited, in which he as much as tells us that there was *something more than natural* in the effects produced by the Gospel on the world, for "it came not in word only, but also in power;" and he means a Divine power, for he adds—" in the Holy Ghost," and therefore also " in much assurance," *i.e.*, with a force and effect of such deep conviction that it gave men the courage of a new faith and hope—carried men right over to the side of Christ, laid the foundations everywhere of Christian and Church life, and commenced in that first Christian century a grand history and progress which has continued unbroken ever since, and is still going on with unexhausted force before the face of the whole world.

Before I break ground upon the argument let me clearly announce the method of using the Epistles which I mean to adopt, and the principles of historical reasoning which I intend to apply.

Remember the nature of the historical documents which are now before us; they are not treatises, they are letters, and not letters addressed to individuals, but to communities—to the Christian communities or societies of Thessalonica, Corinth, Galatia, and Rome. They refer to subjects of common concern between the writer and these communities; they are full of express references to matters of Christian faith and life; and, passing from a Christian Apostle to his Christian disciples and converts, they everywhere assume and proceed upon numerous Christian facts and doctrines and usages and institutes of the Christian life in which he and they believed in common, or to which they were in common attached. We are in presence, therefore, everywhere in these pages not only of what he believed, but of what they believed as well as he; in presence of Christian facts which were not only such to him, but quite as much so to them. For it was upon this basis of common faith and fact that the correspondence between him and them proceeded. But for this common basis—the basis on which these societies were founded—there could have existed no such correspondence of apostolic letters at all; no, nor even any such relation of apostleship and discipleship between the parties.

But here I make a distinction (an important one for my present argument) among these matters of Christian faith and fact common to both the parties in the correspondence. These Christian communities believed in many Christian facts of which they had no independent knowledge from their own observation; such, *e.g.*, as all the facts of Christ's life which the Apostle had communicated to them, or all the facts concerning his own conversion and apostleship, which were known in the first instance only to himself and a very small number of other witnesses. I do not mean to make any use of such facts as these, or of their belief in them, because in relation to these their testimony was of no authority —at least, of no primary authority. They had not been eye-witnesses of them. They had been dependent for all their knowledge of them upon St. Paul's own teaching and testimony; and their reception of them, in the first instance at least, was only the echo of his own voice.

But I am going to point out several facts referred to in these Epistles of quite a different kind—several facts of a supernatural character which the Apostle refers to as having taken place among themselves—before their own eyes, and within the scope of their own independent knowledge—he too having been an eye-witness of them himself. Here then is apparently a common basis of knowledge and conviction between the two parties in regard to facts of a supernatural kind, in which both parties are on equal terms, both having an original, primary, and independent knowledge and conviction of their reality. If this can be shown to be more than an apparency of a common basis of knowledge and conviction—if it can be shown that both parties had and must have had this common knowledge and conviction (otherwise the references to these supernatural facts and experiences could never have occurred in the Epistles), then the argumentative, evidential effect of this will clearly be to prove that these matters of supernatural fact rest on the united testimony both of the Apostle and the churches—that the testimony in both cases was original and of primary authority, and that the Epistles before us become virtually and in effect the joint attestation to these facts of the Apostle as having seen them with his own eyes, and of hundreds of men in Thessalonica, Corinth, Galatia, and Rome, as having seen them and known them to be facts as well as he.

Proceeding now to the substance of the argument itself, I shall be able to do little more than to suggest the chief points as subjects for your own reflection when you turn, as I hope you will be induced to do, to the Epistles themselves, to read them over again in view of the evidential values of their contents which this lecture will point out.

1. First then let us turn to the two Epistles to the Thessalonians to see what is to be found there on the subject of the new Christian character and life which had sprung up in Thessalonica under the Apostle's preaching, and had continued to thrive and grow and develop itself since his recent visit. One or two readings will suffice to set this picture before us :—

(1. Thess. i. 2, 3.) "*We give thanks to God always for you all, making mention of you in our prayers; remembering without ceasing your work of faith, and labour of love, and patience of hope in our Lord Jesus Christ, in the sight of God and our Father.*" (1. Thess. i. 8-10.) "*In every place your faith to God-ward is spread abroad; so that we need not to speak anything. For they themselves shew of us what manner of entering in we had unto you, and how ye turned to God from idols to serve the living and true God; and to wait for His Son from heaven, whom He raised from*

the dead, even *Jesus, which delivered us from the wrath to come.* (1. Thess. ii. 1.) *For yourselves, brethren, know our entrance in unto you, that it was not in vain."*

All at once, on hearing the preaching of Paul, these Thessalonians had abandoned their idolatries and turned to the living and true God, to serve Him in a holy and blameless life, in the power of a new and heavenly hope. All at once they had become men of faith and faith's work—men of love and love's labour—men of hope and of hope's patience, in the midst of persecution and affliction endured on account of their new faith and life.

Nor was this sudden change illusory and transient. Months passed away, and a second letter is despatched to them, beginning in the same strain of warm-hearted thankfulness. (2. Thess. i. 3, 4.) *" We are bound to thank God always for you, brethren, as it is meet, because that your faith groweth exceedingly, and the charity of every one of you all toward each other aboundeth; so that we ourselves glory in you in the churches of God for your patience and faith in all your persecutions and tribulations that ye endure."*

The language seems strong and high-coloured. Was the Apostle flattering them? Did he use such words " as a cloke of coveteousness "—concealing and subserving some selfish ends and designs of his own? Impossible! for what does he say to them on this very point of flattery and cloaked self-seeking? (Chap. ii. 5.) Appealing directly to their own knowledge of him and his ways, he could boldly say, *" For neither at any time used we flattering words, as ye know, nor a cloke of covetousness, as God is witness. Nor of men sought we glory,* neither of you nor yet of others whom we might have been burdensome as the Apostles of Christ." He had never flattered these Thessalonians, and they knew it. All he says here about the rise and growth of the Christian life among them was no more than the truth; for which he might well give fervent and constant thanks to God. But how could he have thanked Him for a flattery and a lie? Would he have dared to appeal to these men as being no flatterer, if he had been conscious that he was even now flattering them in thus describing their character and life? To flatter them, and in the same breath to appeal to their own knowledge of him that he had never been a flatterer, is that conceivable in such a man? And would not such a proceeding have been utterly fatal to his character and credit among them as their religious teacher and guide?

Here then we have virtually a joint testimony from him and from them as to the matter of fact in question— the first appearance in Thessalonica of Christian character and life, and of Church society resting upon these. It is a memorable fact. It marks a grand epoch in the history of Greece and of Europe. Here in Macedonia and in Thessalonica, is the first rise of Christian life under the ministry of the great Apostle of the Gentiles. It is quite a new and strange phenomenon. The like effects of religious and moral teaching had never been seen before—never among the Pagans, never among the Jews. And it was the same wherever the Apostle had been, or was yet to be in the fulfilment of his mission—in Galatia, in Ephesus, in Corinth, and in Rome. His experience everywhere was what he expresses in one of his Epistles to the Corinthians (2 Cor. v. 17, 18): "If any man is in Christ," if any man becomes a real and true Christian, "he is *a new creature;* old things are passed away from him, behold! all things are made new; and all things," he adds, all these things of the Christian man and the Christian life, "are of God."

Yes! All these things, he asserted, were *of God.* They had a Divine source and origin. These spiritual and moral phenomena never seen in the world before, which the Gospel of Christ was everywhere calling forth into view, had a supernatural character and quality about them—not sprung from the lap of mother-nature, but born of a truth and a power which had both descended from heaven, from the love and grace of the Heavenly Father.

The facts of the case defy contradiction. Do you accept also the Apostle's explanation of them? He maintained the facts to have a supernatural cause in two distinct particulars, viz., in a Gospel Divinely revealed and in a Divine presence and power accompanying this Gospel. Do you accept this solution of the origin of the facts in either or in both its parts, or do you disallow and reject it, and substitute another of a naturalistic kind, asserting that even if the facts were really such as we have been looking at, you still see no sufficient reason to think that they had anything in them which was beyond the powers of nature to produce?

2. This brings me to the second link in the chain of proof which I wish to present to you. I invite you to turn with me for our second reading of these Epistles to the First Epistle to the Corinthians.

Let me suppose that your view of the Gospel is that it is a merely human thing, a mere natural product of the age in which it was first preached to the world. In the case of St. Paul in particular, its chief preacher and propagator, your view, I suppose, would be that in his hands the Gospel was nothing more than a complex or mixture of the best things which he had learned in the schools of Tarsus and Jerusalem, with some addition, perhaps, of Oriental ideas from the Greco-Jewish sources of Alexandria. The whole effect of his preaching, you think, was due to this combination of ingredients of human wisdom. It was a great improvement, you admit, upon either Judaism or Heathenism, taken separately. The Alexandrian mixture of the two in such writers as Philo had already made something better than either, and the Pauline mixture of the three was something better still; and this, you think, is sufficient to account for its power to work the effects it did. Well, then, let me bring this way of thinking into comparison with the experiences and the convictions of the most earnest minds at the time when Christianity was making its earliest conquests in Corinth. The situation of matters there was singularly appropriate for such a comparison; for not only the Jewish and the Greek wisdom but also the Alexandrian gnosis or science had its representatives among the Corinthian Christians at that very time; for Apollos of Alexandria had arrrived there shortly after the Apostle's first visit, and his "excellency of speech and of wisdom" had made so great an impression upon those who were able to appreciate them that a party had arisen in the Church who preferred to be called the disciples of Apollos rather than of Paul. It was partly owing to this movement which, without any blame attaching to Apollos, had taken the direction, after he left Corinth, of an undue overvaluing of human wisdom and rhetoric in the things of God, that the Apostle addressed to the Church this very Epistle. And it was with the view of correcting this dangerous tendency that he penned the remarkable passages which we are now to consider:

(1 Cor. i. 17-19.) *"Christ sent me not to baptize, but to preach the Gospel; not with wisdom of words, less the cross of Christ should be made of none effect. For the preaching of the cross is to them that are perishing foolishness; but unto us which are saved, it is the power of God. For it is written, I will destroy the wisdom of the wise, and will bring to nothing the understanding of the prudent."*

You see here how far the Apostle was from thinking that the preaching of the Gospel was only one of the better forms, or the very best extant form of human wisdom, or that human wisdom had anything to do with giving it effect. The very contrary was his conviction on both points. The Gospel was simply the preaching of the Cross of Christ, and the whole power of that preaching lay in its own absolute newness and originality. To mix anything of human wisdom with it was to spoil it, and make it as weak as all mere human wisdom had been. No doubt there was also a "wisdom of the wise," and an "understanding of the prudent," and these were all well enough in their own place and for their own work. But it was never possible that they should have the place and the power of *saving souls*—

of delivering men, that is to say, from the yoke and power, the bondage and the misery of sin, and bringing them back into God's image and God's peace. That is a power, St. Paul thought, which comes forth from God alone, and which is communicated only in the preaching of the Cross. That is a power which " the wisdom of the wise" may put in a claim to possess, and which "the understanding of the prudent" may affect to put forth, but God has said, "I will destroy the wisdom of the wise, I will bring to nothing the understanding of the prudent"—in the sense of exposing to shame their utter emptiness and impotence for any such saving and redeeming work. For such work the wisdom of man is folly, and the strength of man utter weakness and abortion. Not only has God said it, He has also made it good by the demonstration of world-facts and world-history. For mark how the Apostle goes on (vv. 20—25): "*Where is the wise? where is the scribe? where is the disputer of this world? Did not God make foolish* (i.e., *convict of foolishness*) *the wisdom of the world? For when in the wisdom of God* (i.e., *in His wise dispensation and ordering of epochs and events*) *the world through its wisdom knew not God* (i.e., *had failed utterly to reach the knowledge of His mind and will*), *it pleased God through the foolishness of preaching to save them that believe. For the Jews require a sign, and the Greeks seek after wisdom. But we preach Christ crucified, to the Jews a stumbling block and to the Greeks foolishness, but to them which are called, both Jews and Greeks, Christ the power of God and the wisdom of God. Because the foolishness of God is wiser than men; and the weakness of God is stronger than men.*"

In other words, it is proved by the whole history of the world down to the era of Christ that no wisdom of man is able to save the souls of men from sin, and that the Gospel of Christ which is able to do this for mankind, and has already done it in the experience of so many, is not any form or growth or adaptation of human wisdom but a Gospel *of God*—a truth revealed to men from Heaven. In point of fact, and of history, the world at its advent was still unsaved from its sin—in spite of all the boasted wisdom of the schools of Greece, of Jerusalem, and the East. In point of fact it is the preaching of the Cross alone that has brought to the world an epoch of salvation—a way of life and peace. Some men call it indeed foolishness, but none the less it is God's wiser wisdom. Some men scoff at it as weakness, but none the less it is God's stronger strength.

But now mark well what follows next in the Apostle's pleading. He makes his appeal in support of all this to the independent knowledge and experience of the Corinthians themselves. He compares ideas with them, he makes a confident call upon their own consciousness and knowledge and recollection to support his own (vv. 26—end): "*For consider your calling, brethren, how, that not many (of you) were wise men after the flesh (*i.e., *in the sense of human wisdom), not many mighty men, not many noble. But God chose the foolish things of the world that He might put to shame the things that are wise, and God chose the weak things of the world that He might put to shame the things that are mighty, and the base things of the world and the things which are despised did God choose, yea, the things which are not, that*

He might bring to nought the things that are, that no flesh should glory in His presence. But of Him are ye in Christ Jesus, who from God was made unto us wisdom, and righteousness, and sanctification, and redemption. That according as it is written, He that glorieth let him glory in the Lord." What in commoner language is the gist of all this? Simply that the Corinthians themselves were instances and proofs of the truth of what the Apostle had said, and could be appealed to as such. Who and what were these Corinthian Christians? Not many of them were men of high education, or of much rank and influence in the society of their great city. It was not to these advantages that they could ascribe the change that had come over their whole character and life as Christian men. All these advantages had done nothing for the religious and moral condition of the few among them who possessed them, and the great majority of them had never possessed these advantages at all. The preaching of the Cross, and that alone, had done for them what all the wisdom, and teaching, and influence of men had never been able to achieve. They were now for the first time new men—new creatures in character, life-habit, and life-hope; but they had become so only in Christ Jesus—only by the knowledge and faith of His truth and grace, only by the preaching of Christ the power of God, and the wisdom of God. This is what I take to be the true meaning of the Apostle's vigorous words about the confounding of the wise by the foolish, and of the mighty by the weak, and about the bringing to nought of the things that are by the things that are not—of the men that were somethings in the world by the men that were nothings in it, or mere nonentities. For see! (he as much as says) how the tables are turned now by the coming in upon the world of Him "who brings down the mighty from their seats and exalteth the humble and meek." It is the fools now who are made wise in Christ, and the weak strong, and the nobodies somebodies. It is the Christless wise who are fools now, the Christless strong who are weak now, the Christless somebodies who are nobodies now in religion and morals, in the true philosophy of life, in life's true use, and work, and hope.

I beg you, to remember and realise that all this is put by the Apostle in this place, not as a matter of doctrine or theology, but as a matter of fact and history— as a matter of actual experience and observation, and therefore of special value and weight for the purposes of my argument. It is a lesson of history which the Apostle here reads off to us, as it was plainly taught by all that he had read in the annals of the world, by all that he had seen and known of the religious and moral conditions of the nations, and by all that he had experienced in his apostolic travels and labours. The passage has also the great additional value of being a comparison of his own observations and experiences with those of his Corinthian disciples. Both parties had been eye-witnesses of the situation of matters before the Gospel began to be published, and since—and here we have the result which was forced by the demonstration of facts upon both parties alike, viz., that the religion which had wrought the great changes of character and life which as a matter of fact were plain and undeniable, was the wisdom of God, and not the wisdom of man—the truth and revelation of God, and not the speculation or invention of man. As the Apostle so eloquently puts it, " Eye of man had never seen, ear of man had never heard, nor had it ever entered into the heart of man to conceive the things which God hath prepared for them that love Him," the things of the Gospel ; but God hath revealed them to the Church by His Spirit. This wisdom is from above. It could not be Jewish wisdom in a new form, for to the Jews as a nation it was a stumbling-block. And it could not be Greek wisdom brought into a new connexion, for to the Greeks the preaching of Christ crucified was utter foolishness. No! it was a new thing in the earth, it was a new creation in the sphere of religion and morals. It was a new starting-point and beginning in the religious and ethical life of the world. And such a new creation for man, drawing nothing from man himself, could only have sprung out of the life-power of Almighty God. Such a new starting-point for the world, which owed none of its impulses to the world itself, could only have received its impulse from a Supreme hand—from Him who, without Beginning Himself, is the providential and beneficent Beginner of all the grand movements of the world towards light and goodness.

To bring now this section of the argument to a distinct point. We have here the joint testimony of St. Paul and the Corinthian Christians to the supernatural origin of the Gospel of Christ, as proved by the mighty influences of a religious and moral kind which they had seen it produce. Is their testimony valid? Ought it to have weight with us? Ought it to have more weight with us than the opinions of the unbelievers and disbelievers of this nineteenth century? I think in all justice and in all common sense it ought. The conviction of the first Christians on this subject rested upon observation and experience—and these not other men's, but their own. The disbelief of the present age rests on mere speculation and foregone philosophical conclusions. An abstract alleged axiom of philosophy lies at the base of it, viz., that the supernatural is impossible, and that therefore there was and there could be nothing supernatural either in the effects produced by Christianity in the first age, or in the substance and origin of Christianity itself. But such an axiom as this is anything but axiomatic. It needs to be proved before it is applied, and it never has been proved, and never will be, and never can be. Call in question the axiom, and all its *a priori* applications to theological controversy become inept and null at once. I prefer the practical reasoning of St. Paul and his converts—" We and many thousands more," said they, "find ourselves new creatures in Christ; it was the Gospel of Christ that did this for us and nothing else; it is more than the wisdom of the world ever did for us or could do; it is more than ever we were able to do for ourselves. He who did it for us by His Gospel must be greater and mightier than men. He must be what we call Him, 'the Son of God with power;' and His Gospel—the rod of His power, the arm of His strength, must be like himself, Divine." It is a plain, practical kind of reasoning, I admit. It may not sound in some ears very philosophic, but it has the ring none the less of sound common sense; and we should remember that, after all, the philosophy of common sense, the philosophy of observation and experience is acknowledged by philosophers themselves to be the wisest and safest and most fruitful of all philosophies.

Let me now point out to you a *third* and a *fourth* link of evidence supplied by these early Epistles, and bearing specially on the point of the Divine *presence* and *power* which accompanied the preaching of the Gospel in the hands of the Apostles. If this was a reality, it was of course a supernatural element. Do these Epistles contribute anything to prove that it was a real historical thing? Let us see. First, listen to the convictions of St. Paul himself upon the point—a point on which, more than any other man in the world, he was entitled to speak with authority and weight, as it so closely concerned the one great work of his whole life, and penetrated to the very core of its meaning and force. And let it be carefully observed, as before, that in the passage I am now to read from him he is not dogmatizing, not laying down a doctrine or article of faith: he is recalling the circumstances of his first visit to Corinth; he is referring to personal facts and incidents and conditions of that visit of which the Corinthians were cognizant as well as himself. The passage is a bit of St. Paul's autobiography—a bit of early Church history, not of early Church dogma. (1 Cor. ii. 1, 4). "*And I, brethren, when I came to you, came declaring unto you the testimony of God; not with excellency of speech or of wisdom, for I determined not to know anything among you save Jesus Christ and Him crucified; and I was with you in weakness and in fear and in much trembling; and my speech and my preaching was not with persuasive words of man's wisdom, but with demonstration of the Spirit and of power; to the end that your faith might not stand in the wisdom of men, but in the power of God."* That is to say, as he came to Corinth to publish solely a Divine message and not a human one, so his sole confidence for the effect of his publication of it was confidence not in his own power or persuasiveness as a preacher, for he felt nothing but weakness, but in the power of that God whom he served, in the demonstration and manifestation of "the Spirit." If they received his message, their faith was to stand or rest not in any manifestation of the power of man, but only in the manifested power of God. They were to be, as he says in another place, God's own husbandry, not his. It was the presence and power of God's Spirit that was to work their conversion in Christ, and to make them new creatures in Christ. That, he tells them, was his working *programme* when he first came among them; and what was the upshot of his work so projected and planned? It had been an immense success. The power of God had been "demonstrated" among them as he had expected. "God gave the increase; for neither is he that planteth anything; neither he that watereth; but God that giveth the increase"—He is everything in this work, He is all in all.

But here I shall suppose that you stand in doubt of the reality of this supernatural power accompanying the Gospel on the ground of its being an invisible and impalpable power, working unseen in men's minds, if working at all, and not manifesting its presence and force in any undeniable way to the senses. I do not sympathise much with such a doubt, resting upon such a ground, because surely revolutions of character and life and conduct in men are effects of power palpable enough even to men's senses. But let that pass, and rather let me call your attention to two remarkable facts preserved to us by these Epistles to the Corinthians, which prove in the most unanswerable manner that a supernatural presence and power were then at work in Corinth in the most palpable forms possible, and with effects and manifestations of a kind which might even be called sensational. And these two facts are the two additional links of proof to which I referred.

(2 Cor. xii. 12.) "*Truly the signs of an Apostle were wrought among you in all patience, in signs and wonders, and mighty deeds. For what is it wherein ye were inferior to other Churches? Except it be that I myself was not burdensome to you. Forgive me this wrong.*" He plainly means "miracles" of the most palpable kind—he means "mighty deeds," only to be wrought upon nature and the common order of the world by a power above nature herself. Yes! and he refers to them as having taken place before the eyes of the Corinthians themselves—as things which they knew to have taken place, and were as certain of having seen, as he was himself. Could he have written in that manner to them, about miracles done among them, if no such miracles had ever been done? Could he have appealed to these miracles as signs of his Apostleship, if they had been all myths and unrealities! Could he have so appealed to them in a context, where he is finding grave fault with the Corinthians, where he is remonstrating with them for giving too much countenance to men whom

he characterises as false Apostles, transforming themselves into Apostles of Christ? He points to those miracles as the seals of his own Apostleship, as vouchers of its being a true and not a false Apostleship. He is arguing with the Corinthians, he is putting them in the wrong; he is pressing his controversy closely home upon them. And it is in such a connexion and discourse that he is bold to say, "*Truly* the signs of an Apostle were wrought *among you*." This could only be the boldness of conscious truth. This was an appeal which he well knew it was impossible for them to resist. They had seen "the mighty deeds" of God in Corinth as well as he. They were God's witnesses to them as well as he.

The other fact referred to—the remaining link of the argument—is the remarkable one so fully set out in the twelfth chapter of 1 Corinthians, a chapter too long to be quoted in full here, touching the "spiritual gifts" of that church, which he calls "the manifestation of the Spirit, given to every man to profit withal." "*For to one is given by the Spirit the word of wisdom, to another the word of knowledge according to the same Spirit, to another the gifts of healing, to another the working of miracles, to another prophecy, to another discerning of spirits, to another divers kinds of tongues, to another interpretation of tongues. But all these worketh the one and self same Spirit, dividing to every man severally as He willeth.*" Here, verily, was a demonstration of the Spirit of God and of power in the most manifold and palpable forms. If gifts like these did not and could not manifest a supernatural presence and working, I know not what could manifest them. And there was an indubitable and indisputable reality in the whole matter. If I am sure that this letter is from the hand of St. Paul, and was addressed to the hands of the Corinthian Christians—and I may be as sure of these facts as of the genuineness and the date of any letter of Cicero or Pliny—I may be also equally sure that the things which he refers to in these extraordinary terms were real things and no delusions. For he speaks of things of which he claims to have himself large experience. "I thank my God," he exclaims (1 Cor. xiv. 18), I speak with tongues more than you all." Could he be under a delusion as to the reality of a supernatural endowment possessed by himself in so high a degree? or could he have expected the Corinthians to believe at his suggestion that they had been endowed with it too, if they had had no knowledge and experience of the fact themselves, if they had known the exact contrary to be the fact? I am compelled by the inexorable logic of common sense to believe that these gifts of the Spirit were facts of the church-life of Corinth; and the inexorable logic of the facts themselves compels me to believe and confess "that God was in the midst of them of a truth." It was for the sake of this inexorable logic of facts that the facts were brought to pass; they were meant to be "signs to the unbelievers," to heal them of their unbelief. We know that they answered that purpose then (1 Cor. xiv. 24, 25); and such a genuine contemporary original record of them as we have here handed down to us, is well fitted to answer the same evidential purpose still. I know, of course, the difficulties which it is possible to raise upon the collateral points of a subject like this, of which we have nowhere in the New Testament an exhaustive account, and of which we have had no personal experience ourselves. But the difficulties upon collateral points attaching to facts are no disproof of the facts themselves, when the facts are strongly attested and vouched. I know also how easy it is for men to ride off from this whole subject in a contemptuous manner upon the allegation that both St. Paul and his Corinthian converts must have been in a frenzy of enthusiasm, or had fallen into a fit of religious madness. But St. Paul might well have replied at the bar of modern disbelief in the memorable words which he used at the bar of Festus: "I am not mad, but speak forth the words of truth and soberness." Yes, his *soberness of mind* on this very subject vouches for his truthfulness and accuracy upon it. He writes upon the whole matter, supernatural as it was, like a man of sense and of a well-regulated mind; like a man whose judgment was as sound and enlightened as his personal endowments were miraculous. "In the Church," he writes (1 Cor. xiv. 19),. "I had rather speak five words with my understanding that I might teach others also, than ten thousand words in an unknown tongue. Brethren, be not children in understanding, but in understanding be men." Is. not that spoken like a man of sense? Is that the language and bearing of a heated enthusiast, proud of his own imaginary endowments, dazzled by them beyond the power of clear-seeing, and wildly exaggerating and extolling their value? Does not this great teacher, who desires all his friends at

Corinth to be men and not children in understanding, begin by showing that he was such a man himself?—no childish dreamer deluding himself with fond fables and conceits, but a manly thinker with senses well trained and exercised to discern good and evil, truth and error, fact and fable, history and myth, reality and seeming.

Here my present argument must end. But before I quite close this address, will you allow me to throw out one or two suggestions arising naturally from my subject, with the view of correcting one or two very common misapprehensions which, for anything I know, may at this moment be influencing some of yourselves.

You see here how the early Church of Christ was planted and rooted in the world before any part of the New Testament collection was written at all. The Churches of Galatia, Thessalonica, Corinth, and Rome, were all gathered to Christ before the Epistles to these Churches were written, and these Epistles we have seen, are the oldest writings in the New Testament. It is foolish then for men to think that by picking faults with the New Testament here and there they can rid themselves of Christianity altogether. Christianity existed and flourished both in Asia and Europe before any part of the New Testament came into existence. The Gospel of Christ was a spoken and victorious Gospel before it was a written one, and if it was true and triumphant even as a spoken Gospel it must be true and worthy to triumph still.

Again, if you admit, as you cannot help doing, that at least these early Epistles of St. Paul are **genuine** historical documents, do not imagine that you get rid of their historical truth by denying their Divine inspiration. I shall suppose that you do not agree with the Church of Christ upon that matter of inspiration. You think you see many strong objections against such a claim. You think you can break it down by no end of arguments. Very well, but remember that you have here the earliest historical documents of Christianity before you—and these of undoubted genuineness, and of high historic validity—and you have no warrant to neglect or ignore these documents for the uses of history, merely because you do not take them to be inspired. You accept innumerable things of the past as true and important upon the credit of ancient or modern histories—though these had no claim to be given by inspiration of God. Well, then, act in the same way by these early Epistles of St. Paul. To begin with, distinguish between the truth of ancient facts of Christian history and the alleged inspiration of the documents which record and establish them. Convince yourselves first, if you are able, of the truth of the facts contained in the documents viewed simply as materials of history. Afterwards it will be time enough for you to take up and settle the ulterior question of their Divine quality and authority. If Christianity, as we have seen, might have been true and triumphant without a single book of the New Testament being written, it might have been equally so without a single book of the New Testament being inspired.

Last of all, let me suppose that you have one grand *a priori* objection to everything that can be said about supernatural truths, facts, writings, and personages,—viz.

that you see no sufficient reason to think that there is any supernatural being or power in the universe at all, anything above nature, or distinct from it, or able to interfere with it, or either to order it or to dislocate its order.

Well! but I do not suppose you undertake *to prove* that there is no God. That were a Quixotic undertaking. All you mean to say is that as yet you have seen no sufficient proof of God's Being and Power and agency. If so, it is more proof which you are in quest of or should be. If so, I think such historical documents as those we have been speaking of to-night have something to say upon that grand question. I do not see how the supernatural facts there vouched for are to be got rid of by the bare assertion that there is nothing in the universe above nature. That seems to me to be a mere begging of the question. You say you are without evidence enough to prove that there is any God at all. I reply, and am entitled to reply, Well! here at least is some relevant evidence of a historical kind applicable to the question. Impossible! you urge, there is nothing to prove that there is a God in history. Nay, I reply, *not impossible*. It is possible enough that there may be facts of history which admit of no other explanation than by referring them to supernatural Being and Power, and the facts vouched by these earliest of all the Christian documents appear to me to be of that kind. It is no argument to deny and exclude all supernatural solutions *a priori*. You are bound by good logic and by common sense, first, to try whether any naturalistic solution of these facts can be found that will bear a searching criticism, and failing any such, to admit that here at least you have come upon some facts which multitudes not only of intelligent but learned men have interpreted in a supernatural sense, and which cannot be explained or accounted for satisfactorily in any other way.

If the facts of nature are at least relevant materials in arguing the question of God's Being and Work, I do not see why facts of history thoroughly well attested should not be relevant materials also. We have come, I am persuaded, upon some such materials of history tonight, and I commend them to the serious thoughts of any among you who are still debating with yourselves the most fundamental of all questions of Being and Power.

LORD LYTTLETON ON THE CONVERSION OF ST. PAUL.

BY THE
REV. JOHN GRITTON.

Lord Lyttleton on St. Paul.

THE EVIDENTIAL FORCE OF THE CONVERSION OF THE APOSTLE PAUL.

BY reason of the endless variety in the minds of men —as endless possibly as the varieties of human countenances—the same argument will become weighty or weak according to the person to whom it is addressed, and a kind of evidence which affects one person conclusively may fail to influence another person in even the slightest degree. But underlying this variety there is an uniformity of mind—as to its nature and its capacity for for being influenced by evidence—which encourages men to seek in one way or another, by this or that process, to influence their fellows towards the acceptance of beliefs which they themselves have adopted. In consequence of this uniformity, and of this variety, the Christian believer is led to present evidences to the minds of non-believers, and is induced to present many kinds of evidence, and to place the points of evidence in varying proportion and relation, hoping that some kind of evidence, or various evidential elements in varying relations, may beget in the hearer's mind the conviction that the Christian system is Divine in its origin and worthy of the fullest credit.

Some minds are so constituted or are so trained, that if one line of evidence presents itself forcibly, and they are able to grasp it as conclusive, they are never again troubled by difficulties which affect only other lines of evidence. But minds of a different type or habit can never be satisfied by one strong line of argument on a given subject, while objections lie against some other kind of evidence by which also the subject may be exhibited or proved. Let us illustrate this difference. Here is a man who has been persuaded that Christianity is from God, and that the Books of the Old and New Covenant in which that system is contained are given by inspiration of God. He has attained to that conviction, so far as mental exercise is concerned, by observing that in revealed religion there is a wonderful likeness to many things in the order of nature, and by inferring from this likeness that both come from the same hand and have been fashioned by the same wisdom, prevision, and power; or conviction may have resulted from observing the wonderful uniqueness, originality and verisimilitude in the character of Jesus Christ of Nazareth; or the argument from prophecy may have established his confidence in the verity of the Bible as the Word of God : at all events in some way or other he has arrived at that conviction. In the course of after investigation he finds himself face to face with difficulties such as those which exist or seem to exist in reconciling the Mosaic cosmogony with geological fact or geological theory, but he will never be shaken or troubled in mind by such difficulties, knowing that the Book is true whatever may be the case as to geology; and concluding that if the fact in nature fall not in with the apparent statement of the Bible, it is not the Book but the interpretation of the Book which is faulty, and that if the statement in the Book is absolutely contradictory of the supposed fact in science the fact is after all but a theory miscalled. In the same way he deals consciously or unconsciously with biblical difficulties touching on arithmetic, or ethnology, or morals. He has settled the verity of the Book on one clear line of argument, and he considers that his partial knowledge of the whole field in debate fully justifies him in waiting and expecting the solution of difficulties.

Let us take the case of a man who is the type of the other habit of mind to which reference has been made. He has concluded from prophecy or miracles, or the character of Jesus, or the general concensus of differing lines of evidence, that the Bible is of God and that therefore Christianity is Divine. But he too meets with difficulties, numerical, moral, scientific or historical, and they have so much effect on him that he never quite rests in his conviction of the truth and certainty of the Bible because there are these difficulties; and, even when with increasing knowledge he is conscious that the difficulty of yesterday is no difficulty now, he still never learns to conclude that remaining difficulties will disappear before the brighter light of advancing study.

Under these varying circumstances the Christian advocate will learn to deal with many lines of evidence and in many different ways. He will endeavour at one time to present a general view of testimony, and at another will confine himself to some specific and limited line of thought. To-day he will endeavour to place the enquirer where he may obtain a *coup d'œil* of evidence which, however, from its very breadth and fulness will be lacking in definition and sharpness. To-morrow he will place the student at a selected point of view whence he will see some one or some few objects with distinctness, but will see them only.

It is this latter process to which we give ourselves to-night. I wish to lay before you in a brief way the special line of enquiry by which one particular person was led to the conclusion that Christianity is of God. There may be many in this assembly unwilling or even unable to see the full importance and force of the evidence which will be adduced, because pre-engaged with general scepticism or with some special objections; but others may be here who will see in the evidence adduced, the same force and conclusiveness which it presented to the mind of Lord Lyttleton, to whose process of investigation I invite you to-night.

The Lord Lyttleton of whom we speak was an active politician and statesman of the reign of George the Second. He was well acquainted with the world and at the same time studious and reflective. As a poet he enjoys the honour of a place in "Johnson's Lives." His "Dialogues of the Dead" exhibits him as the thoughtful moralist, while his voluminous but heavy "History of Henry the Second" testifies to his ability to investigate fact and weigh evidence.

The period in which he lived was not favourable to

Christian studies or to godly living. General scepticism in sentiment, and abounding profligacy in life marked the whole period in which Lord Lyttleton lived and acted, and he did not escape unscathed in the furnace of evil in which he lived. Johnson who sketches his life testifies "He had, in the pride of youthful confidence, with the help of corrupt conversation, entertained doubts of Christianity," and it was not till he was nearly forty years of age that he was led into that course of reading and reflection of which Johnson writes, "His studies, being honest, ended in conviction."

We do not know with certainty what were the facts which first arrested his attention, or the arguments which overcame his scepticism; but we do know from his own writings that he regarded the conversion of St. Paul, and his after life as an Apostle, taken in connexion with his undisputed writings, as containing on one single and limited line of evidence a force and conclusiveness sufficient to convince an honest enquirer, or, to use his own words, "I thought the conversion and Apostleship of St. Paul alone, duly considered, was of itself a demonstration sufficient to prove Christianity to be a Divine revelation."

It appears that in a conversation with Gilbert West, the author of an invaluable Monograph on the Resurrection of Jesus Christ, Lord Lyttleton had expressed his opinion as given above, and that at his friend's request he engaged to reduce to writing the argument which seemed to his own mind so convincing. This engagement he observed, and sent to his friend his "Observations on the Conversion and Apostleship of St. Paul."

Before I proceed to sketch the argument of his letter

I would remark that it has now been before the world for a hundred and seventeen years, and that while particular expressions and conclusions here and there have been questioned, no opponent of Christianity has ever written a reply to it. It will be well also to notice that, although Lord Lyttleton wrote before the birth of the modern school of scientific criticism of the books of the Bible, he takes for granted only such points as are at the present time regarded as established by the more recent sceptical writers. He postulates nothing beyond the points which Strauss admits, and which Renan in his more recent work takes as certain. I speak of admitted *facts*. Strauss, Paulus, and Renan offer varying and contradictory explanations of the facts, and they differ as to the actuality of certain things lying outside the facts which are taken for granted in the "Observations;" but, with Lord Lyttleton, they admit the existence of Saul of Tarsus—his eminent acquaintance with Judaism and addiction to its most severe form, that of Pharisaic scrupulosity. They admit his persecution of the followers of the Crucified—his journey to Damascus with authority from the Jewish Chief Priests to bind the followers of Jesus whom he might find in that city; and they also admit that from some cause or other this red-handed opponent became a preacher of the faith which before he hated, and a companion and fellow worker with those whom he had sought to destroy. They regard as actual events the incidents in his after life which are contained in the book of the Acts of the Apostles, which history even Renan ascribes to a date not later than A.D. 80; and finally they assert the authenticity of those Epistles to which Lord Lyttleton turns for evidence and illustration, admitting that some of those letters were written by Paul at least as early as the year A.D. 58.

Thus the most destructive schemes of criticism which were ever applied to the books of Scripture have, by a process of mutual destruction and antagonistical admission, left a residuum of confessed fact, which contains all that is necessary for the validity of the argument of the "Observations."

I now proceed to lay the argument before you, not in the fulness of detail given by Lord Lyttleton, but with sufficient fulness and accuracy to convey the general results at which he arrives.

The event with which we have to do is thus narrated by Paul himself at Cæsarea in the presence of Festus the Roman Governor, and Agrippa a Jewish King, and before many of his enemies who knew his history and were ready to detect any error or falsehood in his statement :—

" My manner of life from my youth, which was at the first among mine own nation at Jerusalem, know all the Jews; which knew me from the beginning, if they would testify, that after the most straitest sect of our religion I lived a Pharisee. And now I stand and am judged for the hope of the promise made of God unto our fathers: unto which promise our twelve tribes, instantly serving God day and night, hope to come; for which hope's sake, King Agrippa, I am accused of the Jews. Why should it be thought a thing incredible with you, that God should raise the dead? I verily thought with myself, that I ought to do many things contrary to the name of Jesus of Nazareth. Which thing I also did in Jerusalem: and many of the saints did I shut up in prison, having received authority from the chief priests; and when they were put to death I gave my voice against them. And I punished them oft in every synagogue, and compelled them to blaspheme; and being exceedingly mad against them, I persecuted them even unto strange cities. Whereupon as I went to Damascus with authority and commission from the chief priests, at mid-day, O King, I saw in the way a light from heaven, above the brightness of the sun, shining round about me and them which journeyed with me. And when we were all fallen to the earth, I heard a voice speaking unto me, and saying in the Hebrew tongue, Saul, Saul, why persecutest thou me? It is hard for thee to kick against the pricks. And I said, Who art thou, Lord? And He said, I am Jesus whom thou persecutest. But rise, and stand upon thy feet: for I have appeared unto thee for this purpose, to make thee a minister and a witness both of these things which thou hast seen, and of those things in the which I will appear unto thee; delivering thee from the people, and from the Gentiles, unto whom now I send thee, to open their eyes, and to turn them from darkness to light, and from the power of Satan unto God, that they may receive forgiveness of sins, and inheritance among them which are sanctified by faith that is in me. Whereupon, O King Agrippa, I was not disobedient unto the heavenly vision: but shewed first unto them of Damascus, and at Jerusalem, and throughout all the coasts of Judea, and then to the Gentiles, that they should repent and turn to God, and do works meet for repentance." (Acts xxvi. 4—20.)

On another occasion, defending himself before the Jews

in Jerusalem he gives in substance the same statement but adds other particulars :—

" And I said, What shall I do, Lord? And the Lord said unto me, Arise and go into Damascus; and there it shall be told thee of all things which are appointed for thee to do. And when I could not see for the glory of that light, being led by the hand of them that were with me, I came into Damascus. And one Ananias, a devout man according to the law, having a good report of all the Jews which dwelt there, came unto me, and stood, and said unto me, Brother Saul receive thy sight. And the same hour I looked up upon him. And he said, The God of our fathers hath chosen thee, that thou shouldest know His will, and see that Just One, and shouldest hear the voice of His mouth. For thou shalt be His witness unto all men of what thou hast seen and heard. And now why tarriest thou? Arise, and be baptized, and wash away thy sins, calling on the name of the Lord." (Acts xxii. 10—16.)

The same historian who records these statements of the convert, and was himself a companion of Paul in much of his life of ministry, narrates the incident in another chapter of the book of the Acts, mentioning other circumstances besides those recounted by Paul in his apologies before his enemies—as that Saul in a vision saw Ananias before he came to him, coming in and putting his hand on him, that he might receive his sight. And that when Ananias had spoken to him, "immediately there fell from his eyes as it had been scales." (Acts ix. 12 18.) All these statements are in the book of the Acts of the Apostles. Statements made by Paul in letters which he addressed to various Churches and persons are agreeable to them, and they occur in letters of which Lord Lyttleton says their authenticity " cannot be doubted without overturning all rules by which the authority and genuineness of any writings can be proved or confirmed," and which since the writing of the " Observations " have been subjected to the test of modern criticism in the hands of Paulus, Strauss, Renan and others, and have stood that test beyond all question. Writing to the Christian Churches which he had founded in Galatia, Paul says, " I certify you brethren that the Gospel which was preached of me is not after man. For I neither received it of man, neither was I taught it, but by the revelation of Jesus Christ. For ye have heard of my conversation in time past in the Jews' religion, how that beyond measure I persecuted the Church of God, and wasted it. ....But when it pleased God, who separated me from my mother's womb, and called me by His grace, to reveal His Son in me, that I might preach Him among the heathen, immediately I conferred not with flesh and blood." (Gal. i. 11—16.)

To the Philippians he writes, " If any other man thinketh that he hath whereof he might trust in the flesh, I more: Circumcised the eighth day, of the stock of Israel, of the tribe of Benjamin, an Hebrew of the Hebrews; as touching the law, a Pharisee; concerning zeal, persecuting the Church; ....But what things were gain to me, those I counted loss for Christ." (Philipp. iii. 4-7.)

In a letter to Timothy, who was one of his converts and a fellow-labourer in the Gospel, he writes, " I thank

Christ Jesus, our Lord, who hath enabled me, for that He counted me faithful, putting me into the ministry; who was before a blasphemer, and a persecutor, and injurious." (1 Tim. i. 12-13.)

Elsewhere he calls himself "An apostle by the will of God, by the commandment of God our Saviour, and an apostle, not of men, neither by men, but by Jesus Christ and God the Father, who raised Him from the dead," (2 Cor. i. 1; Col. i. 1; 1 Tim. i. 1; Gal. i. 1.) and concerning Jesus Christ, he asserts in a letter to Corinth, "Last of all He was seen of me also, as of one born out of due time." (1 Cor. xv. 8.)

Here are assertions made to his enemies and his friends in public apologies and private letters, to Churches which he had gathered and to friends who were fellow workers. These assertions were made before and to those who had the best means for ascertaining their truth or falsehood. They were made in the emotion of public debate and in the quiet hours of imprisonment. They were not disproved then. They have never been disproved since. What is the great point which they all include? If words have any meaning, Paul asserts for himself, and the historian Luke asserts for him, a "miraculous call which made him an apostle."

In that call we have the beginning of a life of ministry lasting for, certainly, more than thirty years, during which period it may be followed in the book of the Acts, and by the light of the information contained in many letters which he wrote.

The account which Christian believers give of the matter is that it was true,—true, not only in the incidents which even sceptical criticism admits, but true also in the miraculous element, in the revelation of Jesus Christ, the manifested glory of God—the voice from the brightness—the conversation between the prostrate persecutor and the exalted Jesus—the sudden blindness—the vision of Ananias—the message from God—and the instantaneous recovery of sight.

But believers know that there are many persons who do not admit this, and who endeavour to account for the admitted facts of the case on one assumption or another which excludes the miraculous elements.

Lord Lyttleton enumerates three suppositions which may possibly be made to account for the facts of the case without admitting the miraculous element, and we may feel secure in saying that no other solution is possible. Our author thus states the case :—

"It must of necessity be that the person asserting these things of himself, and of whom they are related in so authentic a manner, either was an impostor who said what he knew to be false with an intent to deceive; or he was an enthusiast, who by the force of an over heated imagination imposed on himself; or he was deceived by the fraud of others, and all that he said must be imputed to the power of this deceit; or what he declared to be the cause of his conversion, and to have happened in consequence of it, did all really happen, and therefore the Christian religion is a Divine revelation."

The three first of these suppositions are those which we have to examine. If they fail I shall be fully justified in accepting the fourth, unless my hearers will suggest some other solution not covered by these, a task to which I seriously invite them, and which they will have to perform, or be led to the conclusion that Paul's conversion was miraculous; and, in connexion with the events which followed, is a sufficient evidence that the Christian religion is from God.

First then we have to examine the assumption of imposture, that is to say that Paul said what he knew not to be true with intent to deceive. This assumption raises two difficulties, for it cannot be shown either that he could have any rational motives to undertake such an imposture, or that he could possibly have carried it on with any success by the means we know him to have employed.

When we search for motives to such an imposture, we are shut up to one of two—either the hope of advancing himself in his temporal interests, credit or power; or the gratification of some of his passions under the authority of it by the means it afforded.

What hope of temporal interest had Saul the Persecutor when he became Paul the Apostle? Jesus had been crucified as an impostor and blasphemer; and by that crucifixion the Jewish conviction that He was not their promised Messiah and King had been confirmed. His disciples indeed asserted that He was risen from the dead, and confirmed or seemed to confirm their statement by miracles; but the Jewish rulers were not convinced, and by imprisonment, beating and persecution unto death manifested their implacable rage against the believers. Paul concurred in these cruelties, voted for the death of the Christians in judicial assemblies, aided at their martyrdom, and in the intensity of his zeal persecutes them to strange cities, going with authority and commission to Damascus, to hale them to prison and death. Then it was and under those circumstances that Paul became a Christian. What wealth could he anticipate? All wealth and the power of conferring wealth were with the party he left. Those whom he joined were indigent men, oppressed and kept down from all means of improving their fortune. Some few disciples were better provided than others and aided the poorer, but during the lifetime of Paul, the whole community were not more than barely supplied with the necessaries of life, and Paul so far from availing himself of their veneration for him to secure wealth, refused oftentimes, even in the Churches he had founded, to accept ought at their hands. Of this abundant evidence exists in his own statements made to the various Churches. Thus he writes twenty-four years after his conversion in a letter to Corinth, "Even unto this present hour we both hunger, and thirst, and are naked, and are buffeted, and have no certain dwelling-place; and labour, working with our own hands." (1 Cor. iv. 11, 12.) A year later in A.D. 60, he writes again to Corinth thus, "I will not be burdensome to you: for I seek not yours, but you." (2 Cor. xii. 14.) Appealing to the Christians in Thessalonica, at a somewhat earlier date, he says, "Neither at any time used we flattering words, as ye know, nor a cloak of covetousness; God is witness.......For ye remember brethren, our labours and travail, for labouring night and day, because we would not be chargeable to any of you, we preached unto you the Gospel of God." (1 Thess. ii. 5, 9.) And face to face with the ministers of the Ephesian

Church, he thus appeals to them : " I have coveted no man's silver, or gold, or apparel. Yea, ye yourselves know, that these hands have ministered unto my necessities, and to them that were with me." (Acts xx. 33, 34.)

It is clear then that neither could Paul have anticipated wealth as the reward of submission to the Gospel, nor did he care to take even such support and emolument as the poor Christians might have been able to confer on him. The hope of fortune would have bound him to the Jewish rulers. When he broke with them he faced and he found poverty.

But perhaps contemning wealth he was animated by the prospects of credit or reputation. That also rested with those whom he left. "The sect he embraced was under the greatest and most universal contempt of any then in the world." What gain of reputation could come to the disciple of Gamaliel, the member for the Sanhedrim, the trusted ambassador of the rulers of the people, by joining himself to a party without birth, education or rank—whose works were attributed to imposture or magic, whose founder had died a felon's death, and whose central and fundamental preaching, Christ crucified, was to the Jew a stumbling block, and to the Greek foolishness? (1 Cor. i. 23.) Experience did but confirm his necessary anticipation of shame and reproach. A quarter of a century after the vision at Damascus, he wrote to the Corinthians. "We are made as the filth of the world—the offscouring ($περικαθάρματα$ refuse—offal), of all things unto this day." (1 Cor. iv. 13.) Very certainly the bubble reputation could neither have lured him nor rewarded him.

But perhaps it was the love of power—that "infirmity of noble minds!" "Power? Over whom? Over a flock of sheep driven to the slaughter, whose Shepherd Himself had been murdered a little before!" What power could he dare to hope for which would be of any avail against the power, now energized and sharpened by hatred to one who had forsaken and betrayed them, which was on the side of those he left? Nor will his after life and teaching shew that he sought or regarded power. He affected no superiority over the other Apostles. He termed himself "the least of them," (1 Cor. xv. 9), and "less than the least of all saints," (Ephs. iii. 8). Did he try to form a party for himself or to elevate himself to primacy? Hear his appeal, "was Paul crucified for you? or were ye baptized in the name of Paul? I thank God that I baptized none of you, but Crispus and Gaius; lest any should say that I had baptized in mine own name." (1 Cor. i. 13—15.) "Who then is Paul, and who is Apollos, but ministers by whom ye believed, even as the Lord gave to every man?" (1 Cor. iii. 5.) "For we preach not ourselves, but Christ Jesus the Lord; and ourselves your servants for Jesus' sake." (2 Cor. iv. 5.) Moreover Paul affected no earthly power. " He innovated nothing in government or civil affairs, he meddled not with legislation, he formed no commonwealths, he raised no seditions." "Obedience to rulers was the doctrine he taught to the Churches he founded; and what he taught he himself practised." (Rom. xiii.) It is certain that his higher birth, and better education and knowledge of the world gave him opportunities for pre-eminence; but it is **not** less certain that he made even light of these **advantages** esteeming those with whom he was associated as "fellow-labourers" and "fellow-servants," and distinctly affirming, "I came not with excellency of speech or of wisdom, but determined to know nothing among you, save Jesus Christ, and Him crucified. That your faith should not stand in the wisdom of men, but in the power of God." (1 Cor. ii. 1, 2, 5.)

On the other hand, while the Gospel could not tempt Paul by promises of wealth or reputation, or power, and he found in effect that in serving Christ he embraced poverty and shame, he did by the very fact of submitting himself to Jesus as Master and Lord put from him wealth and reputation and power which were actually his in possession, or were the certain reward of continuance in his course as an opponent of the Gospel.

"Upon the whole then," says Lord Lyttleton, at this point, "I think I have proved that the desire of wealth, or fame, or power could be no motive to make St. Paul a convert to Christ; but that on the contrary he must have been checked by that desire, as well as by the just apprehension of many inevitable and insupportable evils, from taking a part so contradictory to his past life, to all the principles he had imbibed, and all the habits he had contracted."

But it may be said Paul was actuated by the desire of gratifying some irregular passion under cover of the Christian religion, and by the means which it afforded. Undoubtedly such persons have been—men who have desired to set themselves free from the restraints of government, law, and morality—but there is nothing in the teaching or in the life of the Apostle to give the slightest strength to this objection. "His writings breathe nothing but the strictest morality, obedience to magistrates, order and government, with the utmost abhorrence of all licentiousness, idleness, or loose behaviour, under the cloak of religion." As confessedly among the Jews, so among the Christians his conversation and manners are blameless. (See Rom. xi. and xiii.) It was no libertine who could appeal to those among whom he had lived, and whom he had won to the Gospel, " Our exhortation was not of deceit, nor of uncleanness, nor of guile. Ye are witnesses, and God also, how holily and justly and unblameably we behaved ourselves among you that believe." (1 Thes. ii. 3, 10.) "We have wronged no man, we have corrupted no man, we have defrauded no man." (2 Cor. vii. 2 ; see also 2 Cor. i. 12, and iv. 2.)

Is it said that all this notwithstanding, Paul might have been an impostor in that for the sake of advancing the morality of the Gospel he gave himself to pious frauds —doing evil that he might promote good? It is true here also that some men have thus acted, as Lycurgus in the case of the Spartans, or Numa in the case of the Romans, who lent themselves to superstitions which they did not believe, that they might advance things which they held to be useful; but let it be noted that neither their superstition nor their teaching brought on them persecution and enmity : while in the case of Paul not only was the morality he taught unpalateable, but the persecution he endured sprang from enmity to the *facts* on which he *based* the morality. Nor must it be forgotten that he of whom this supposition is hinted wrote these words : " There are those who say, Let us do evil, that good may come ? whose damnation is just." (Rom. iii. 8.)

We may then safely conclude that no *rational* motive existed which could impel Saul of Tarsus to become, as an impostor, Paul the Apostle; and if any motive existed to such a course it must have been simply *capricious*, as men sometimes act on absurd impulses, they know not why. But to this the answer is simple. There is absolutely nothing in the conduct or the writing of the Apostle which can for a moment justify the thought. Nothing capricious or unreasoning appears in the methods by which he promoted the Gospel. On the contrary his is a life constantly guided by thoughtfulness, prudence and sustained purpose.

But if any one, in the face of evidence given thus far, should still insist that Paul was in his conversion an impostor unmixed, or an impostor who was a strange specimen of a capricious fool to boot, let him consider that "he could not possibly have carried on his imposture to success by the means that we know he employed."

Paul did not found Christianity. He accepted an existing religion, and did not draw the doctrines he proclaimed from his imagination. He had not learned of Jesus, nor had he had any connexion with the Apostles except as their persecutor. How could he obtain a sufficiently accurate knowledge of their teaching but by intercourse with them? He set up as an Apostle of their faith, but with such ignorance of the teaching of the other Apostles, that either they must have been forced to ruin his credit or he would have ruined theirs. They could not but have detected the variance, in a thousand points, between his fancies and the teaching which they had received from Jesus Himself. He must therefore act in confederacy with the Apostles, not only to gain an accurate acquaintance with the Gospel, but also to learn the secret arts with which they beguiled men into the common belief that they worked miracles. Now how did he incline them to communicate with him on these essential matters? By furiously persecuting them and their brethren to the moment of his conversion? This he did, and then they immediately entrust their capital enemy with all the secrets of their imposture.

"Would men so secret, as not to be drawn by the most severe persecutions to say one word which would convict them of being impostors, confess themselves such to their persecutor in hopes of his being their accomplice?"

Not this only, if his conversion was unreal, and the events connected with it non-existent, consider the risk of exposure from those who journeyed with him—employed with him by the Jewish rulers to extirpate Christianity—and breathing his old temper of opposition to the faith to which he now addicted himself. Again he was to be instructed by one at Damascus, and the teacher and his disciple met as absolute strangers each to the other; and this man, Ananias, "who had goodly report of all the Jews who dwelt in Damascus," and an excellent character, must have been confederate with the impostor in his guilt. But on the supposition of imposture how futile this connexion with Ananias, who appearing this once in the affair is never heard of afterwards—their whole known intercourse having been private, and Ananias having knowledge of his own and Paul's dishonesty.

But consider also how, some years afterwards, when pleading before Agrippa, in the presence of Festus, he was bold enough to appeal to him upon his own knowledge of the truth of his story, and that in the presence of many only too ready and desirous of convicting him of falsehood and crime—"a very remarkable proof both of the notoriety of the facts, and the integrity of the man, who with so fearless a confidence could call upon a king to give testimony for him even while he was sitting in judgment upon him."

Then, inasmuch as he must secure his recognition as an Apostle by the Apostles and bring them to admit him into a participation of all their mysteries, doctrines, and designs, he was necessitated to court their society and win their good favour: but this he did not do, for he went away to Arabia and then, returning to Damascus, did not go to Jerusalem till after three years (Gal. i. 17-18.); and while on the supposition of imposture, the Apostles and Churches must have known how and when he gained his knowledge of the Gospel, he ventured to assure the Galatians that he neither received his knowledge of men, nor was he taught it, but by revelation of Jesus Christ. (Gal. i. 12.) Consider again how by rebuking his fellow Apostle Peter openly at Antioch, and defending that rebuke in his letter to the Galatians (Gal. ii. 11—14.) he incited Peter to reveal, in self-defence or in anger, any want of righteousness in himself. "Accomplices in fraud are obliged to shew greater regards to each other; such freedom (of rebuke) belongs to truth alone."

The supposition of imposture cannot be adequately judged unless it be also remembered that Paul was devoted mainly to the propagation of the Gospel among the Gentiles, in which enterprise he would have to contend with four adverse influences against which the help and presence of God could help him, but against which, on the supposition of imposture, he was utterly unprovided. He had to contend : 1. With the policy and power of the magistrates. 2. With the interests, credit, and craft of the priests. 3. With the prejudices and passions of the people. 4. With the wisdom and pride of philosophers.

Heathen magistrates permitted considerable laxity in the choice and worship of gods, but certainly did not endure so exclusive a system as that of Christianity, which not only demanded a place and recognition, but asserted itself as true, and alone true. It did not ask a nich in the Pantheon, but set to work to rase the Pantheon with all its gods, and to erect on its ruins the temple of the true God. Judge then what chance of success Paul had at Ephesus, Corinth, and Athens, at all which places he founded Churches which presently after swept the idols away altogether.

Consider also the difficulty arising from the priesthood who, finding their craft in danger, could wield all the power of the State for the repression of the teaching they abhorred. These men might tolerate the easy atheistical philosopher who would be content with theorizing against religion and yet maintain the popular religions as useful cheats ; but they would have no patience with the aggressive system which Paul propounded, which endured no rival near its throne.

And again consider the difficulties springing from

the prejudices and passions of the people. In Judea the voice of the people often restrained the violence of the rulers in their opposition to Christianity; but in the case of the Gentiles, intense and violent prejudices existed in favour of the popular religions, and were more than ever intense when opposing anything taught by a Jew—one of a nation on whom the then world looked with unutterable scorn. Such an one carried only new ideas when he appealed to the Gentiles, and told them that Jesus was the Christ of God. They expected no Christ, they allowed no such Scriptures as those to which Paul made his appeal. They had to be taught the New Testament, but were ignorant of the book of the old covenant on which the Apostles turned for evidence when seeking to convince the Jew. There was not even the common ground of Monotheism on which Paul and the Gentile populations could take their stand. Thus he must come before them with no political, or social, or religious authority, and bid them surrender the idolatry which gratified their tastes, ministered to their passions, and satisfied their lower nature. He bade them forsake these idolatries for the spiritual worship of " one invisible God, and to accept salvation by the death and sufferings of a crucified Jew "—to their view such an one as a condemned criminal executed at Newgate would be to us.

To these accumulated difficulties must be added those springing from the wisdom and pride of the philosophers. They had prejudices of their own still more repugnant to the doctrines of the Gospel than those of the vulgar, more deeply rooted, and more obstinately fixed in the mind. The wisdom on which they prided themselves—" their vain metaphysical speculations, their logical subtleties—their endless disputes—their high flown conceits of the perfection and self-sufficiency of human wisdom—their dogmatical positiveness about doubtful opinion—their sceptical doubts about the most clear and certain truths" made the soil in which a humble stranger, a despised Jew, and in their eyes a contemptible apostate had to sow the seeds of the doctrine of Christ. "If St. Paul had had nothing to trust to but his own natural faculties, his own understanding, knowledge, and eloquence, could he have hoped to be, singly, a match for all theirs united against him? Could a teacher unheard of before, from an obscure and unlearned part of the world, have withstood the authority of Plato, Aristotle, Epicurus, Zeno, Arcesilaus, Carneades, and all the great names which held the first rank of human wisdom?"

"From all this it may I think be concluded that no human means employed by St. Paul in his design of converting the Gentiles were, or could be, adequate to the great difficulties he had to contend with, or to the success that we know attended his work; and we can in reason ascribe that success to no other cause but the power of God, going along with and aiding his ministry, because no other was equal to the effects."

And on this follows the conclusion, that whatever Paul may have been besides, he was no impostor.

But while many yield this point, they are yet unable to accept the miraculous element in the history of his conversion; they fall back on the assumption that he "was an enthusiast, who by the force of an overheated imagination imposed on himself." Probably this opinion will impose on men only so long as they rest in generals, and fancy to themselves an enthusiast who is void of the qualities which constitute enthusiasm. The general ingredients of enthusiasm, as men use the word, are great heats of temper, melancholy, ignorance, credulity and vanity, or self conceit. But of all these one only, that of a quick and warm disposition, is to be found in Paul as it was in the Gracchi, in Cato, in Brutus, and in many of the best and wisest of men. And even this quality never had such command of the mind of Paul as to rule and darken his understanding. The best test is this, that in things where principle was not concerned, he was so easy as to "become all things to all men." (1 Cor. ix. 20, 22.) And that in moments of the most trying and exciting character he manifested prudence, and had regard to the civilities and decorums of society, as appears clearly in his behaviour when defending himself before Agrippa, Felix, and Festus. His was a zeal ever tempered by prudence.

Where again is the proof that he was a sour, melancholy enthusiast? Remorse he felt indeed for his former life as a persecutor, but it led him only to a new life of unwearied and cheerful labour. He inflicted on himself no gloomy penances or extravagant mortifications. His holiness was the simplicity of a good life and the industry of a devoted Apostle. He bore sufferings cheerfully, but he did not court them—even pleading his Roman citizenship to avoid being beaten, and at Athens he avoided the application of a capital law which forbad the introduction of a new god by prudently laying hold on the presence of an altar to the Unknown God, and thus connecting his teaching of the living and true God with a recognised but unknown being: "whom therefore ye ignorantly worship, him declare I unto you." (Acts xvii. and Josephus cont. Apion. Book II. Ch. 37.) Paul indeed desired "to depart and to be with Christ," which he knew to be better than his life of sorrow and suffering; but he sought not to die, and was ready to remain with the Churches he had founded, because his presence and leadership was an advantage to them. Willing to labour, ready to rest, and impressing the same condition of mind on multitudes, he cannot in any fairness be called a melancholy enthusiast.

Again is there proof that Paul had the mark of ignorance? Hardly so when he was master of Jewish and Grecian learning, and in this respect commanded the enforced commendation of Festus, and on their own ground could cope with the Athenians on Areopagus. Nor is credulity—as distinguished from assent to truth on sufficient evidence—observable in Paul. He was in fact slow and hard of belief. The miracles done by the Saviour, the resurrection of Him who was crucified and buried, miracles wrought by Peter and John—even that well known and much canvassed marvel the healing the lame man at the Beautiful Gate of the Temple (Acts iii.) had not persuaded him to believe. Other miracles and several proclamations of the Gospel (Acts v. 18, 32), with the eloquent defence of Stephen before the council had left him untouched—left him to attend the martyrdom of Stephen as consenting to his death (Acts viii. and ix.)— left him with his zeal against Christ only embittered and deepened, so that he set forth to Damascus, " breathing out threatenings and slaughter" against the disciples. All evidence up to this point he had resisted, "so that his mind far from being disposed to a credulous faith, or a too easy reception of any miracle worked in proof of the Christian religion, appears to have been barred against it by the most obstinate prejudices, as much as any man's could possibly be; and from hence we may fairly conclude, that nothing less than the irresistible evidence of his own senses, clear from the possibility of doubt, could have overcome his unbelief."

But these points failing, may not the position and work of Paul be accounted for by self-conceit, a quality which often places men in extraordinary circumstances, and urges them to amazing doings? With high conceits of their importance, such men may mistake the workings of their own folly as the will of God, and may persuade themselves that, as favourites of heaven, they are the recipients of Divine revelations. Such were Montanus, Santa Theresa, Catharine of Sienna, Francis of Assisi, and others famous in the martyrology and sanctology of the Romish Church. But was Paul such an one, eaten up by self-conceit of knowledge, goodness and favour: vain of personal gifts, higher genius, or Divine communications? Listen to his words to the Ephesians, the Corinthians, and to his beloved fellow-worker Timothy. I who am "less than the least of all saints." (Eph. iii. 8.) "I am the least of the Apostles, that am not meet to be called an Apostle, because I persecuted the Church of God." (1 Cor. xv. 9.) "Jesus Christ came into the world to save sinners, of whom I am chief. Howbeit for this cause I obtained mercy, that in me first Jesus Christ might show forth all long-suffering, for a pattern to them which should hereafter believe on him to life everlasting." (1 Tim. i. 15, 16.) Only once does he use language opposed to this, saying, "I was not a whit behind the very chiefest Apostles." (2 Cor. xi. 5.) And then the very safety of the Corinthian Church—their deliverance from false teachers—necessitated a strong assertion of his authority among them; and even then he does it in such a way that his very boasting becomes the most evident humility, and does in no wise counteract his deliberate statements to the same Church. (Vide 2 Cor. xi. 16-19, 30; 2 Cor. xii. 2, 6, 7.) "Who then is Paul and who is Apollos, but ministers by whom ye believed, even as the Lord gave to every man? I have planted, Apollos watered, but God gave the increase. So then neither is he that planteth anything, neither he that watereth, but God that giveth the increase." "By the grace of God I am what I am, and His grace which was bestowed upon me was not in vain, but I laboured more abundantly than they all; yet not I, but the grace of God which was with me." (2 Cor. xii. 1-5; 1 Cor. iii. 5-7; 1 Cor. xv. 10.) And lastly, let us listen to the lesson which he laboured to impress on his followers, exalting a self renouncing love above all other things.

"Though I speak with the tongues of men and of angels and have not love, I am become as sounding brass or a tinkling cymbal. And though I have the gift of prophecy, and understand all mysteries and all knowledge; and though I have all faith, so that I could remove mountains, and have not love, I am nothing. And though I bestow all my goods to feed the poor, and though I give my body to be burned and have not love, it profiteth me nothing." (1 Cor. xiii. 1-4.) He who can read this and trace the example which illustrates it in the life of the Apostle, and yet attribute his conversion and his Apostleship to self-conceit, must either mistake the sense of words, or be very determined to bring the Apostle in guilty. Since therefore we do not find in the writings or acts of Paul those characteristics which mark the hot headed enthusiast, we may conclude he was not such an one. But even did we find in him these qualities of mere enthusiasm it can be proved, "That he could not possibly have imposed on himself by any power of enthusiasm, either in regard to the miracle which caused his conversion, or to the consequential effects of it, or to some other circumstances which he bears testimony to in his epistles." Imagination is doubtless very strong, but it is strong in the direction imprinted on it by opinions held at the time of its working. Now Paul on his journey to Damascus was undoubtedly possessed of opinions utterly hostile to Christianity, and his passions were at that time inflamed by the irritating consciousness of his past treatment of them, the pride of continuing in a line of conduct on which he had voluntarily and publicly entered, and the credit and praise that line of conduct obtained from him among the rulers of his nation.

In this state of mind visions, marvels, alarms, and any other thing acting on his imagination only, would not undo the whole current and tide of his life and his opinions. Everything within him hurried him along in opposition to Jesus Christ; and when his imagination is impressed it is in a direction utterly hostile to his every opinion, passion, and line of conduct. But even were this self deception under the force of mere imagination possible in Paul, how can it be explained that his fancy should be so real to others; that his companions also, nothing actually happening, should see the light and hear the voice, and fall from their horses, and be speechless with terror." (Acts ix. 3 ; Acts xxii. 9 ; Acts ix. 7 ; Acts xxvi. 14.)

But it may be said, "something did happen. A storm broke, or a meteor of unusual brilliancy fell." But how did this storm frame articulate voice and carry on a conversation in Hebrew? and how can the meteoric light have given visions to Paul and Ananias simultaneously, and in such wise that each was led to a course of action fitting in with that of the other, and exactly corresponding ; and how could the thunder and the meteoric light combined have both struck Paul blind and have given to Ananias the power of restoring his sight suddenly and effectually? Moreover the fact of Paul's conversion and the miracle of Ananias were but parts in a long series of wonderful events. Could imagination thus excited shew to Paul the vision of Jesus Christ many times? Could a power of marvel-working, thus originated, have enabled Paul to preach the Gospel among the Gentiles from Jerusalem round about to Illyricum (that is to say in Judea, Samaria, Galilee, Syria, the Lesser Asia, Pontus Galatia, Cappadocia, Bithynia, in Greece, and away to the confines of Northern Italy), "with mighty signs and wonders wrought by the power of the Spirit of God, to make the Gentiles obedient to his preaching." (Acts ix. 17,

18; xxii. 13, 17, 18; xi., xxi., xxii., and xxiii.; and Rom. xv. 18, 19.) "Surely such a series of miraculous acts, all consequential to and dependent on the first revelation, puts the truth of that revelation beyond the possibility of doubt or deceit." The supposition is that Paul was an enthusiastic madman; but "if the difficulties which have been shewn to have obstructed that work which he did were such as the ablest impostor could not overcome, how much more insurmountable were they to a madman?" Indeed, however difficult it may be to account for the conversion and Apostleship of Paul on the supposition that he was an impostor, it is a harder task to give an account of things on the assumption that he was a mad enthusiast. His "madness" in its unreasoning, honest blundering did things too wonderful. His fellow travellers, Ananias at Damascus, Sergius Paulus the prudent deputy at Paphos, Elymas the sorcerer, Eutychus at Troas, the priests and people at Lystra, the jailor at Philippi, the barbarian Maltese, Erastus the city treasurer at Corinth, and Dionysius the learned areopagite at Athens, must have all been equally mad, and mad with marvellous uniformity; mad too with a madness which gave feet to the lame, eyes to the blind, healing to the sick, freedom to ironbound captives, and life to the dead; mad with a madness which subdued to the faith of Christ men and women of many nations, of various religions, of every kind of intellectual and educational degree, and of all ranks of society. Men here and there however still ascribe to immagination that which Paul ascribes to the power of God, not perceiving that "they ascribe to imagination the same omnipotency which he ascribes to God."

One other enquiry remains. Was Paul the victim of others' deceit, and can all he said and did be referred to the power of that deceit.

" But I," to quote the words of Lord Lyttleton, " need say little to show the absurdity of this supposition. It was morally impossible for the disciples of Christ to conceive such a thought as that of turning His persecutor into His Apostle, and to do this by a fraud in the very instant of his greatest fury against them and their Lord. But could they have been so extravagant as to conceive such a thought, it was physically impossible for them to execute it in the manner we find his conversion to have been effected. Could they produce a light in the air which at mid-day was brighter than that of the sun? Could they make Saul hear words from out of that light which were not heard by the rest of the company? Could they make him blind for three days after that vision? and then make scales fall from off his eyes, and restore him to his sight by a word? Beyond dispute no fraud could do these things; but much less still could the fraud of others produce those miracles subsequent to his conversion, in which he was not passive but active, which he did himself and appeals to in his epistles as a proof of his Divine mission. I shall then take it for granted that he was not deceived by the frauds of others, and that what he said of himself cannot be imputed to the power of that deceit, no more than to wilful imposture or to enthusiasm; and then it follows that what he related to have been the cause of his conversion, and to have happened in consequence of it, did all really happen, THEREFORE THE CHRISTIAN RELIGION IS A DIVINE REVELATION."

To the mind of the Christian believer the conclusion is absolute : but even in the case of the sincere but sceptical enquirer, it ought to carry so much at least of force and probability as will make him very cautious and watchful before he rejects it ; and will lead him to give a truly humble and kindly attention to the exhortation of Paul, which in all love and brotherly kindness, I adopt as my own, "Believe in the Lord Jesus Christ and thou shalt be saved."

ALLEGED DIFFICULTIES IN THE MORAL TEACHING OF THE NEW TESTAMENT.

BY THE
REV. C. A. ROW, M.A.,

Prebendary of St. Paul's,
Author of "The Nature and Extent of Divine Inspiration," "The Jesus of the Evangelists," "The Moral Teaching of the New Testament," etc.

Alleged Difficulties in the Moral Teaching of the New Testament.

IN treating of this subject within the limits of an hour's lecture, it will be necessary for me only to deal with objections which are urged by writers of high literary reputation. It would be simply impossible to meet every conceivable objection in the space allotted to me. Nor is it necessary that I should do so, for we may conclude that difficulties which eminent writers, who do not believe in Christianity, pass over in silence, exist only in the imagination of those who adduce them. Just in the same way it would be quite a legitimate answer to make to me, who am profoundly ignorant of the various mechanical arts, if I were to attempt to instruct an experienced workman how to do his work better,—Pray try to master the very elements of the trade, and try your own hand at it, before you presume to lecture us, who have been in the business all our lives.

There are two well-known writers in this country, whom we are quite ready to recognise as men of unquestionable ability, who have raised exceptions against certain aspects of the moral teaching of the New Testament—Mr. F. W. Newman and the late Mr. J. S. Mill. Among other things, the first of these has published a tract, evidently intended to be widely circulated, directly inculpating it; and the second has published opinions which, while he directly asserts that he does not think that there is anything in its teaching contrary to sound morality, yet he implies that he considers it defective.

On one point I cordially agree with Mr. Newman, and I solicit the attention of all unbelievers to it, for it is one which in controversy they greatly overlook. "Our sole concern," says he, "here is with the New Testament as it stands, as it is popularly received, and is read in the Church." This is the only correct principle. Let it be understood therefore, that in dealing with the moral teaching of the New Testament, we are are not concerned with that of anything which stands outside its pages. We have neither to discuss the practice of Christians, nor to deal with the teaching of any other book. Mr. Newman's principle is thoroughly sound: I only regret that he does not always abide by it.

The following passage will explain Mr. Newman's general opinions on this subject:

"If one is asked to specify the defects in the New Testament morality, the difficulty of reply is caused by the too great abundance of material. The defects are not partial, but total. They pervade the entire moral system, and are the greater in each part, the greater its importance. Fully to enumerate the defects would be equivalent to writing a complete moral treatise. . . It must be added, that the defectiveness here complained of is sometimes that of total omission; sometimes that of precepts contrary to those of right and truth. In fact, the latter is the common case."

I think that it will be conceded that Mr. Mill was a far more profound philosopher than Mr. Newman. On the most important portion of this charge he is hopelessly at issue with him. Having pointed out the clear distinction which exists between the moral teaching of the New Testament and what Mr. Mill designates "Theological Morality,"—by which he means various systems of morality evolved during the centuries of the Church's history, and which he charges with various defects,—Mr. Mill says: "I am as far as anyone from pretending that these defects are necessarily inherent in Christian Ethics, in any manner in which it can be conceived; or that the many requisites of a complete moral doctrine which it does not contain do not admit of being reconciled with it. Far less would I insinuate this of the doctrines and precepts of Christ himself. I believe that the sayings of Christ contain all that I can see any evidence of their having been intended to be; that they are irreconcilable with nothing which a comprehensive morality requires; that everything which is excellent in Ethics may be brought within them with no greater violence to their language than has been done to it, by all who have attempted to deduce from them any practical system whatever." (Essay on "Liberty.")

Mr. Newman affirms that principles contrary to truth and right preponderate in the teaching of the New Testament; and in making this affirmation he includes many of the sayings of Jesus Christ. Mr. Mill, however, is of opinion that "the sayings of Christ are irreconcilable with nothing which a comprehensive morality requires." No contradiction can be more complete. Mr. Mill is certainly the higher authority on moral questions.

Still, however, I apprehend that they agree in considering that the moral teaching of the New Testament is defective—*i.e.*, that it does not fulfil the requirements of our present form of civilization. Yet there is an obscurity in Mr. Mill's language on this subject. Strictly speaking, he is charging this defect on "Theological Morality" alone ; but as at page 90 he refers expressly to the New Testament, I think that it will be the most candid course for me to conclude that he intended to include the teaching of the New Testament in this charge of deficiency, while he expressly absolves it from that of immorality.

Before examining the positions of either of these writers, I must lay down what I mean when I use the expression "a system of moral teaching," and when I affirm that that in the New Testament is adequate to meet the requirements of every stage of civilization. By this expression is frequently understood not only a body of principles, but of precepts, which should give suitable directions as to what is the correct line of duty in every emergency in which we can be placed. I restrict it to a body of principles, from which the correct line of duty may be evolved in all special cases ; and I also include under the term those various moral and spiritual forces, powers, and motives which are adequate to make the moral law predominate over the mind of man. If I understand Mr. Newman rightly, he is of opinion that the New

Testament ought also to have contained a body of precepts elaborated so as to meet the various circumstances of life, if it is to be entitled to be considered an effective moral guide to man in every stage of civilization. The number of questions which he considers that it ought to have solved is very numerous. Thus he complains that its political teachings are very obscure and inadequate. He charges it with having omitted several most important questions of individual and social morality altogether, or with having dealt with them on false principles. Judging by the special instances adduced by him, he seems to consider that it ought to have contained solutions of all the individual, social, and political questions of morality which can arise. I am not sure that he would not add a complete body of casuistry. I reply that a system of moral teaching may be complete and wholly adequate which leaves unattempted the various things of which Mr. Newman demands that the New Testament should contain a complete solution.

I am happy to say that the pages of the New Testament make no pretensions whatever to solve every conceivable detail of duty or doubtful moral question which may arise. If they had done so, it would have constituted an objection against it far more formidable than the strongest which can be urged by unbelievers. The writers would have attempted to do what is impossible to be done, and what, if done, would degrade man from a free moral agent into a machine. In proof that it makes no such pretension, I shall quote the authority of Mr. Mill. "If it [Christian Morality] means," says he, "the teaching of the New Testament, I wonder that anyone who derives his knowledge of this from the book itself, can suppose that it was announced, or intended, as a complete doctrine of morals." In this expression of wonder I heartily concur, whether the contrary has been affirmed by Christians or unbelievers. It contains all the great principles of moral teaching, but leaves the elaboration of them, and their application to specific cases, to be determined by the enlightened conscience of the individual.

Yet such an attempt has been made, and the result only shows that it is incapable of realization. The Jewish Talmud is a movement in that direction. Its bulk is about fourteen folio volumes, yet it contains very little which is applicable to our Western civilization. The Scribes and Pharisees, the predecessors of the Talmudists, expended their powers in refinements on moral duties, which led to a disregard of the weightiest obligations. Many Christian writers have been guilty of the same folly, into which heathen ones had fallen before them. The treatise of the great Roman orator Cicero, entitled "De Officiis," gives us many specimens of this mode of raising curious questions on moral subjects, as for instance whether, in case of a loss at sea, a man should save a worthless slave or a valuable horse; whether a wise man when in the water should wrench a plank from a fool; also, in case two wise men are shipwrecked, and there is only a single plank sufficient to support one, which of the two should seize the plank, and which should yield it to the other. The mode of settling this last question is somewhat curious. The two wise men are to determine in the water whose life is most valuable for his own sake or for that of the republic.

Having settled this rather complicated problem in the water, the man whose life is the most valuable is to retain the plank, and the other to go quietly to the bottom. Such questions will only be discussed where there is little or no moral earnestness.

Instead of attempting to settle questions of casuistry, or to lay down rules of conduct, which can be applied mechanically to the ever-varying circumstances of life, Mr. Mill says, and says truly, " The Gospel always refers to a pre-existing morality, and confines its precepts to the particulars in which that morality was to be corrected or superseded by a wider and a higher." He would have described the case more correctly, if he had said that it contents itself with laying down the great fundamental principles of duty, and then appeals to the conscience enlightened by its teaching, as the only adequate guide to direct us as to what is the course of duty in the innumerable and often conflicting circumstances in which we are placed. Instead of attempting to lay down a set of rules as guides to conduct, it announces the utter worthlessness of such systems. The seat of all sound morality it places in man's spirit. Its precepts are intended as illustrations of its great principles under existing circumstances. Above all things let it be observed that Christianity professes to be a law of liberty, and not of slavish adhesion to a mere literal commandment.

Still, however, the New Testament professes to be, and is a moral guide adequate to meet the wants of man in every condition of civilization. How then, if the case be as I have stated, is this possible? Ought not it to contain what Mr. Mill designates a complete system of Ethical doctrine? I answer that it effects its purpose much better by laying down great principles, which embrace every possibility of moral obligation. It also brings a number of mighty forces to bear on the heart and the spirit of man. It directs its appeals to every principle of our nature which can be enlisted into the service of holiness. When these principles are kindled into activity, it constitutes the enlightened conscience a law to itself.

I will at once lay down the great principles which constitute the essence of Christian morality, and which, when they have thoroughly penetrated our being, are adequate to be the guide of life. First, the moral law as proclaimed by Jesus Christ is announced as consisting of two great commandments, which are the foundations of all moral obligation. The first of these flows from man's relationship to his Creator. Being His creature, he is bound to love Him with every affection which he possesses, and to devote to Him his entire being. By laying down this as the great fundamental principle of His teaching, Jesus Christ did what the whole of the ancient philosophers failed to accomplish. He brought to bear on man's moral nature the whole force of his religious being, and presented the idea of duty on the widest and most comprehensive principle. On this duty of man to God, He erected the second great principle on which all obligation between man and man must rest, and which embraces every possible duty in its all-comprehensive sweep, "Thou shalt love thy neighbour as thyself." He then proclaimed that the idea of neigh bourhood as between man and man was not limited by the ties of country, citizenship, sect, or race, but that its essence was, man wherever met with in need of help. Neighbourhood in Christ's teaching consists in the power of performing acts of kindness on the one hand, and the presence of necessity on the other. This great law of obligation of man to man was not limited by one single selfish consideration. This is plainly and definitely taught in the parable of the man who fell among thieves, in which Jesus Christ broke down all the narrow distinctions which separated man from man in the ancient world. Let it be particularly observed that He has extended this obligation by further teaching that Christians are bound to love one another, not only as they love themselves, but as He has loved them. So wide has He laid down the principle of obligation.

This principle of self-sacrifice is the central position of the moral teaching of the New Testament. It is one most wide and all-embracing. I will cite a single passage as an illustration of it. "None of us," says St. Paul, "liveth to himself, and no man dieth to himself; for whether we live, we live unto the Lord; and whether we die, we die to the Lord: whether we live therefore, or die, we are the Lord's; for to this end Christ both died and rose, that He might be the Lord of the dead and living." This principle is adequate to determine every question of moral obligation. It demands the most absolute sacrifice of self in the service of Jesus Christ. If a doubt arises whether this or that line of conduct is a duty, or what is the amount of self-sacrifice which is required at our hands in the discharge of it, we have only to ask ourselves two questions, and the answer will at once determine the line of conduct which ought to be pursued, and the degree of self-sacrifice required. The first of these questions is, What do I wish that another should do to me, if I were in his place? The second is, To what extent has Jesus Christ sacrificed Himself for me? I owe a similar sacrifice of self to Him. In whatever position of life a Christian may be placed, he is Christ's, bound to discharge every duty which it requires for His sake; and that not grudgingly, but measured only, as to the extent of the obligation, by the self-sacrifice of Jesus Christ for him.

It is quite evident that both Mr. Mill and Mr. Newman have overlooked this great and fundamental principle of the moral teaching of the New Testament, without the deepest attention to which it is impossible to form a correct estimate of its scope and bearing. At any rate I can find no reference to it in their estimate of its moral teaching. It is to this that their complaint that its teaching is inadequate in reference to the requirements of advancing civilization is due. I maintain, on the contrary, that it is adequate to guide us on every question of individual, social, or political morality which can arise. Jesus Christ claims, not only our religious duties, but every portion of our secular calling. The distinction between them is destroyed by Christianity. In its view all secular duties have become religious ones. Christ demands as His the entire life, nothing short of it. The Christian is to continue in the calling in which he is called of God. There is no injunction in the New Testament that a man, when he became a Christian, was to leave his secular calling, unless it positively ministered to vice. On the contrary, it contains many exhortations to discharge it faithfully as to the Lord, and not unto man. Whenever good is to be done, he is bound to do it. Whenever the condition of man can be ameliorated, the morality of Christianity teaches that we are bound to exert our utmost efforts to effect it, as due not only to our brother man, but unto the Lord. "Ye are not your own," writes St. Paul; "therefore glorify God in your body and in your spirit, which are God's."

But while the New Testament appeals to this as the fundamental groundwork of its teaching, let it be observed that it has invoked every other principle of our nature which can be enlisted into the service of holiness. In proof of this I quote a single passage, but it is a very comprehensive one. "Finally," writes St. Paul, "whatsoever things are true, whatsoever things are honest, whatsoever things are pure, whatsoever things are lovely, whatsoever things are just, whatsoever things are of good report; if there be any virtue, if there be any praise, think of these things." Here we find the principle of truth, of honour, of justice, of the morally beautiful, that of the approbation of society, man's love of excellence, and even his desire for praise, appealed to, to excite us in the pursuit of what is good and virtuous. I ask whether any teaching can be more comprehensive?

It is satisfactory to observe that Mr. Mill deals with the teaching of the New Testament in a spirit very different from that of Mr. Newman. While the Tract before me is an attack upon it of the strongest character, it does not contain a single allusion to the fact that its teaching is based on the widest and most comprehensive principles which I have enumerated, and which are indelibly stamped on its pages. Yet to judge the teaching of a book, without estimating the principles on which it is founded, is impossible. They assign to the subordinate details their entire meaning. I ask emphatically whether such a mode of dealing with questions can be conducive to the interests of truth?

I will now deal with as many of the special objections before me as my space will allow. Mr. Newman objects that the views of the writers of the New Testament as to the nearness of the future world must have rendered them inadequate moral teachers. I believe that it is an idea widely spread among unbelievers, and is certainly entertained by very many in this hall, that a Christian's interest in this life is so short, and that his desire to effect his own salvation ought to be so absorbing, as necessarily to make the consistent Christian indifferent to all the higher interests of humanity.

I reply, that this opinion is not founded on anything contained in the New Testament. Whatever may be the assertions of unbelievers with respect to the expectation of the followers of Jesus Christ as to the speedy end of the present dispensation, it is a plain fact that many of our Lord's parables, in which He explained the nature of His kingdom, assert that it would be one of a slow and gradual growth, and that human nature would become penetrated with Christian principles only by means of a slow and gradual progress. Of this the parables in Matt. xiii. are a striking example.

Whatever views may be entertained about the relative nearness or distance of the period of the end, there is one very palpable fact on which we must all agree, that human life is short. In a moral point of view there can be little difference whether we are firmly persuaded that life is short, or the coming of Christ's kingdom near. It is a plain fact both to Christians and unbelievers, whether they like to think about it or not, that at best our time for doing any important work here is very limited, and that our interest in earthly things may pass away at any hour. The objection applies to both alike.

Next, Christianity expressly teaches that a man's interest in the world to come will be best provided for by a diligent discharge of the duties of the present. Where is it said, I ask, that a man should neglect his duties to save his soul? On the contrary, he is expressly told that his best mode of promoting his interests in the world to come, is by the diligent discharge of every known duty in the present life. Does not the New Testament expressly teach that every opportunity of doing good, every faculty, and every endowment, is a stewardship entrusted to the Christian by his Master? Surely, if there is a great deal to be done, and but a short time to do it in, the harder one works, the better. If a railway station is a mile off, and I have only fourteen minutes before the arrival of the train, I think this an urgent reason for mending my pace. As the parable teaches, it is only the slothful servant who hides his talent in the earth. I fully concede that the New Testament lays down that the next world is vastly more important than the present one. So is the subsequent period of our lives, compared with the interval of five or six years which we pass at school. But those who have spent their school-days in idleness have inflicted an irreparable damage on their interests in their future life, and frequently the deepest repentance is unable to repair the mischief. The more important are our interests in the world to come, the more important is it for us rightly to use the present life as a preparation for it.

But Mr. Newman further observes: "That St. Paul's teaching should not be definite concerning the rights and duties of citizens, concerning war, concerning slavery, and the rights of man, followed necessarily from his belief that the end of all things was so close at hand. No time was left to improve the world, to regenerate politics, to enfranchise slave castes; radical change was impossible; palliation of evil was only to be thought of."

I reply, first, that if it is necessary to render a system of moral teaching an adequate guide, that it should contain definite information on all these points, it would involve the production of a library of considerable size. Nor is this all: it would be necessary that it should be constantly enlarged, to meet the ever varying circumstances of our political and social life. Yet this is really what it would have been necessary that the writers of the New Testament should have done if the absence of these subjects is to be viewed as an objection against the adequacy of their teaching. They have acted more wisely by enunciating great principles of morality which render the entering on such subjects entirely unnecessary.

Next, as I have observed, the shortness of the time is an additional reason for the diligent discharge of duty. Its teaching is, that duties are to be discharged at all hazards, without reference to results. The measuring duties by results belongs to the modern utilitarian gospel, and not to that of Jesus Christ. Mr. Newman imagines that no man with the views which he attributes to the first Christians could be in favour of radical changes, but would only attempt palliations of existing evils. I find this nowhere hinted in the pages of the New Testament. The opponents of Christianity in the first century took a very different view of the subject, and mistook the apostles for a species of radicals. The charge which they preferred against them was, "Those who have turned the world upside down, have come hither also." Christianity really seeks to effect a most radical change in human nature.

There is doubtless a great diversity of view between the writers of the New Testament and modern unbelievers as to the most effectual mode of acting on man. Both alike are animated by a desire to effect a radical change in his condition, and seek to effect his elevation. The one were of opinion that the right way to effect this was to begin with that which is inward, and to work from the inward to his outward condition. The other think that the correct method of procedure is to reverse this process. The difference is one of method, not of principle I assert that all experience is in favour of that pursued by Christ and His apostles, and that all great and beneficial changes have been effected by bringing mighty forces to bear on man's inmost being, and that all moral and spiritual regeneration must originate from within.

I will now take Mr. Newman's points seriatim.

If I understand him rightly, he considers that the New Testament ought to have laid down a positive doctrine, as to what is right and wrong in our political relations. On the contrary, I have always considered that its abstinence from attempting to do this constitutes one of the particular excellences of its teaching. By this alone it has been able to accommodate its teaching to the universal condition of man. What would have been the result if it had been the duty of the Church of Jesus Christ to meddle with political questions? When it has unwisely attempted to do this the results have been disastrous. Nothing is more certain than that the different races of men require different forms of political government. The laws and constitutions which fit one nation do not suit another, just in the same way as it is impossible to manufacture a coat which will fit every man's figure and size. We have had abundance of evidence that the attempt to foist the institutions of one nation on another have ended in failure. Its freedom from advocating any particular form of political constitution has adapted Christianity to every nation under heaven.

Next, if they had commenced their labours by endeavouring to regenerate the faulty political constitutions around them, they would have ensured the active opposition of every existing government, and brought them to a speedy termination. In this respect the contrast between it and Judaism is remarkable. Judaism was designed for a single nation, and it contains the outlines of a political constitution suited to its requirements. Christianity was intended to exert a mighty moral and spiritual influence over every nation under heaven, and it contains none. Yet the writers of the New Testament were Jews, who felt for the Old Testament a profound veneration; and yet they have deliberately abandoned its political institutions, and substituted no others in their place. Nearly every ancient philosopher, at the conclusion of his writings on morals, favoured the world with his ideas on the laws and constitution of a republic, through which he hoped to effect the regeneration of society. But it always fell still-born; and neither the men of his own age, nor of any subsequent one, have been persuaded to adopt it. Mahomet fell into the error of uniting with his moral code a body of political legislation. The result is that Mahometanism is only fitted for Orientals. The Koran will never extend its influence beyond the unprogressive races of mankind. The same remark is true respecting Hindooism. Its caste system is both destructive to itself, and unfit for every other nation.

Yet the New Testament lays down a few broad principles respecting political duties. It teaches that political society is an ordinance of God; that to public authorities obedience is to be rendered conscientiously; that the end of political society is the good of the governed; and that there are certain limits within which civil government has no right to interfere. In ancient States political and religious obligations were frequently confounded, and no respect was shown in their legislation for the rights of conscience. Jesus Christ laid down clearly that man is bound by higher obligations than those due to the State. "Render to Cæsar," says He, "the things which are Cæsar's, and to God the things which are God's." In no work of any ancient philosopher is there any so clear a distinction as to the limits of civil obedience. If Jesus Christ and

His apostles had been the fanatics which unbelievers charge them with having been, they would have dealt with political questions in a very different spirit. Fanatics have so done in all times. Their mode of referring to them is one of the strongest proofs of their calmness of judgment.

Mr. Newman next asserts that the New Testament contains no precept regulating the practice of war. I am astonished at this assertion, for I have read it to little purpose if it does not contain many which have the closest bearing on it. The only thing which is true is, that it does not contain a formal treatise on the law of nations, or one regulating the duties of belligerents. What! Nothing about war, when every virtue which it pronounces to be preeminently Christian is utterly opposed to its practice? Nothing about war, when it contains a direct precept to feed one's enemy? Let its moral teaching become an actuality, and war will become an impossibility. This peculiarity of its teaching is all the more striking when we take into consideration the fact that ancient writers do not say one word in condemnation of war, but many in its praise, and that the martial virtues received their highest commendation. The most eminent men of ancient times had no compunction to kill,to enslave, or to destroy.

A similar objection is made, because it contains no precept directly commanding the abolition of slavery. Is it the only, or even the most efficacious way, I ask, to bring about the extinction of an institution deeply interwoven with the whole fabric of society, by commanding its abolition by direct precept? Is not the inevitable result of the great principles of its teaching, when they have thoroughly penetrated the mind of man, its certain and gradual destruction? What mean, I ask, its reiterated declarations, that all men are brothers in Jesus Christ? What is the meaning of its positive assertion, that in Jesus Christ there is no distinction between bond nor free, and between one race and another, but that all are children of a common father? I should simply weary you if I were to quote passages which assert the elevation of the humbler classes of mankind, and multitudes of others which utterly conflict with every principle on which slavery is built. Some of the grandest exhibitions of Christian martyrdom were exhibited in the persons of slaves. Renan tells us that the Neronian persecution of the Church commenced the elevation of both slave and woman.

I assert that nothing more exhibits the sobriety of the teaching of the New Testament, than the mode in which it deals with the question of slavery. It has been objected, that its greatest missionary tolerated it. He did, and he acted wisely in so doing. There were elements in society enough for stirring up a servile war. There had been many such in the previous history of Rome. With what result had they been attended? The aggravation of the slave's condition, and the suspension of thousands of slaves on crosses on the public roads of Italy. Would the Christian missionary have promoted the interest of the slave, by stirring up a servile war, while the emperor was the master of forty legions? The writers of the New Testament acted wisely, in laying down principles which could not help sapping slavery to its centre. Unbelievers are always anxious to refer to the teachings of ancient philosophy. What philosopher, I ask, has laid down any principle which was subversive of slavery? On the contrary, some of the greatest of them expressly taught that slavery was the natural condition of society. An eminent Roman, I mean Cato the Censor, left his worn-out slaves to perish and die. St. Paul says, "Masters, give to your slaves that which is just and equal, knowing that you have a Master in heaven." Please to observe his words, "just and equal;" do you except against this as the right principle for regulating the relations of the capitalist and the workman? He tells the Christian slave, if he had the opportunity of getting his freedom, to embrace it. He sent back to his master, it is true, a runaway slave, whom he had converted, but accompanied with a letter compared with which there is nothing more pathetic in the whole range of literature—the Epistle to Philemon. It is worth your reading as an exquisite piece of composition, though somewhat marred in our translation He promises under his hand to pay any debt he might have contracted; and then hinting that he had a right to command, he entreats his liberty by every pathetic consideration which could weigh on a sensitive mind. "Receive him," says he, " not as a slave, but above a slave, a brother beloved, specially to me; but how much more unto thee, both in the flesh, and in the Lord." He designates him as "his son, born in his bonds, his own heart." Are not these facts subversive of the fundamental principles on which slavery rests?

I cannot forbear drawing your attention to a striking contrast. A great philosopher, justly admired by unbelievers, the Emperor Marcus Aurelius Antoninus, sat on the imperial throne of the Roman Empire during the middle of the second century of our era. He was influenced by a deep sense of duty, but he issued no edict enjoining the manumission of the slave. In our day an emperor who is not a philosopher, but a Christian, has issued an edict abolishing slavery throughout the wide extent of his dominions. He has liberated serfs by tens of millions, and for so doing he deserves the gratitude of mankind. I fearlessly put the question, Which is more favourable to liberty, that philosophy which teaches that all mankind are descended from an ape; or Christianity which teaches that all men have a common father, even **God?**

But Mr. Newman further objects, St. Paul's teaching is deficient in not enunciating the rights of man. Does he mean deliberately to affirm, that it would have been an improvement to the pages of the New Testament if they had contained a direct discussion on this subject? It has done better. Although it may not have said much about the rights, it has said much about the duties of man. But adds Mr. Newman, "Better irrigation, or cultivation, better roads, better laws of land, better condition for the poor, better government, equally with improved astronomy or other science, were matters of little worth to one who expected a Divine Governor and Avenger, shortly to appear in the clouds of heaven." Does Mr. Newman mean to imply that for the purpose of constituting the New Testament an adequate guide as to the duties of life, that it ought to have contained a treatise on road making, or agriculture, or astronomy, or exhortations enjoining special diligence in these pursuits? But it will be objected, nothing is more suited to prevent attention to such subjects than the expectation of the nearness of the end of the world? I reply, that the shortness of life is a fact; if man perishes with his body, all earthly interest may be over to us at any moment, and cannot endure long. Why should not a full realization of this unquestionable fact, on the part of unbelievers, produce a similar result? There are passages in St. Paul's writings which show that he was far from being indifferent to the evils by which society is afflicted. He was very far from being insensible to the perils to which the traveller was exposed, the wrongs inflicted by magistrates, or the dangers arising from mobs, and he uniformly dealt with such questions with practical wisdom. One thing is certain, that the Author of Christianity laid down, whether His coming was near or remote, that diligence in their respective callings was the great duty of His followers; that He would call them to account for everything with which He had entrusted them; and that those who simply endeavoured to preserve what they had, without actively using it, would be visited with His heaviest censure. If it is a man's duty to cut a road, or to improve a piece of land, or to study astronomy, the teaching of the New Testament requires that he should do it with his utmost diligence. "Whatsoever ye do, do it heartily as unto the Lord, and not unto men."

Mr. Newman's complaints of the defectiveness of the teaching of the New Testament on the principles of social and political morality are widely scattered throughout this Tract. Among them, is the old charge of its omission to enforce the duty of patriotism. Mr. Mill also seems to be of opinon, that it greatly ignores our public duties. At page 90 of his Essay on Liberty, he writes as follows: "And while in the morality of the best pagan nations, duty to the State held a most disproportionate place, infringing on the just liberty of the individual, in purely Christian Ethics, that grand department of duty is scarcely noticed or acknowedged." If I were to understand the words "Christian Ethics" in this passage, as meaning what Mr. Mill has elsewhere laid down as its meaning, viz. "Theological Morality," as contradistinguished from the teaching of the New Testament, the observation before me would lie beyond the purpose of this lecture. But he adds: "It is in the Koran, and not in the New Testament, that we read the maxim, a ruler who appoints any man to an office, when there is another man in his dominions better qualified for it, sins against God and against the State. What little recognition the idea of obligation to the public obtains in modern morality, is derived from Greek and Roman sources, not from Christian; as even in the morality of private life, whatever exists of magnanimity, high-mindedness, personal dignity, even the sense of honour, is derived from the purely human, not from the religious side of our education." It seems to me that in this passage Mr. Mill intended to include the moral teaching of the New Testament in his charge of defectiveness, and not simply "Theological Morality."

I concur with Mr. Mill in thinking that in the ancient systems of morality the duty of patriotism occupied a **very** disproportionate place. In fact, ancient moralists viewed morality as a branch of politics. When, however, he censures Christianity for disregarding this duty, he has committed an oversight, of which his own account in his autobiography of his early training affords an adequate solution. I propose the following answer:—

First, as to the general principle. Patriotism as a virtue is far from being one which admits of an indiscriminate commendation. As it was exhibited in the ancient world (nor is the modern world blameless), the evils which were connected with it were enormous. What did it mean in the mouth of a Roman? A ruthless disregard of the rights of those who were not citizens, and the trampling on a conquered world. What were the views entertained respecting it by the Greek? A devotion to the interests of a little state consisting of 30,000 citizens, and rarely coming up to that number; a disregard of the interests of the vast servile class and of neighbouring states; the right to consign enemies to death or slavery; and a contemptuous trampling on every one whom he considered a barbarian, whom he might enslave or plunder at his pleasure. What effects had it on the Jew? It shrivelled up his character into an exclusive narrowness, such as we have it described in the classic writers. In the midst of the weary mass of selfishness with which the pages of history are filled, I own that I cannot help feeling a certain amount of admiration for the self-sacrifice which it envoked, even in the midst of the manifold evils with which its practice was attended. There is always something noble in the sacrifice of self, in whatever form it may be exhibited. The inscription placed over the 400 Spartans and their companions, who perished at Thermypolæ, is one of grand simplicity: "We lie here, obeying her laws." The laws of Sparta told the citizen not to turn his back on his enemy, but to die. Still it is impossible to close our eyes to the enormous evils which were wrought in the name of patriotism. The New Testament therefore is right in not taking notice of this quality as a virtue. It has consecrated as the first of virtues all that was essentially good and great in it, the principle of the sacrifice of self for the good of others, and placed it the highest among duties. It gives us all that was noble in it, without any of its defects.

I have never read a work written by an unbeliever, in which the duty of self-sacrifice has been recognised as the great and all-distinguishing principle of Christian teaching, or in which a proper place has been assigned to it in estimating its teaching as a whole. Yet it is evident to every careful reader of the New Testament that it forms the corner-stone of Christian morality, and that it is impossible to do it justice without deeply considering the place which it holds in it. While this is the case, it must be carefully observed that those principles of our moral nature which terminate in self, have their proper place assigned to them in the New Testament. But above them, regulating them, and controlling them, stands this great duty of self-sacrifice. A holy Christ seats Himself down in the place, which in ancient morality was occupied by citizenship and race. He calls forth the highest sacrifice of our selfish nature; He claims the entire man, body, soul, and spirit, to be consecrated to His service, and to be engaged in doing His work. That work is to do good with all his power, and with all his means; no act is too great, none too lowly, not to be demanded by this great principle.

I assert then that this duty constitutes a great principle, which is adequate to guide us in all the requirements of political or social morality. By it the Christian is bound to do to his brother man all the good he can; and he is to do it with the best light which his understanding imparts. The Christian politician is bound to feel an entire responsibility to do his duty with his utmost powers in the situation in which he is placed. So is the magistrate, and every public officer. The Christian landlord is bound by it to exert the influence of his position for the good of those dependent on him; so is the Christian capitalist; so is the Christian merchant; so is the Christian in every possible calling. So, let me add, is the Christian workman bound to do his work honestly and well, and not, as Carlyle says, to manufacture shoddy, and to worship Beelzebub. There is no social or political duty which this principle does not require the Christian to perform, and to perform well. Slightly altering Mr. Mill's precept from the Koran, I affirm if a Christian ruler were to appoint a man to an office, while there is another man better qualified to discharge it, and he was aware of the fact, it requires no special precept to inform him that he sins against this great duty.

Mr. Mill's next assertion, that whatever recognition the idea of obligation to the public obtains in modern morality " is derived from Greek and Roman sources, not from Christian ones," is surely owing to his want of appreciation of the all-comprehensive duty of which I have been speaking. No inconsiderable portion of the teaching of the New Testament is occupied in enforcing on us the duties we owe to others, *i.e.* to the public. "Look not," says St. Paul, "every man to his own things, but every man to the things of others." This duty is in the strongest manner enforced by example, " I would gladly," says he, "spend and be spent for you, though the more earnestly I love you, the less I be loved." The whole life of the apostle was occupied in the discharge of public as distinct from private duties. Ordinary men and women are far more indebted to such teaching, as the source of their obligations to society, than anything which they have learned from Greek or Roman writers. All that can be said is, that the New Testament contains no chapter specially devoted to the elaboration of our political or social duties, though it lays down principles abundantly adequate to guide us in the discharge of them, and to excite us to their practice.

I am still more astonished at the following passage, which I can only attribute to the prepossessions produced by Mr. Mill's early education, as set forth in his autobiography : " As even in the morality of private life, whatever exists of magnanimity, high-mindedness, personal dignity, even the sense of honour, is derived from the purely human, not from the religious part of our education."

I ask boldly, is this a fact ? The New Testament forms the most important ingredient in the training of ordinary men and women. Its principles have largely modified modern society. Is not high-mindedness to be found therein ? Is not personal dignity ? Is not a sense of honour ? Doubtless it teaches humility ; but the most perfect humility is consistent with all these qualities.

The human side of the character of Jesus Christ is a perfect exhibition of magnanimity, high-mindedness, and personal dignity. Was not the man who would not intrude himself on other men's labours, but who worked with his own hands to support himself and his companions, instead of allowing his converts to contribute to it, a high-minded man? Was he ever deficient in showing self-respect or dignity? Has he not appealed to the highest principles of human nature, to our love of truth, of honourable conduct, justice, purity, moral beauty, to the enlightened opinion of society, even to our love of approbation? This man expressly writes, " Be ye followers of me."

I now address myself to that numerous class of objections which may be summed up in the assertion, that the teaching of the New Testament contradicts that of the science called Political Economy.

Probably many in this room do not consider this a very grievous charge, for I suspect that in some of its principles you are far from being hearty believers. Thomas Carlyle, as you know, has designated it "the dismal science;" and if its teachings are the sole message of good news which we have to address to degraded man, I shall not dispute that it is dismal enough. I will state my own opinion. This science is an exhibition of a number of partial truths respecting human nature; but it contemplates only one aspect of it, and if it is propounded as the sole means of regenerating or elevating mankind, or as adequate to the entire wants of our moral nature, or as the sole physician of our condition morally and physically, it becomes a cruel parody. Man has wants and aspirations which this science can never meet, and is subject to disasters which it cannot remedy.

The following, I apprehend, contains the real point of the objection. Christianity is so earnest in teaching the duties of benevolence, kindness, and almsgiving, that it must come into collision with those of industry, saving, accumulation of capital, and the production of wealth, without which advancement in civilization is impossible ; and that it is even adverse to the accumulation of the fund necessary for the payment of wages.

First, I observe that mankind are subject to dire calamities, with which the principles of this science are wholly inadequate to grapple. Let us consider an instance or two. A man who is the sole support of his family dies suddenly, and leaves them destitute, or is seized with sickness which utterly incapacitates him ; or his children are idiots, and otherwise incapable of earning their bread. I need not enumerate to you the ten thousand calamities to which life is liable. Multitudes of men also are sunk into a profound state of moral degradation. All these things can only be adequately provided for by the stimulation of those virtues and affections, to which Christian moral teaching directs its most earnest appeals.

I think that you will agree with me, that the selfish affections in man are far stronger than the benevolent ones. If men could be cured of the vices which Christianity pre-eminently denounces, the affections which terminate in self are quite adequate to take care of themselves, and require no stimulation. Our benevolent feelings, under which head I include all those which prompt us to self-sacrifice, are comparatively feeble. The idea presented to my mind when quietly surveying the most crowded parts of the City during the most active hours of business is, The weakest to the wall. Sorrow, misery, or misfortune do not expect relief or attention here. When, then, the moral teaching of the New Testament throws all its energy into the attempt to quicken the benevolent feelings of our nature, and leaves the selfish ones comparatively uncared for, I think that you will not take exception to this portion of its teaching. I will examine a few of the objections in detail.

First, Mr. Newman affirms that all the precepts of Jesus Christ were intended to be taken literally. On this point Mr. Mill disagrees with him; and he also thinks that they are irreconcilable with nothing which a comprehensive morality requires. Mr. Newman endeavours to support his position by affirming that His first followers so understood Him, referring to the opening chapters of the Acts of the Apostles. These undoubtedly tell us, that under the peculiar circumstances in which the infant Church was placed, large numbers of its members contributed their property to a common fund. But there is a portion of the narrative which he has omitted to notice, and which is conclusive against his position. Peter is represented as saying, "Ananias, why hath Satan filled thine heart to lie to the Holy Ghost? Whiles it (*i.e.* the land) remained, was it not thine own? and after it was sold, was it not in thine own power?" These words make it clear that the act of contributing to the common stock was a purely voluntary one; that it formed no condition of Church membership, nor was it any portion of the law of Christ. The circumstances of the times rendered it necessary to support large numbers out of the common fund, precisely as you yourselves do when a strike takes place. In their zeal large numbers of the converts sold their possessions for the purpose of contributing to this. What Ananias did was that he professed to give up the whole, and thus to entitle himself to support from the fund, whereas he only surrendered a part of the proceeds of the sale. The epistle of St. James proves that the state of things mentioned by St. Luke was only designed to serve a temporary purpose. It had then ceased.

Again, many of the precepts of the New Testament are uttered in opposition to some corrupt moral principle then extensively prevalent, or are addressed to men under particular circumstances; to take an instance, that given to the rich young ruler. What is there in the context to imply that it was intended for any other purpose than to test him, or that it was designed for universal application? All such precepts no doubt involve a great moral principle which is of universal obligation ; but it is simply absurd mechanically to apply the mere letter of a precept to all states and conditions of mankind. Against this practice the New Testament emphatically protests. To do so is to imitate those quacks, who pretend that they have found out a universal medicine, able to cure every malady. You will probably ask, How are we to determine when this is the case? I answer, By the use of a little common sense and common candour; by entering into the spirit of its teaching, and viewing its subordinate parts in relation to it. I need hardly say, that this is necessary to enable us to get hold of the meaning of every writer.

But you will object, Does not the teaching of the New Testament utterly discourage saving? Does it not absolutely forbid us to make provision for the future? What can you say to such a precept as this, " Consider the ravens, which have neither storehouse nor barn, yet God feeds them. Are ye not much better than they?"

Yes, truly, we are much better than the ravens. We possess reason and foresight, which they do not, and this makes all the difference. God provides for both men and ravens within the range of their respective faculties. The raven, according to the faculties which God has given it, is provided for. In a similar way man shall be provided for within the range of his. This forms a good reason why men should not be devoured with anxiety for the future; but none for taking no care about it. It were absurd to argue because God provides for a raven to whom He has given no faculty like foresight, that therefore He will provide for men, to whom He has given it, and who neglect to use it. What the speaker intended to teach is the great truth that we ought to trust in providence, after we have used the best faculties which God has given us.

But it will be urged, that the precepts respecting almsgiving are without the smallest limitation. They say nothing about looking out for deserving objects. So are numerous other duties in the New Testament. If all the qualifying circumstances had been inserted, the book would have been swollen into a library. The duties are strenuously affirmed, and each individual is left to fill up the details by the aid of common sense and an enlightened Christian judgment.

But it will be objected, the charge has not been met that Christian teaching is antagonistic to the principle of prudent saving, and that it renders the accumulation of capital impossible. I reply—

First. The New Testament teaches that a man is bound to act as God's steward, in whatever position in society he may be placed by providence. This is distinctly recognised in the parables of the Talents, the Pounds, and the Unjust Steward. All waste is strongly discouraged. Idleness is forbidden. Diligence in business is expressly commanded. So is laying by for charitable purposes. So is making a suitable provision for a man's family. It was needless for it to teach directly the duty of accumulating capital, for the desire to do so is one of the strongest in human nature; so strong is it, that instead of requiring encouragement, there is the greatest danger of its absorbing every noble and generous principle.

Secondly. Christian teaching wages an internecine war against those vices which tempt men to extravagance. I need not draw your attention to them, for their injurious consequences no one can mistake. They are the fruitful sources of the misery of mankind. It also in the most emphatic manner enjoins moderation in all things. If then its injunctions were obeyed, we should see an end of misery, squalor, and rags. Savings would be as large as the political economist could desire, and the most ample provision made for providing the requisite wages fund. Get rid of these vices, practice the opposite virtues, and all the supposed collision between Christian teaching and social science will cease; all its demands will be complied with, and in addition society will have at its command all the resources necessary for the exercise of the benevolent affections.

I cannot here help noticing a charge which Mr. Newman brings against Christ and His apostles as being mendicants. This is simply invidious. They are described as devoting their lives to the work of doing good. Is it mendicancy, I ask, to receive a simple maintenance for doing so, and to eke this out by labouring with one's own hands, as St. Paul did? Is every popular lecturer who receives maintenance for devoting himself to the work of lecturing, a mendicant?

There is nothing therefore in the principles of the New Testament, if these were fully, and not partially carried out, which is adverse to such reasonable accumulation as is requisite for the purposes of social progress. I say emphatically, *if they were fully, and not merely partially, carried out;* for it is not possible to form a correct judgment of any system by dwelling only on one half of its teaching. Let its teaching respecting benevolence, and its utter denunciation of the vices tending to extravagance be set side by side, and then estimate the result. Selfishness in man is pre-eminently strong. It therefore exerts all its efforts to call into activity our benevolent feelings. That numbers of evils exist in the world which no principle founded on self-love can adequately meet is no theory, but a fact. It addresses itself strongly to those principles of our nature, whose proper function is to palliate those evils. It wages internecine war against those vices which impel men to extravagance. Its demands of self-sacrifice in the work of doing good are one of its strongest characteristics; but let it be observed in proportion as the evils of the world are got rid of, the sacrifice of capital necessary to effect this will diminish likewise. I ask you not to survey one portion of the teaching of the New Testament without the other.

I do not think that there are many persons in this room who will find fault with the New Testament because it teaches that there is something more in the relation between the employer and the employed than a mere pecuniary bargain, and that the mere inspection of the rate of wages in the labour market, is not the full discharge of the duties which they owe to each other. In this portion of the subject, Mr. Newman is guilty of an incredible unfairness. He affirms that St. Paul teaches the unqualified obedience of slaves to their masters, of children to their parents, and of wives to their husbands. What shall we say of a writer who quotes a line or two in which such duties are enjoined, and omits even to notice the context, which enjoins the duties correlative to these. It is perfectly true that there is such a passage in St. Paul's writings, as "Servants, obey in all things your masters according to the flesh." Here Mr. Newman stops. But the Apostle adds, "not with eye-service, as men-pleasers, but as doing the will of God from the heart; for of the Lord ye shall receive the inheritance, for ye serve the Lord Christ." The same apostle has a very strong precept for masters, enjoining their corresponding duties. "Masters," says he, "give to your servants that which is just and equal, knowing that ye have a Master who is in heaven, and there is no respect of persons with Him." Faithful service on the part of the employed; just and equal treatment on the part of the employer, is St. Paul's golden rule to regulate the relations between these two classes. Do you except against it? Is it not a far better one than the squeezing as much labour as possible out of the employed on the one hand, and the rendering the smallest amount of loyal service as he can to the employer on the other? There is a morality in conducting an argument as well as in striking a bargain. What shall I say of a writer who affirms that St. Paul taught unlimited obedience to servants, and who has omitted all mention of his teaching to masters, to give that which is "just and equal"?

Mr. Newman also asserts that St. Paul teaches, without the smallest qualification, the duty of absolute submission of wives to husbands. Will it be believed that in the direct context he has enjoined on husbands "to love their wives, as Christ has loved the Church, and has given Himself for it"? Observe the last words, and "*gave Himself for it.*" As Christ then gave His life for the Church, so it is the duty of the husband to give his life for the wife. Yet this writer affirms that St. Paul held a degraded view of the married state. You will find no such teaching in any work of ancient moralists. In the ancient world the wife was degraded into a chattel. The woman who flouted herself before the world's eye, and had comparative freedom was the courtezan. The Christian husband is to love his wife as Christ loved the Church, and gave His life for her. The Christian husband is therefore bound, not only to sacrifice himself, but if need be, to give his life for his wife. Where will you find the rights of women so effectually vindicated as by this teaching; or the marriage union placed on so high an elevation?

There are many other subjects which I would have gladly treated of in this lecture, but my space is exhausted. My selection has been regulated by their importance. If I have succeeded in showing that those difficulties which I have discussed are devoid of any real foundation, or have arisen from misconception of the great principles on which the teaching of the New Testament is based, the less important ones may be solved by the application of the same line of reasoning. I believe that the great principles which I have laid down are adequate to meet every difficulty. I ask you first to ascertain what those principles are, and then to apply them to the investigation of its subordinate details. Above all, do not be guilty of a course so utterly unphilosophical, as to apply a precept intended for one condition of society to a wholly different one, or to except against one portion of its teaching, while you have utterly neglected to take into account the other, which is its legitimate complement.

Finally, let me observe that there is one portion of the moral teaching of the New Testament which the limits assigned to this lecture have only permitted me to allude to. To give it an effective treatment has been simply impossible. Yet it constitutes the most distinguishing feature of its teaching. I allude to the all-important fact, that Christianity not only professes to lay down a number of moral principles, which are adequate to guide man in every advancing stage of his civilization; but to create a moral and spiritual power, which is able to rescue unholy men from their unholiness, degraded men from their degradation, and to elevate men whose virtue is imperfect to higher degrees of purity and goodness. Unless we keep this fact steadily in view, it is impossible to form a right estimate of its moral teaching. I repeat it, this forms its most distinguishing characteristic. Philosophers sighed for such a power, but they found it not; they left the degraded masses of mankind in their degradation, and contemplated their condition with despair. The lowest haunts of humanity formed the subject of the special care of Jesus Christ. They heard the voice of no philosopher; but they heard His. At His call multitudes have forsaken their evil ways, and have striven to follow Him. The wisest, the best, and the holiest of men, have proclaimed Him their Master and their Lord. The influence which has been exerted by Jesus Christ has exceeded that of all philosophers and moralists united. No personal influence which has been brought to bear on the world has been equally mighty. In proof of this I adduce the authority of Mr. Lecky, in his History of Morals from Augustus to Charlemagne. With this quotation I will conclude: " It was reserved for Christianity to present to the world an ideal character, which through all the changes of eighteen centuries, has inspired the hearts of men with an impassioned love, and has shown itself capable of acting on all ages, nations, temperaments, and conditions; has not only been the highest pattern of virtue, but the highest incentive to its practice; and has exercised so deep an influence, that it may be truly said that the simple record of three short years of active life has done more to regenerate and soften mankind, than all the disquisitions of philosophers, and all the exhortations of moralists "

THE COMBINATION OF UNITY WITH PROGRESSIVENESS OF THOUGHT IN THE BOOKS OF THE BIBLE,

An Argument in Favour of Divine Revelation.

BY THE
REV. J. H. TITCOMB, M.A.,

Vicar of St. Stephen's, South Lambeth, and Rural Dean of Clapham.

The Combination of Unity with Progressiveness of Thought in the Books of the Bible,

AN ARGUMENT IN FAVOUR OF DIVINE REVELATION.

THERE is one element of consideration underlying this subject which is not at first sight conspicuous, I mean the element of time, or the fact of there having been an interval of *at least* one thousand years between the publication of the earliest Old Testament literature and the birth of our Lord Jesus Christ. We who receive the whole Scripture as containing an authentic revelation from God, of course believe this interval to have been longer; but, in view of the question now to be raised, that variation of opinion is not of much consequence. For, even assuming that no portions of the Old Testament were written before the time of David or Solomon (B.C. 1,000), it is now admitted on all hands that many very ancient documents must have been preserved to the times of the Hebrew monarchy; and that notwithstanding the forms into which such documents were afterwards thrown, they must still have enshrined the faith and feelings of previous generations which had not only dated historically from Abraham, but had looked back traditionally even into earlier and more remote periods.

I do not enter, therefore, into any arguments about the authenticity of the books of Moses; nor do I even take for granted their Divine inspiration. I only lay down as the basis of my position, that the Old Testament Scriptures, whatever may have been the dates of their various publication, practically represent the religious faith and hope of one continuous stream of people from the time of Abraham to Christ. Which faith was briefly this: that as soon as the human race first felt the curse and misery of sin, it had been cheered by a revelation from God, which promised it a final victory of good over evil, and of happiness over sorrow, by means of some coming Deliverer who should one day be born as "*the Seed of the woman.*" Upon that simple thought the Hebrew people ever looked back as to the first bud of promise, and the first germ of hope which had gladdened the world in its sufferings—a hope which they had not only inherited from their forefathers, but which had never ceased to be the theme of a long series of *sacred* writers, whose literature professed to have been Divinely inspired.

It is this fact, gentlemen, to which I now desire to call your attention. I ask you to follow me in an argument by which I shall endeavour to show (1) that the Sacred Scriptures contain a unity, combined with progressiveness of thought, running over a prodigious lapse of time, making up one harmonious and perfect whole. I shall then (2) inquire whether such a fact finds a single counterpart in any other religion of the world. And (3) whether, taking all circumstances into consideration, the conviction is not forced upon us, that this must have involved a great deal more than what was merely natural or human; and that the only solution of the matter left to us is a belief of its having been really the result of Divine Revelation.

I. Let us INQUIRE, WHETHER THERE IS NOT A UNITY COMBINED WITH PROGRESSIVENESS OF THOUGHT IN THE SCRIPTURES, RUNNING OVER A PRODIGIOUS LAPSE OF TIME, YET MAKING UP ONE HARMONIOUS AND PERFECT WHOLE.

We may look at this subject either *Historically* or *Doctrinally*.

1. Regarding the *Historical* development of the promised "Seed," it may be enough to say that the Hebrews dated a tradition of it from the beginning of human woe; believing that, however much of this idea may have been gradually overlaid by idolatry and unbelief, it was, nevertheless, always to some minds the germ of a living hope. Mark you, I am not assuming this tradition to have been an actually supernatural revelation. I am only treating it now as a floating opinion which was handed down from generation to generation, with the view of tracing it out briefly in regard to its historical growth.

In the first place, then, you will please to observe that this traditional hope belonged to the whole race of man. It simply announced the coming of a human Redeemer, without the slightest reference either to time, or to place, or to family. It said that the "Seed of the woman" was to bruise the Serpent's head (Gen. iii. 15). From the date of Abraham, however, we gather that this belief became handed down under a more limited form, inasmuch as the Promised Seed was then made a special gift to that patriarch's house; the word of promise being "In *thee* shall all families of the earth be blessed" (Gen. xii. 3). Call this hope superstition if you like, it was, at any rate, the Hebrew belief. And so it passed on, through Isaac and Jacob, until we reach the twelve tribes of Israel, and the kingdom of David; when a revelation was alleged to have been given, announcing that the covenant of God with that king's house should be inalienable, and his dynasty established for ever. "And when thy days be fulfilled, and thou shalt sleep with thy fathers, I will set up thy Seed after thee which shall proceed out of thy bowels, and I will establish His kingdom. He shall build an house for My name, and I will establish the throne of His kingdom for ever" (2 Sam. vii. 12, 13). By and by, the manner in which this Son of David was to make His appearance became still more distinctively marked. One prophet taught the Church that He would come out of Bethlehem: "But thou, Bethlehem Ephratah, though thou be little among the thousands of Judah, yet out of thee shall He come forth unto Me, that is to be Ruler in Israel; whose goings forth have been from of old, from everlasting" (Mic. v. 2). Another prophet announced that the monarchy which was to be overthrown by Babylon should continue to be humbled by its enemies till the birth of this long looked for Ruler: "I will overturn, overturn, overturn it; and it shall be no more until He come whose right it is; and I will give it Him" (Ezek. xxi. 27). Another prophet declared that when He did come there would be a breaking up of the whole Jewish nationality: "After threescore and two weeks shall Messiah be cut off, but not for Himself; and the people of the prince that shall come shall destroy the city and the sanctuary; and the end thereof shall be with a flood, and unto the end of the war desolations are determined" (Dan. ix. 26). In the same strain spake Malachi, the last of the prophets: "But who may abide the day of His coming? And who shall stand when He appeareth? For He is like a refiner's fire, and like fullers' soap. And He shall sit as a refiner and purifier of silver; and He shall purify the sons of Levi, and purge them as gold and silver" (Mal. iii. 2, 3). At length, after 400 years, there appeared One in whom all these characteristics were alleged to have been combined. Now, of course, as Christian believers, we feel sure they were combined. We believe that Christ *did* come of Abraham's seed, and of David's house; that He *was* born in Bethlehem, and at a time when the royal dynasty *was* in ruins; and that the issue of His coming *was* the actual destruction of Jerusalem, and the scattering of the nation, and the purging of the priesthood by fire. As for yourselves, gentlemen, all I wish to press upon you, for the present, is this: that here is a long-continuous development of one idea, progressively evolved, and harmoniously sustained by a number of different writers lasting from at least the time of Abraham to the first century of our own era. And just notice also how this unity of belief is expressed in the Gospel of

St. Luke: "Blessed be the Lord God of Israel; for He hath visited and redeemed His people, and hath raised up an horn of salvation for us in the house of His servant David; as He spake by the mouth of His holy prophets, which have been since the world began: that we should be saved from our enemies, and from the hand of all that hate us; to perform the mercy promised to our fathers, and to remember His holy covenant, the oath which He sware to our father Abraham" (Luke i. 68-73). In other words, one continuous and progressive hope is described as having travelled through a period of about 2,000 years, living on freshly to the last, with a permanence which was incapable of destruction.

2. I might have said very much more upon this part of the subject, but the whole question is so vast that I must hurry on rather to the *Doctrinal* hopes which gathered around this promised Redeemer; inasmuch as the preservation of those hopes, in their unity yet growing fulness, throughout so long a period and by so many different witnesses, is one of the greatest human marvels. According to the oldest tradition of the Hebrew race, the Promised Seed was to be looked for as a Redeemer from sin and its attendant curse. Not a word, however, was at first stated as to the *means* by which that conquest should be effected. Those particulars were opened out gradually—grouping themselves around three aspects of character, namely, the Prophetic, Kingly, and Priestly offices. I am afraid it will be only on the two former of these that I shall now have time to enlarge.

First, then, let us view Him in His PROPHETIC or TEACHING OFFICE.

This was distinctly announced by Moses. I say by him; for although you may deny that Moses was the actual penman of the whole Pentateuch, yet you can scarcely deny that it was in the main a compilation of traditionary, if not documentary, fragments which had been handed down to the Church through that lawgiver. What, then, are the recorded or traditional words of Moses upon this point? He says: "The Lord thy God will raise up unto thee a *Prophet* from the midst of thee, of thy brethren, like unto me; unto Him shall ye hearken" (Deut. xviii. 15). Whether the full meaning of those words was detected by the Hebrews at once, and the hope thereby engendered of any ultimate abrogation of the burdensome law through the coming in of a greater Prophet who should bestow upon them a higher, holier, and more permanent covenant, we cannot say; but certainly that view was gradually introduced afterwards. For example, David hinted at it when he described in the 40th Psalm how "burnt offering and sin offering" were not to be required for ever; and how One *was* to come who should say: "I delight to do Thy will, O my God, yea Thy law is within my heart. I have preached righteousness in the great congregation" (Ps. xl. 6—9). Isaiah brought it out still more clearly when he said, "It shall come to pass in the last days that the mountain of the Lord's house shall be established in the top of the mountains . . . and *all nations shall flow into it. And many people* shall go and say: Come ye, and let us go up to the mountain of the Lord, to the house of the God of Jacob; and *He will teach us of His ways*, and we will walk in His paths: for *out of*

Zion shall go forth the law, and the word of the Lord from Jerusalem*" (Is. ii. 2, 3). In other words, this promised Prophet was to be, like Moses, a new lawgiver, teaching not only the Hebrews, but many nations also in the spirit of the freest possible education. For which reason Joel, speaking, as we believe, in the name of the Lord, said: "And it shall come to pass afterwards that I will pour out My Spirit upon *all flesh.* . . . . . . Also upon the servants and upon the handmaids in those days will I pour out My Spirit" (Joel ii. 28). And afterwards Jeremiah, still more plainly: "Behold the days come, saith the Lord, that I will make *a new covenant* with the house of Israel, and with the house of Judah. . . . This shall be the covenant that I will make with the house of Israel: After those days, saith the Lord, I will put My law in their inward part, and write it in their hearts, and I will be their God, and they shall be My people" (Jer. xxxi. 31, 33). So in an earlier chapter: "It shall come to pass in those days, saith the Lord, they shall *no more* say, The ark of the covenant of the Lord; neither shall it come to mind; neither shall they remember it. At that time they shall call Jerusalem the throne of the Lord, *and all nations shall be gathered into it, in the name of the Lord*" (iii. 16, 17). Could any truth, then, be more continuously evolved through successive centuries than this? If Moses said that the coming Prophet was to be a lawgiver like himself, and Isaiah that He should give His law from Jerusalem to all nations (*i.e.* the Gentiles), Jeremiah enlarged the picture by proclaiming it, not only a new covenant, but so new that the ancient ark, as a symbol of their then worship, should be known no more. In other words, the whole basis of their worship was to be altered. It was no longer to be represented by one local symbol, and to be confined to the Hebrew people, but to consist in the worship of God by the whole Gentile world, based upon a perfectly new dispensation. How changed this new dispensation was to be under this new Prophet, Malachi also made known 200 years after Jeremiah, when he said: "From the rising of the sun even unto the going down of the same My name shall be *great among the Gentiles*, and in *every place* incense shall be offered unto Me, saith the Lord of Hosts" (Mal. i. 11). Four hundred more years passed away after Malachi, and yet this doctrinal hope of the coming Prophet survived. You may not believe the testimony of the Gospels as to the miracles of Jesus. But granting even that those miracles were never performed and that the Jews who thought so were mere credulous enthusiasts, still their exclamation, "This is of a truth that Prophet that should come into the world" (St. John vi. 14), exhibits the survival of a strong national hope upon this subject. At any rate, the New Testament covenant, as it has actually been handed down to us, is in wonderful accordance with this long-continued development of Old Testament thought. Believers or unbelievers, Christians or infidels, no one can fail to see that New Testament thought here fits into Old Testament thought with the same propriety and neatness that a well-made key fits into a complex and elaborate lock; and that although it was the work of many centuries, yet the hope and its fulfilment were, from first to last, coherent.

Secondly, let us now view this promised Hope of Israel in relation to His KINGLY office.

For some reasons this should, perhaps, have come first, inasmuch as the primeval tradition of Eden, which is recorded in the book of Genesis (viz., that the Seed of the woman should bruise the Serpent's head), fundamentally involved the idea of an universal dominion over the powers of evil. That is to say, it embodied the belief that as man had ruined his own race, so One of that race should hereafter rise up to extricate and deliver it from ruin. Hence the thought of conquest and kingship had been an underlying element in this traditional hope of a coming Redeemer, even from the beginning. Abraham (*e.g.*) had beheld Him as blessing the whole human family (Gen. xii. 3); Jacob as gathering the nations under one great dominion (Gen. xlix. 10); and Balaam as smiting down all the opposition of his enemies (Numb. xxiv. 17). In this way the picture was unfolded with unswerving fidelity through all the roll of the prophets. Isaiah said: "The government shall be upon His shoulders; and His name shall be called Wonderful, Counsellor, the mighty God, the everlasting Father, the Prince of Peace. Of the increase of His government and peace there shall be no end, upon the throne of David, and upon His kingdom, to order it, and to establish it with judgment and with justice from henceforth even for ever" (Is. ix. 6). Jeremiah said: I will raise unto David a righteous Branch, and a King shall reign and prosper, and shall execute judgment and justice in the earth" (Jer. xxiii. 5). Ezekiel said: "I will set up one Shepherd over them, and He shall feed them, even my servant David; He shall feed them, and He shall be their Shepherd; and I the Lord will be their God, and My servant David a prince among them" (Ezek. xxxiv. 23). Daniel said: "Behold one like the Son of Man came with the clouds of heaven, and came to the Ancient of days, and they brought Him near before Him. And there was given Him dominion, and glory, and a kingdom, that all people, nations, and languages should serve Him: His dominion is an everlasting dominion which shall not pass away, and His kingdom that which shall not be destroyed" (Dan. vii. 13). The same prophet also stated the same symbolically, when he represented "a stone cut out without hands smiting the image upon his feet and breaking it to pieces;" and then interpreted it thus: "In the days of these kings shall the God of heaven set up a kingdom which shall never be destroyed; and the kingdom shall not be left to other people, but it shall break in pieces and consume all the kingdoms, and it shall stand for ever" (Dan. ii. 34, 44). Zechariah also said: "Rejoice greatly, O daughter of Zion; shout, O daughter of Jerusalem, behold thy King cometh unto thee; He is just and having salvation; He shall speak peace unto the heathen, and His dominion shall be from sea to sea" (Zec. ix. 9).

How strongly these hopes still abode among the Jews at the time of Christ's appearing no one can doubt. We do not need the New Testament to prove this, because the whole bulk of ancient Jewish literature does so. Whether, therefore, those words recorded by St. Luke were a true revelation from God or not, they were, at any rate, an embodiment of the national belief.

"He shall be great, and shall be called the Son of the Highest, and the Lord God shall give unto Him the throne of His father David: and He shall reign over the house of Jacob for ever; and of His kingdom there shall be no end" (Luke i. 32, 33). Now this is all I want for my present purpose. I am simply pressing on your attention the fact that one living hope of a coming King had been nursed among the Hebrew race from the beginning, and that not a single epoch in its history can be pointed to in which that thought had ever been lost sight of. I will not say that *every* feature in the prophetic portrait of this King was equally nursed up to the last moment in the national heart. For it was with the Jews as with most of ourselves; they clung to what was joyous and pleasant, but ignored the painful and unpropitious. David had first brought out to view the fact, that just as his own pathway to the crown of Zion had been opened through sufferings and persecutions, so the ideal David of his own house—the promised King of Israel, could only be exalted to the throne of Zion in the same manner. This was the picture in the 2nd Psalm: "Why do the heathen rage and the people imagine a vain thing? The kings of the earth set themselves, and the rulers take counsel together against the Lord and against His Anointed. . . . . . *Yet* have I set My King upon My holy hill of Zion." The same idea came out in other Psalms, such as the 22nd, which said: "They pierced My hands and My feet. They part My garments among them, and cast lots upon My vesture" (*ver.* 16, 18)—words which, never having been personally fulfilled in David, are necessarily held as prophetic of

David's ideal—the promised King of Israel; and no less in the 118th Psalm which said: "The stone which the builders refused is become the Head stone of the corner" (*ver.* 22). Not, however, till the time of Isaiah was the whole picture openly manifested. "My Servant shall deal prudently; He shall be exalted and extolled" (Is. lii. 13). Nevertheless, it was added :—He shall "grow up as a tender plant and as a root out of a dry ground." He must be "bruised" and "put to grief," and be brought "as a lamb to the slaughter, and as a sheep before her shearers is dumb, so He opened not His mouth" (Is. liii. 2, 7, 10). Thus the exaltation and glory of the Redeemer's kingship were to be preceded by the antagonism of an unrighteous world. Only through the pathway of suffering could He finally and effectually overcome the powers of evil, and redeem the world itself from its sufferings on account of sin. Daniel said the same thing:—"Messiah shall be *cut off*, but *not for Himself*" (Dan. ix. 26). Zechariah also repeated it: "Awake, O sword, against My Shepherd, and against the man that is My fellow, saith the Lord of Hosts. Smite the Shepherd, and the sheep shall be scattered" (Zech. xiii. 7). If time allowed other texts might be quoted. These were points, I say, which, though plainly painted in the sacred writings as part and parcel of the professed revelations of God, were yet neglected and forgotten by the nation at the appearing of Christ, because unpalatable and difficult of apprehension. Nevertheless, if you will only calmly read the New Testament, you will see that the teaching of the Gospels exactly harmonised with these pictures of the Redeemer's kingship. For without entering into any critical question as to the credibility of the claim, it is undoubted and certain that the Jesus of the Evangelists *did* claim to be Israel's promised King; that He *was* opposed by a persecuting world, and rejected alike by the heathen and Jewish rulers; that His hands and feet *were* pierced, and His garments divided among His enemies; that He *was* "bruised," and "put to grief;" that the Shepherd *was* smitten, and His sheep scattered; and that He *did* claim to come forth as conqueror of Death, and afterwards to be exalted to the throne of Zion. And on that throne we Christians believe Him to be still resting—according to another prophecy: "Sit thou on My right hand, till I make Thine enemies Thy footstool" (Ps. cx. 1).

I regret that I have only time to take up these two points, viz., the Prophetic and Kingly offices of this long looked for Redeemer, as illustrations of my argument. They do but form parts of a mighty subject which would rather require a volume to unfold than a lecture. Yet they are enough to indicate what remains behind. They show how one continuous stream of ever developing but united thought went sweeping on through successive generations in the shape of predicted hopes; and how accurately those hopes harmonised at last with the doctrinal and historical teaching of the New Testament in reference to Him who claimed to have appeared as the promised Redeemer.

Now mark, gentlemen, I am not asking you to believe that He was your Redeemer because the Evangelists say so; nor yet because they tell you that He proved His commission by miracles; nor because we assert the Gospels to have been really written by the men whose names they bear; nor because the Church of Christ has handed them down to us with an authority which demands our faith. You may smile as much as you please at all these points of Christian evidence. You may stamp upon them, and tread them under foot as you like. But this you cannot deny: that for a thousand years or more the Hebrew race, as exhibited in the various writings of the Old Testament, held to one great hope—ever the same, yet ever expanding—which hope became accurately re-exhibited in the writings of the New Testament as having been actually fulfilled.

The wonderful extent to which that fulfilment goes might occupy us all night, especially if I applied it to the typical ceremonial of the law of Moses, and to the way in which the recorded life, death, and resurrection of Christ satisfied the moral purport of that law, and explained its final abrogation. Could we employ one hour expressly for that subject, I might show you how the Christian doctrine of redemption interprets all the sacerdotalism of the Mosaic institutions, and explains their hidden meaning with a beauty and perspicuity which are marvellous. Whether that doctrine be true or false is not now under debate. All I contend for is that, taking it as it is written, it fits like a golden key into the ceremonial ordinances of the Old Testament, and harmonises with that faith and hope which had been gradually developing among a people who had been in professed covenant with God for at least 2,000 years or more previously.

II. Let us now INQUIRE WHETHER ANYTHING SIMILAR TO THIS CAN BE FOUND IN CONNECTION WITH OTHER RELIGIONS OF THE WORLD.

(1.) Take ancient Egypt for example. It is true there existed in that country a pantheon or assemblage of gods and goddesses, which lasted for 3,000 years. So far, we allow, there was a certain well sustained unity of thought in its religion. But there was no progressiveness of thought in it. There was not the vaguest semblance of any historical or prophetic belief in a coming Person who should embody in Himself the hope and happiness of all nations, and who should ultimately bring back the world into an universal empire of peace, love, and righteousness. Thoughts and hopes like those had never entered into the religion of any other country upon the face of the globe, except Palestine; still less were they ingrained into a sacred literature, which (always consistent with the expression of such thoughts and hopes) went on century after century in portraying them with increasing minuteness, and with growing fulness. If you tell us that among the philosophers of ancient Greece and Rome there was, notwithstanding, great progressiveness of thought, we reply—Yes, because all philosophy implies a seeking after truth; and where truth is honestly searched after, there cannot but be more or less of mental progress. But, on the other hand, those philosophers exhibited little or no unity in the midst of their progressiveness. Some of them believed in the mythological deities of their country, and some did not. Some began their search after truth by the study of external nature; others by denying the reality of matter. Some held that God and the universe were one; others that God and the universe were eternally distinct. Some believed that the Divinity took no interest in the affairs of men; others just the opposite. It would be endless to narrate the utter incoherences which separated even the best of these philosophers from one another, through the different centuries during which they flourished. Scarcely any truth of importance was settled and fixed. And as for writings which were homogeneous in the texture of their thought, or progressive in their descriptions of even *one* religious belief respecting the future, you might search on for ever without discovering them. No one pretends to do so. All those religions or philosophical productions were just what you might have expected them to be as the mere offspring of natural enlightenment. Many of them were acute, subtle, refined, and even noble. But they were continually discordant and hostile to each other; bearing marks upon their very forefront that they were the outcome of independent minds and judgments, without any supernatural inspiration to weld them together into one common web.

(2.) What shall we say of China, whose authentic annals far exceed in duration those of ancient Greece or Rome—stretching back from the present moment to about the seventh century before Christ? In some respects the religion of this great empire is more like that of ancient Egypt than of Greece or Rome, and is analogous even to that of the Hebrews. For it possesses a sacred literature; it has inherited holy books. The first of these books, the *Yih-king*, is a mysterious treatise upon the nature of the universe, and the action of the elements in creation. The second, called the *Shu-king*, is more historic. The third, called the *She-king*, is chiefly lyrical, and for the most part moral and ethical. Another is the *Li-ki*, or book of rites and manners, prescribing rules for society. Confucius, the second founder of the Chinese state religion, revived the teaching of these old books, and established them on a firmer basis, upon which basis they still rest. One thing is certain, however, in the midst of all this unity of purpose—viz., that, from first to last, it was simply utilitarian and materialistic; rejecting everything which could not be comprehended by the natural understanding. It was pre-eminently an appeal to reason, subordinated to the wants and welfare of society—a system in which the emperor was the fountain-head of order, and the parental relationship its living soul.

You will see, then, that while the sacred literature of China possessed a certain amount of social and ethical unity within itself, yet it was essentially fixed and stationary. It admitted of no new development, and never looked out beyond the world of sense and sight. It lacked the intellectual progressiveness of Grecian thought, because it tied men down to the rigid rules of sacred books which were, after all, more political than religious, and which were so completely utilitarian as to choke all imagination and speculation. There was nothing, therefore, analogous in this country to the Hebrew literature, whose sacred books were not only much more numerous, but, while social, political, and ethical, like the Chinese, were also full of enthusiastic hopes prophetical of the time to come.

(3.) Let us turn now to Buddhism. If this is not the oldest it is, at any rate, the widest-spread religion of the world; not perhaps geographically, but numerically without a doubt. It boasts of three hundred millions of disciples.

It too can boast of its sacred books, such as the Sútras, the Vinaya, and Abhidharma. But, like the Chinese books, they are without any elements of a future hope for this world; still less of a hope which was continually getting more and more definite with increasing years. There is but one idea of supreme happiness in the creed of Buddhism—Nirvána; *i.e.*, deliverance from existence into a state of impenetrable apathy, or absolute annihilation. With the deepest convictions of present wretchedness in the world, the only ultimate hope which it sets before man is extrication from the bonds of individuality. True, there is much that is noble, mild, and lofty in its attention to the charities and duties of life; in its cultivation of meekness, forgiveness of injuries, and resignation under suffering. But, speaking of it as containing a creed for the future, what parallel is there between its sacred books with those of Hebrew Scripture? The latter, in full view of the same wretchedness as that which Buddhism contemplated, were always expanding and developing the portrait of one living Person who should come to deliver the world from its suffering—teacher after teacher rising up to add some fresh touch to the picture, which made its historical fulfilment all the more complex and difficult. The former, on the other hand, had no hope to communicate concerning a living Person who was to come; nothing that could be brought to the test of an actual historical proof; nothing which could be proved or disproved by identification with the predicted delineations of previous teachers. Anything of that kind was as much unknown among the Buddhists as it had been among the Confucians of China, or the old Egyptians, and Greeks and Romans.

(4.) Was it different with Brahminism in Hindustan? This religion can boast indeed of its sacred books—the Vedas, the Puranas, the Shastras. But what unity of thought is there in them? There is plenty of progressiveness we allow, but little unity. In the Vedas there are many prayers and hymns addressed to the powers of nature, which exhibit noble thoughts, representing the Brahmin seeking after nearer approaches to the Divine Spirit. In the subsequent Puranas, and other sacred books, however, we pass on to deities and immoralities which it is shameful even to think of. At one time worship is given to Brahma; at another time it is superseded by Vishnu worship; then comes the stern and cruel Siva worship; and out of all has followed a pantheon in which deities may be reckoned by the million. The voice of such a religion is truly a testimony to the inner cravings of mankind after some sort of revelation from God; and the contents of all these books doubtless embody, with more or less of fulness, the longing of the human heart to have converse with the unseen world. In the Avatars, or incarnations of Vishnu, for example—who is represented in the Bhagavat Gita to say—" As often as there is a decline of virtue, and an insurrection of vice in the world, I make myself evident; and thus I appear from age to age for the preservation of the just, the destruction of the wicked, and the establishment of virtue,"—we see a faint trace of something like the Hebrew hope. Yet what comparison is there between the two, when you examine the literature of these religions in detail? In the earliest Vedas you trace Monotheistic hope and aspirations. In the latter books you have hope rising up for man through the grossest Polytheism. And if Vishnu be represented in these books as revealing himself from time to time for the world's good, yet what continuity of thought combined with progressiveness of portraiture is ever given by successive Hindoo writers respecting his appearance, through two thousand years or more before his arrival, followed also by an historical narrative of that appearance, in broad harmony with such forecast outlines of his portrait? None but a madman would attempt even to look for it. In the Hebrew theology alone do we find any such phenomenon. Just where all the future of hope for a world of sin and sorrow is, in other religions, at the best vague, shadowy, and undefined, in the Bible it is clear and distinct. Mind, I am not saying at present that these its utterances were supernaturally inspired. But, at all events, those utterances for centuries went on expanding with a growing breadth and definitiveness, which cannot be gainsaid; and they stand out now amongst the religions of the world as absolutely separate from anything and everything which ever existed by their side.

Having said thus much, let us

III. INQUIRE, WHETHER, TAKING ALL CIRCUMSTANCES

INTO CONSIDERATION, THE CONVICTION IS NOT FORCED UPON US THAT THIS FACT MUST HAVE INVOLVED A GREAT DEAL MORE THAN WHAT WAS MERELY NATURAL OR HUMAN, AND THAT THE ONLY SOLUTION OF THE MATTER LEFT TO US IS A BELIEF IN ITS HAVING BEEN REALLY THE RESULT OF DIVINE REVELATION.

First. *As to the Fact itself, which divides itself into three parts.*

(1.) There are thirty-nine books of the Old Testament, which were certainly all in existence in the time of Antiochus Epiphanes, nearly two hundred years before Christ. The most unbelieving critic does not deny this. It is as much an historical truth as that of the existence of the British Museum Library in the reign of Queen Victoria.

(2.) Assuming (for the sake of argument) that these thirty-nine books were not all necessarily written by the authors to whom they are popularly assigned, it is nevertheless perfectly incontrovertible that they represent the progressive faith and hope of one continuous stream of people from the time of Abraham to Christ. Allowing, for example, that the Pentateuch was only finally thrown into its present form during the latest age of the Hebrew monarchy it is nevertheless confessed, even by the most remorseless of critics, that the materials of which it is composed belonged to various antecedent ages, running back through many ancient documents and traditions. Some of those accounts may be rejected by unbelievers as fabulous; the belief in a coming Personal Redeemer, which they nursed within the Hebrew race, may be laughed at as superstition; their miraculous elements may all, for the time being, be obliterated; yet it is acknowledged that they still embalm the remains of an actual faith and hope which never became extinguished in Israel.

(3.) It was the peculiarity of this religious hope of the Hebrews not only to fix itself steadily on the coming of one living Personal Redeemer, who should through their race bring in salvation for the entire world, but to be gradually confirmed and enlarged by a succession of religious teachers, and by a variety of distinct methods, which made any guesses at what should happen extremely hazardous, and any accurate fulfilment more and more improbable.

This fact, I maintain, constitutes a phenomenon unlike anything else in the religious history of the world. The more so when we look minutely into the whole case. Hence a few words further.

Secondly. *As to the* CIRCUMSTANCES *which attend this fact.*

(1.) The people who so tenaciously clung to this fixed yet growing hope were subject to the greatest vicissitudes of fortune. Mind, I am not relying at present upon any of the miraculous elements of the Hebrew narrative, but only on that plain outline of Hebrew history which is so abundantly confirmed by profane authors, and by monumental remains. I do not stay to inquire how this people got into the land of Canaan. Authentic history undoubtedly finds them there. It finds them there established as a strong monarchy. It finds them there closely attacked by foreign enemies, and afterwards carried for a long period of exile into the heathen empire of Babylon. It finds them again restored to their own land, but distressed and discouraged by new foes. It finds them there alike ravaged by the Greeks and Romans, and reduced into a miserable state of vassalship to the latter power. Nevertheless, throughout all these political changes we see the same great hope abiding in the national heart. Nor is that hope stationary. Instead of being suppressed it rises higher, and expands more fully, and becomes portrayed with more and more of minuteness.

(2.) The writers who developed this hope were men of various orders—kings, priests, prophets, statesmen herdsmen. Yet with all these antecedent grounds for expecting their witness to be different, it was practically the same. Separated as they were from each other by education, by position, by modes and habits of thought, and by variations in national experience, they all had in view the same living picture of one coming Redeemer; and without variation or contradiction they painted Him in colours of increasing brightness.

(3.) Some of the points brought out in this developed portraiture were of the most strikingly practical character, admitting of the plainest possible refutation, supposing the result should not agree therewith. Moreover, this picture of the living Man and His times was confessedly finished off and stereotyped about 200 years before the time when a new set of writers proclaimed its fulfilment in the person of Jesus Christ. In the prolonged unity, therefore, of this wonderful chronicle of predicted hope, there was a wide front of thought open to the charge of misconception and error if events should not correspond with the description.

(4.) Fully 250 years after the time of Antiochus Epiphanes, when every one admits the thirty-nine books of the Old Testament had been written, it is now most fully conceded, even by infidel writers like Renan and others, that St. Paul wrote the epistles to the Romans, Galatians, and Corinthians, containing many historical allusions to the existence of Jesus of Nazareth. For argument sake, therefore, I will exclude all that was miraculous in these epistles, and take up only those points which belong to simple and actual fact. I will treat them for the moment, that is to say, as merely human compositions, and see how far they bear witness to what you may be pleased to call the surmises of the Old Testament writers.

Not to be too diffuse, let me name only *three* points of singularly clear and undoubted harmony between these epistles and the Old Testament teaching previously referred to.

(1.) St. Paul here declares it to be the belief of the Church, that although Christ was of the seed of David, the long promised King of the Old Testament prophets (Rom. i. 2, 3), yet that He had been despised and rejected by His own nation (1 Cor. ii. 8, and i. 23).

(2.) He shows that Christ was not only acknowledged by believers in His *Prophetic* office (*i.e.* as a great spiritual teacher), but that the result of His teaching had introduced them into a new covenant, under which certain old Jewish ordinances (*e.g.* Circumcision and the Passover) had disappeared as obligatory (Gal. v. 2, 6; vi. 12, 15; 1 Cor. v. 7, 8), and the law of Moses had been set aside for a new Gospel dispensation where

Gentiles stood as welcome as Jews (Rom. ix. 24-30; x. 12, 13; xv. 16).

(3.) He teaches that this changed dispensation was in the course of actually breaking up the whole Jewish nationality (Rom. xi. 7-10), and of thus bringing upon it all the woes predicted by the prophets—circumstances which, I need not say, were fulfilled in the destruction of Jerusalem by Titus, and in the "scattering and peeling" of the people through the whole world.

Here then were, at least, three undeniable facts, entirely removed from the region of myth or miracle,—three actual and historical circumstances which were as plainly authentic as any that were ever recorded by the pen of a contemporary writer. And these three facts, moreover, were in absolute harmony with certain Old Testament statements made from 200 to 2,000 years before they happened.

I have mentioned only these three, because time alone allows of it; otherwise I might have adduced more. But taking these three as sufficient for my purpose, I now ask you to rise up and account for this unity combined with progressiveness of thought, running on through 2,000 years and more, and all winding up harmoniously in the historical Christ just as it had been portrayed, on any other principle than that of Divine Revelation.

You have already seen that there was nothing like it in any other religion of the world. What, then, accounts for this unique phenomenon in the religion of the Hebrews? How is it that in the sacred books of the Old Testament—separated, at least, by 200 years from the first authentic books of the New Testament—there is one golden thread of thought which runs on through both; one great hope predicted, and then fulfilled; one distinct web of events prophetically announced, and afterwards as plainly woven together into actual history? I ask you, gentlemen, to account for this by any natural law of human probabilities.

Consider, first, that in the ordinary phases and changes of human thought (subject as they are to all sorts of disturbing elements from rival schools of teachers, and from different idiosyncracies of mind) this unity and continuity of hope in one coming Redeemer, throughout many centuries, would be naturally most improbable. Assuming there was no external revelation, and that nothing gave rise to such a style of writing except the inspiration of human genius, and the surmisings of men's imagination,—I ask you to account for this uniformity of witness to one thought, and for the gradual development of this one prophetic portrait through successive centuries, without any mutual contradiction or incoherence. As I have remarked before, these writers were men of various orders, and of different dates; and belonged to a nation whose political and religious life was subject to many convulsions. Everything, therefore, was calculated to disturb their unity of sentiment. Yet nothing broke it. If you can produce one single case even approaching to such a phenomenon in any other religion, we will say no more; but as we know you cannot, we maintain it to be a marvel of mental unanimity which, in itself, so reaches the miraculous as to be only capable of explanation upon the supposition of its having resulted from the gift of Divine Revelation.

This, at least, is *our* explanation. We ask *you* to find a better.

The case, nevertheless, becomes stronger—very much stronger—when you consider—

Secondly. That there was not merely a correspondence of *sentiment* in relation to this Promised Hope of Israel between the books of the Old Testament and the first authentic books of the New Testament, notwithstanding an agitated interval of two or three hundred years; but that there was also a perfect agreement between *the prediction of actual events relating to Him* in the one, and the *fulfilment of such events* in the other.

You will remember that, to meet your own objections, I have eliminated all the miraculous elements of Scripture; and that I have placed no weight in my argument upon the necessary authenticity of the Old Testament records. I have taken them, for the moment, as mere human compositions, which, somehow or other, no matter by whom, were confessedly written at different periods of Hebrew history, and were gathered at all events into one sacred canon by the time of Antiochus Epiphanes, or nearly 200 years before the birth of Jesus Christ. Even on this naked basis, however, you have seen that the Old Testament records pledged their veracity to the fulfilment of three coming events—viz., (1) That the Redeemer when He appeared would be opposed and persecuted, and rejected and slain by His own people. (2) That the result of His ministerial teaching would be to introduce a new covenant, by which the law of Moses would be set aside for a new dispensation, granting equal privilege to the Gentiles as to the Jews. And (3) that this changed dispensation would have the effect of breaking up the Jewish nationality. You have also seen, on the authority of four New Testament books, whose authenticity is now universally admitted, written about 250 years after the time of Antiochus Epiphanes, that those events were in the course of an actual historical fulfilment. Now those events were not miraculous. You cannot treat them as myths. They are ordinary historical events which still remain uncontradicted and indisputable. We therefore call upon you to give us some reasonable explanation, upon natural grounds and on human laws of probability, for this wonderful harmony between the events as predicted and the events as fulfilled.

To do this you will be driven to one or other of the three following alternatives: either (1) to prove that these sayings of the Old Testament have no proper application to the coming of a Redeemer; or (2) that, if they had, they were only the surmisings of genius—the forecasts of penetrating minds as to future probabilities, which were strangely and unexpectedly brought about by a series of lucky coincidences; or (3) that being mere guesses and speculations, subsequent events were so moulded by Christ and His apostles as purposely to bring about the fulfilment of them.

If you take the *first* of these alternatives, then I confront you with a literary difficulty. For it runs clean contrary to the whole current of the most ancient Jewish interpretation. Take the 53rd chapter of Isaiah, for example, the Messianic interpretation of which was only abandoned by later Rabbis, such as Abenezra, Jarchi, and Abarbanel. Gesenius says: "It was only the later Jews who abandoned this interpretation; no doubt in consequence of their controversies with the Christians." This is the interpretation, for instance, in the Chaldee Paraphrast. And even some of the later Rabbis assent to it. Thus *Rabbi Alschech*, in his commentary on that chapter says: "Upon the testimony of tradition, our old Rabbis have unanimously admitted that king Messiah is here the subject of discussion." In a similar manner *Jonathan Ben Uzziel*, the author of the Chaldee Targum, who lived a little before the time of Christ, says, in allusion to Daniel, when speaking on the prophet Habakkuk, that "the four great kingdoms of the earth should be destroyed in turns, and be succeeded by the kingdom of Messiah." It would be endless to adduce proof upon this point, and needless too; for however much our modern rationalists may argue to the contrary, it is simply a matter of fact that all the opinions of the ancient Jewish Church are against them.*

If you adopt the *second* alternative, maintaining that these predictions of the coming Messiah were merely the surmisings of natural genius, which were strangely and unexpectedly brought about by a series of lucky circumstances; then I challenge you to prove that there was anything in the state of the Jewish mind, even for a thousand years before Christ, that naturally led to such a development of thought. On the contrary, was not everything directed against it? Did it flatter any national hopes? Was it in keeping with any feeling of patriot-

---

* See *Dr. Allix*, "On the Judgment of the Ancient Jewish Church."

ism? Was there any one element in the Mosaic theology which led up to it? Were not all the hopes which clustered around this expected King of Israel naturally of a joyous and triumphant nature? What teacher of a people having such hopes could have ever instinctively had the slightest antecedent ground for prognosticating that the arrival of their King would issue in the downfall of their nation? Or that when He appeared, it would be to overthrow their temple, and abrogate their laws, and introduce a totally new dispensation? Or that the coming of such a King would be signalised by his rejection and death? Such predictions were no outcome of human genius—no forecasts of probabilities founded upon astute observation. We look in vain for any natural germ of such thoughts. At all events, if there were any, we ask you to produce them, and we challenge you to bring them forward.

If you adopt the *third* alternative, viz., that these thoughts were mere rough guesses, first originated as speculations, then elaborated artificially, and afterwards moulded into realities by the determined conduct of Christ and His apostles, who purposely brought them about in order to make their fulfilment agreeable with the prediction—then we bid you explain how it was done. That line of reasoning might, perhaps, be applied to some points of the evangelistic narratives, such as our Lord's entrance into Jerusalem on "a colt, the foal of an ass" (see Zech. ix. 9), or to the commencement of His ministry in Galilee (see Is. ix. 1)—circumstances which were perfectly within His own control, and which, therefore, might possibly be alleged as having been effected to secure the fulfilment of Jewish prophecy. But these instances of which we speak were very different. They were perfectly beyond the control of any individual will of man. You will tell me, perhaps, that any one might have risen up as a teacher in Israel, and by setting forth claims which were opposed to the prejudices of the Jewish rulers, have brought about his own death. Doubtless. But will you have the kindness to inform me how a man by those means could have forced on, after his death, a series of gigantic events so as to produce a disruption of Jewish nationality, just because such a catastrophe had been fancifully sketched out some hundred years before as a consequence of the coming of the King whose claims that teacher had ambitiously assumed? You will reply, perhaps, that the time was well selected, inasmuch as Palestine, already in captivity, was already giving preliminary signs of an expiring nationality; and that, therefore, its final conquest by the Romans was sufficiently probable to justify its speedy expectation. But even this subtle argument fails you. For the voice of that continuous and progressive teaching throughout the Old Testament, of which I have been speaking—though in one point of its development it foretold the breaking up of Jewish nationality as a consequence of the rejection of its promised King—yet did not let that fact stand alone. It predicted the going forth of a new law from Jerusalem, by which all nations were to be gathered into it, as into a spiritual metropolis for the world. The King, whose rejection was to bring ruin on that city literally, was also to be a Teacher or Prophet whose doctrine and influences after death should spiritually restore it for ever, by making it a common centre round which the affections of the converted heathen were to be gathered, and into which their forces should flow. The testimony of past centuries, we repeat, was not merely to the breaking up of the old Jewish nationality, but to the coincident uprising of an universal though spiritual empire, in which the long promised King and Prophet of the Jews should administer His kingdom under new laws and statutes, fitted to the moral and spiritual wants of humanity at large. Now such a kingdom we actually behold in the Christian Church; not as a matter of speculation, but as a hard, dry fact. You may ridicule our faith as superstition, you may deny the personal resurrection of Jesus as a delusive sham; but you cannot deny that through the teaching of apostles and evangelists there came forth a risen power from Christ which lived after He had disappeared, and which, coincidently with the dissolution of the Jewish nationality, peacefully opened a new kingdom of faith to all nations. I say peacefully opened it; because however much you may retort that it was debased by violence in later times, yet it should be ever remembered that the kingdom of Christ was not set up like Mahomet's, by the power of the sword, but simply by that of argument, of faith, of patience, and of love. Its victories through the first few centuries were purely moral and spiritual. Nevertheless, it triumphantly ran throughout many nations, and so fulfilled the predictions of the ancient prophets. is in the union then of these two facts which are both strictly historical, and each of which survives (be it observed) up to this very day; it is the union of these two facts, each so difficult of achievement yet so widely spread, so established and permanent, that we see how utterly impossible it must have been for any one will to have personally planned and carried them into execution. If any of you think this complicated moulding of public events according to a preconceived programme possible, let him try the experiment. Let Mr. Bradlaugh, for example, so set himself against the rulers of this country that he is obliged to lay down his life as the penalty. Let him and his principles then rise up, as it were, from the dead, and so reassert themselves through the pages of the *National Reformer*, as to bring on a total collapse of the British empire by means of foreign invasion and conquest. Let his followers then manage simply by moral and intellectual means, without the slightest violence or turbulence, to get rid of Christianity in Europe, so that its churches perish and all its institutions fall. When you have done this, gentlemen, as the simple result of your own will and pleasure, we will give you a right to the argument now propounded. But meanwhile, whether you like to hear it or not, we maintain that Christianity is a supernatural continuation of the Old Testament church of the Hebrews—the predicted evolution of its prophecies—the only key which unlocks with reasonableness the full meaning of its sacred books; a continuation up to the present moment of the same line of thought which had been in one long course of progressive development from the beginning. I remind you once more that this continuation of Church life is not an arbitrary assumption; it is a fact. Apart from religion altogether, it takes the shape of an historical and literary truth which can neither be gainsaid nor got rid of. All other religions are ideal and speculative. The Hebrew faith is historical. Its sacred books are a deposit of national literature, bristling with every form and variety of style, and extending over a vast period; yet never deviating from one witness in religious hope and thought. You have, therefore, to account for this fact. As for ourselves, we contend that the phenomena here presented to us were above all human causation; that there is not only nothing like them in the history of any other religion in the world, but that no other theory except that of supernatural revelation is left to us, if we fairly wish to account for them. Upon that theory everything is clear. There is then an intelligible connection between cause and effect; but without it, we search in vain for a solution. If you think you can give us a better solution, gentlemen, try your hands upon it now; and I promise we will listen to you patiently.

THE AUTOBIOGRAPHY OF JOHN STUART MILL.

BY

W. R. BROWNE, M.A.,

Fellow of Trinity College, Cambridge.

The Autobiography of John Stuart Mill.

I MUST begin this lecture upon the Autobiography of John Stuart Mill by observing that I have already published a review of that work in the first number of the *Christian Evidence Journal*. In this review are contained the chief conclusions and reflections to which the study of the book had then led me. I have, however, followed a somewhat different path in this investigation, and it is therefore only a few phrases and arguments contained in the review which I have found occasion to reproduce; but I allude to the fact lest there should be anyone here present who has read the review, and might be surprised to hear some parts of it repeated without explanation.

The very first point I wish to note is one which has already been alluded to in the review, and that is the exceeding value of the book before me. No thoughtful man should, in my opinion, neglect to read it, whether he agree or disagree with the opinions of its author. We live so much to ourselves, each in his own little world of thought and feeling and experience, that we should always seize the opportunity to look into another man's mind and see how the problems of life appeared to him, and what means he took to solve them. Now there is no such opportunity to be compared with that of reading an autobiography, if only the writer sets forth faithfully the history of his convictions, of the causes which led to them, and the effects on life and character which they produced. This holds true even if the writer is an ordinary man like ourselves, with no special talents or high qualities. But the value is of course far greater where the writer is no ordinary man, but a leader of his age, either in thought or in action, and perhaps in the former case more than in the latter. Now this John Stuart Mill undoubtedly was. Whatever may be the estimate of his powers into which the world will finally settle down, he, more than any one man, moulded and influenced on all abstract questions the *thought* of the age in which he lived. And here we have the record of this man's own thoughts—the picture of his inner life—traced out, as all must admit, with simplicity and frankness and truth. I think no one reading the book can doubt that what he there describes himself to have thought and felt that he really did feel and think; and although there was probably much in his life which he does not tell us, yet that what he does say may be fully relied on. Therefore, as I said before, this book is one which all thoughtful men should read ; one from which many lessons may be learnt, and on many subjects. But my business to-night is not with the book as a whole, nor with all the pursuits —political and social and literary—in which its author was immersed. I am going to look at the life of John Stuart Mill from one point of view only, and that is the point of view of religion. The one question which we have to discuss in this hall—to my mind the one question which the world has to discuss—is the question whether Christianity be true or false. I am going to examine this man's life in order to see how it bears upon that one question; what evidence it furnishes, what lessons we may draw from it that may help us to that question's solution.

I need hardly stop to explain why the life of this particular man is specially suited to furnish such evidence. The reason is not far to seek. John Stuart Mill was one of the keenest, the clearest, the most influential thinkers of his day. He was also a man much beloved by his friends—(Heaven forbid that I should stint a word that can be uttered in praise of the dead)—devoted to the welfare of his fellow men, regular and temperate in his life, honest, upright, sincere; and he was an utter unbeliever in any form of religion whatsoever. This fact, which was tolerably well known in his lifetime, is made perfectly clear and certain by the volume before us. He was all that I have described, morally and intellectually, either in consequence of or in spite of his rejection of all which Christians hold true and sacred. Which of these is the case? There can be no denying that at first sight his life makes against the party of religion. I know that it has been felt to be so by many; I have felt it to some extent myself. Can that be true which a thinker so careful and so brilliant—the greatest master, in this age at least, of the science of logic and the laws of evidence—pronounced unhesitatingly to be false? This is the question which men have asked themselves in looking at the fact of John Mill's unbelief before light was thrown upon the subject by the appearance of this volume. I ask that question again to-night, and in the light so afforded I will try to answer it.

With this object I turn to the book itself, in order to learn (1) what John Mill's religious opinions really were; (2) what were the causes which produced them, and the grounds on which they rested. And here I am met by a very striking fact. The subject of religious opinion is the only subject which does not run through the book. There is one passage near the beginning where, in giving a general account of his education, he states at length and distinctly what were the religious views held by his father and impressed from earliest childhood on himself; and from that time forward we hear no more on the topic, except in a few casual allusions, referring more to others than to himself. Considering how minutely he describes the change and development of his views upon politics, social science, and mental philosophy, this silence is certainly remarkable. It must mean one of two things—either that his religious views underwent no change throughout his life, or that the changes were such as for some reason he thought proper to conceal. The latter supposition—that he did alter his opinions but would not say so—is opposed to all we know of him otherwise, and to what we may glean from the book itself. We must therefore fall back on the first supposition—that his religious views remained throughout exactly what they were in his boyhood. And on looking again at the book, I think we may see very clearly why this was so, and at the same time of how little weight his authority is on this matter. I must here quote the one important passage which I have already mentioned. Having described the extraordinary course of mental training to which he was subjected, he goes on to speak of moral influences, and introduces the subject of religion thus:—

(P. 38.) "I was brought up from the first without any religious belief, in the ordinary acceptation of the term. My father, educated in the creed of Scotch Presbyterianism, had by his own studies and reflections been early led to reject not only the belief in Revelation, but also the foundations of what is commonly called Natural Religion..... Finding no halting place in Deism, he remained in a state of perplexity until, doubtless after many struggles, he yielded to the conviction that *concerning the origin of things nothing whatever can be known.* This is the only correct statement of his opinion: for dogmatic Atheism he looked upon as absurd; as most of those whom the world has considered Atheists have always done. These particulars are important, because they show that my father's rejection of all that is called religious belief was not, as many might suppose, primarily a matter of logic and evidence: the grounds of it were moral still more than intellectual. He found it impossible to believe that a world so full of evil was the work of an Author combining infinite power with perfect wisdom and righteousness.... His aversion to religion, in the sense usually attached to the term, was of the same kind with that of Lucretius: he regarded it with the feelings due not to a mere mental delusion, but to a great moral evil. He looked upon it as the greatest enemy of morality: first by setting up fictitious excellences—belief in creeds, devotional feelings, and ceremonies, not connected with the good of human kind—and causing them to be accepted as substitutes for genuine virtues: but above all by radically vitiating the standard of morals: making it consist in doing the will of a being, on whom it lavishes all the phrases of adulation, but whom in sober truth it depicts as eminently hateful. I have a hundred times heard him say that all ages and nations have represented their gods as wicked, in a constantly increasing progression; that mankind have gone on adding trait after trait till they reached the most perfect conception of wickedness which the human mind can devise, and have called this God and prostrated themselves before it. This *ne plus ultra* of wickedness he considered to be embodied in what is commonly presented to mankind as the creed of Christianity. Think (he used to say) of a being who would make a Hell—who would create the human race with the infallible foreknowledge, and therefore with the intention, that the great majority of them were to be consigned to horrible and everlasting torment."

Such then were the opinions of the father. Were they imparted to and acquiesced in by the son? On this head we are not left in doubt. A little further on we read:—

"It would have been wholly inconsistent with my father's ideas of duty to allow me to acquire impressions contrary to his convictions and feelings respecting religion: and he impressed upon me from the first, that the manner in which the world came into existence was a subject on which nothing was known: that the question 'Who made me?' cannot be answered, because we have no experience or authentic information from which to answer it: and that any answer only throws the difficulty a step further back, since the question immediately presents itself, 'Who made God?' He at the same time took care that I should be acquainted with what had been thought by mankind on these impenetrable problems."

It is thus certain that no pains were spared to impress upon John Mill the religious opinions of his father. That he retained those opinions through life there can be, as I have already said, as little doubt. Not merely does he here quote them with manifest approval, but the few scattered notices further on in the book are all in the same tone. Thus in the course of an eulogy on the character of unbelievers (p. 46) he speaks of them as men "who think the proof incomplete that the universe is the work of design, and assuredly disbelieve that it can have an Author and Governor who is *absolute* in power, as well as perfect in goodness." This then may be taken as the creed, or rather the no-creed of James Mill and his son. Looking into it we are at once struck by this fact, that the grounds of unbelief in this case have nothing whatever to do with what are commonly called the Evidences of Religion natural or revealed; nothing whatever to do with the claims of Christianity as compared with those of other forms of belief. What we are dealing with is simply a sweeping rejection of everything that we call supernatural, a rejection made on *a priori* grounds, which are quite independent of the positive evidence, however strong, that may be offered on its behalf. All such evidence is in fact shut out of court and barred by the position that the world being evil, cannot have an Author absolute in power and goodness. The strength of that position I shall consider presently. What I now wish to point out is the effect that it exercises on the minds of its supporters. It is my full belief that John Mill never fairly studied the Evidences of Christianity at all. I expect to be told that this is inconceivable: that a man of his powerful intellect and grasp of mind could not but have made a thorough investigation of so weighty a matter. It is well therefore that I should state clearly my reasons for making such an assertion; and they are these.

(1.) He never in any part of the book gives any hint of his having made such an investigation. Considering the full information given us as to all he did and thought, this omission is very significant: at any rate it throws on my opponents the burden of proving that such an investigation was made. There is one passage of the Autobiography where we should certainly have expected some notice of the kind: and that is the description in ch. v. of the mental crisis through which he went in early manhood. In the full tide of youthful zeal and ambition to be a reformer of the world he suddenly asked himself whether, if all the objects for which he was working could be completely realised at the instant, this would be a great joy and happiness to him: and an irrepressible self-consciousness answered "No." On this he fell into a state of utter and hopeless dejection, which lasted for some months. It is in such circumstances that many men have recourse to religion, and we might have expected that John Mill would at least have made an effort to do so: but though the whole crisis is minutely detailed, there is no hint of his even entertaining the idea. He at last found a refuge from his state of despair in the enjoyment derived from the contemplation of nature, from books, conversation, and in general the cheap and quiet resources of life; and it may fairly be questioned whether any man having passed through such a crisis without the aid of religion is likely ever afterwards to have recourse to it.

(2.) The early training of John Mill is sufficient in itself to account for his never giving any thought to the subject of Christian Evidences. What this training was we have already seen. The effect produced may be described in his own words (p. 43): "I am one who has not thrown off religious belief, but never had it: I grew up in a negative state with regard to it. I looked upon the modern exactly as I did upon the ancient religion, as something which in no way concerned me. It did not seem to me more strange that English people should believe what I did not than that the men I read of in Herodotus should have done so." In fact John Mill's attitude towards Christianity was precisely that of a learned and thoughtful Christian towards Mahometanism: an exhaustive inquiry into the subject would not appear necessary in the one case any more than in the other. The powerful influence of such early training is allowed on all hands—by none more than by the sceptical school. The only possible means they can take to explain the fact that the great bulk of mankind, even of the clever and intellectual, profess a belief in religion—the only justification of their outcry as to the evils of prejudice and priestcraft and superstition—is the fact that men are as a rule very slow to give up the opinions that have been impressed on them in childhood and youth. It may be objected that this applies rather to the stupid and ignorant; that the keener and more cultivated minds find much less difficulty in shaking off the trammels in which they have been bred. But whatever force there may be in this objection, there is an influence on the opposite side which much more than counterbalances it —the influence of that subtle snare, intellectual pride. It must be confessed that there is no credit to one's intellect in being a Christian. It is a conviction shared with the dullest, the humblest, the most ignorant of mankind. The founder of our faith openly thanked God that he " had hid these things from the wise and prudent and had revealed them unto babes." But it seems obviously and on the face of it a grand thing to be a doubter. It shows that we are wiser than our parents and teachers: clever enough to see the weakness of arguments which they think conclusive; too clear-sighted to be blinded by the mists of prescription and authority. This is to march with the age and rise superior to the antiquated superstitions of the past. Therefore it is a matter of common observation that a clever, shallow, half-instructed man is always more or less of a sceptic in religion. Of course this character does not apply to John Mill. But there are evidences enough even in the book before us of a calm abiding sense of superiority, not at all the same thing as vanity and conceit, but quite as great a hindrance to the real grasping of truth. He had been taught, and had taught himself to believe, that he stood by training and instruction on a higher level than the mass of mankind; on their narrow views and sordid interests he looked down as from an eminence with pity, and not without contempt. Was it likely that such men should have the key to a mystery which defied his powers to penetrate? Is there wisdom in such as these?

But I may be reminded that these causes, however far they may go towards accounting for the scepticism of John Mill, do not apply to the case of his father. Be it so. I will show you another cause, more powerful than any of those I have named, and affecting father and son alike; a fatal error on what may seem a mere abstract metaphysical question, but is really of the most tremendous and vital import. These two men were unbelievers, essentially and directly because they did not admit the freedom of the will. Once allow that man is free, and the whole ground on which they stand is cut away from them. To show this let us state their view of religion, look it fairly in the face and see what it amounts to. Religion cannot be true (this is what they say in effect) because the world is evil. "You tell us that all things are under the rule of an unseen Being, boundless in power, perfect in goodness. But, in fact, men find themselves living under an empire, not of good, but of evil. They have to struggle against pain and sickness, and poverty and oppression, and all manner of adversities. Why should this be? If God desires his creatures to be happy, why does he not make them so? Nor is this all. As if the misery of this world was not enough for him, he has prolonged it into eternity. He has made a hell—has created the human race with the infallible foreknowledge, and therefore with the intention that the great majority of them are to be consigned to horrible and everlasting torment. Is not this the most perfect conception of wickedness which the human mind can devise? Is it not a palpable contradiction to assert that a Being who would so act can at the same time be perfectly good? And if so, must not a system which involves such an assertion be utterly false? But all modern religious systems do involve such an assertion, and therefore all such systems stand self-condemned, apart from any evidence that may exist for or against their historical truth."

This, put as briefly and plainly as I can, I believe to be the position held by James and John Mill. I think all will acknowledge its strength. It is at any rate clear and definite. The argument appears to me faultless; the conclusion to be, on one assumption, undeniable. That assumption, though not expressed, underlies the whole, and it is utterly false. It is the assumption that man is not a free agent, that he is in the hands of God exactly as a machine is in the hands of its maker, only that he is a machine capable of feeling pleasure and pain. God being almighty must do all things, and if man is miserable it must be because God of his own pleasure makes him so, and for no other reason. That God being almighty could make man free; that he could put before him good and evil, and leave him to choose between them, such choice being the one end for which he existed, and for which existence was worth having; and that if he chose evil he suffered, not from God's act, but from his own: these are conceptions which such a theory as Mill's can never embrace, or even conceive. We know that it must have been so. I need hardly remind you that John Mill has done more than any other man of this century to advance the modern theory of Necessity, and present it in its most complete and plausible form. That theory, as set forth in his "Logic," is quite different from the Fatalist doctrine which has been largely held both in ancient and modern times. The Fatalist believes in a great overruling power that settles man's destiny beforehand, and brings it to pass without fail; but it does not fetter man's will, it only conquers it. If a man is predestined to be drowned he will be drowned, do what he may; but he still is free to struggle, only he will assuredly struggle in vain. Such a belief, though it may deaden man's energy, does not relieve his conscience. The modern theory is much more subtle and much more dangerous. According to this theory man is simply the connecting link in a chain of unalterable sequences. He is born with a certain disposition and tendencies, for which, of course, he is not responsible; the outward circumstances with which he is surrounded act upon this disposition, and inevitably produce certain special actions on the man's part. These actions by the like fixed law issue in certain habits, and so the man's whole life goes on in a fixed mechanical succession of events, which could be calculated beforehand by any one knowing the complex forces which act on it just as accurately as astronomers can calculate the complex path of a planet. The essence of the theory is in fact just this: that the reign of law—of fixed invariable succession—which has been proved to hold in the world of matter extends also to the world of mind. Now, to discuss this great question fully would be impossible to-night. But to the theory I have described there is this one fatal objection—that it is clean against man's consciousness, or rather I should perhaps say against my consciousness, since each man can speak only for himself. But for myself (and I think that I must speak also for every one here present) I know that I am free, that I am not the slave of circumstances, that I may act according to a motive, but do not obey it any more than a king obeys the councillor whose advice he follows. When I move my hand near a flame, the consciousness of heat is no whit more clear or certain than the consciousness that such movement was my own free act alone, and not due to any power whatsoever; and you are as likely to persuade me to disbelieve the one fact as the other. Further, what is still more to my purpose to remark is that this theory is utter destruction to all that we call morality. It asserts that the life of man is just as much the product of certain causes as the life of a plant; that knowing all the conditions you could describe it beforehand just as exactly as you could describe the life of a plant if you knew the nature of the seed and all the conditions of soil, weather, and so forth under which it sprang up and grew. Then if so, how can man be more responsible for his actions than a plant is? He did not make his own nature nor the circumstances in which he lived; how did he in any sense make what that nature and those circumstances produced? How can we possibly honour this man for his truth and virtue, blame that man for his baseness and infamy? May we not just as well honour the rose for its sweetness, or blame the hemlock for its poison? This is so plain and obvious that even the opponents of free will find it very hard to shut their eyes to it. I appeal on this head to the witness of John Mill himself. The difficulty pressed hard upon him, and he got rid of it by an evasion as shallow and as flagrant as was ever used by the votary of superstition in the attempt to reconcile reason with faith. After telling us (p. 168) that he felt as if he was scientifically proved to be the helpless slave of antecedent circumstances—as if his character and that of all others had been formed for us by agencies beyond our own control, and was wholly out of our own power—he goes on to say, " I pondered painfully on the subject, till gradually I saw light through it. . . . I saw that though our character is formed by circumstances, our own desires can do much to shape those circumstances ; and that what is really inspiriting and ennobling in the doctrine of free will is the conviction that we have real power over the formation of our own character: that our will, by influencing some of our circumstances, can modify our future habits or capabilities of willing." Our desires can do much to shape our circumstances. But what have we to do with our desires? Do they not rise unbidden in our minds, just as the outward circumstances rise unbidden around us? It is true that our actions, by which alone we can influence circumstances, do modify our future desires, and produce habits. But if each action from the first moment of our existence was the simple result of whatever desires and circumstances existed at that moment, how are we responsible for such modification? Unless at some point at least of the chain of events our own independent will has come in, that " power over the formation of our own characters" of which Mr. Mill speaks is not a reality but a phantom. And it *is* a phantom, because this independent action is exactly what Mr. Mill and his school deny. Therefore his escape from the difficulty is a mere paltry evasion. Therefore on the doctrine of free will, and of free will alone, has man any responsibility for his actions, or such words as right, duty, and morality any proper meaning whatever.

I hold therefore as a certain truth this great axiom of the freedom of the will. And now I will show you how utterly it changes the face of the question as to the possibility of believing in religion. I have already sketched out for you the scheme of religion as it appeared to James Mill and to his son: I will now sketch it out again, as it appears to me. It is a fact accepted by all wise and true men, that happiness without virtue is poor and worthless : that virtue without happiness is noble, but too hard to bear; lastly, that happiness with virtue is the one good thing which man desires, for which he is fitted, for which alone it is worth while to live, to dare and to suffer all things. But what do you mean by virtue? Not merely doing acts which are useful and beneficial to others? If so, a machine could be virtuous. If you think of what you mean by virtue it is this : to do good when you might do evil ; **to** walk steadfastly in the narrow road when the broad lies open before you. There is the clue to the mystery which has so puzzled men in all ages, the mystery of evil. Choose any virtue you please, and you will see that but for the presence of evil it could not exist. Where would be the merit of truthfulness, if it were impossible to lie? of courage if there were nothing to fear? Where would benevolence be, if all were happy? or trustfulness, if none were false? Even love itself, the crowning grace, the message of the Gospel, is not a virtue so long as it is a mere natural feeling for those who are near to us, and contribute to our happiness: it becomes such only when it extends to the unknown and the outcast, and to our enemies themselves. Evil is necessary to the growth, nay to the very existence of virtue; to overcome evil with good is the grandest thing, is the one only grand thing, which the mind of man can conceive. And doubtless, grand though it be to us, it is far grander in the sight of God. God who made the world and all things therein would have the reasonable service of free men, rather than the blind obedience of slaves. Therefore he has created a world of mingled good and evil, pleasure and pain; therefore he has placed man in that world, having given him from the treasure of his own omnipotence the supreme gift of will; and setting before him good and evil, blessing and cursing, he leaves him to choose between them. As his choice is so is he virtuous or vicious, happy or miserable. Here comes in the explanation of moral evil, as distinct from physical. Once admit that man is free to choose, and you must admit the possibility of his choosing wrong. Once admit this to be possible, and there can be no cause for surprise that it has actually happened, or that it has happened any number of times. And whilst to those who choose and cleave to the good, there is an end ere long of trial and discipline, and virtue perfected receives its exceeding great reward: so those who wilfully give themselves to evil, must sooner or later reap the just recompense of their deeds, as even by the working of natural law, guilt brings in general its own punishment. Sin when it hath conceived, bringeth forth death.

Hitherto I have spoken in the language of natural religion only, and the Jew, the Deist, the Mahometan, may all go with me thus far. But we Christians claim for this doctrine of the majesty of suffering a witness such as no other creed knows of, no philosophy has conceived. The God whom we worship has not given us precepts of virtue merely: he has also " left us an example that we should follow in his steps." The fiery trial of adversity was in his eyes a thing so precious that even his own perfections he deemed imperfect until they had thus been tried. When man in his weakness chose evil rather than good, and fell ever deeper and deeper into the gulf of sin, then God not willing that any should perish found out a remedy by the sacrifice of himself. He descended from his secure throne above into the forefront of the battle, and dying gave to us in one act pardon for past failure, and strength for victories to come. Therefore is he not our Lord only, but also our pattern and our guide; how often so ever we fall, yet in his name we may arise; he was tempted in all our temptations, and in all our sorrows we are filling up the measure of the sufferings of Christ. What have other religions to offer in comparison with this? They may paint the unapproachable splendour of their deity, the immutability of his repose, and invest him with the poor attributes of wisdom and strength: but we know Jesus Christ and him crucified. Ours is a God who went about doing good; who had not where to lay his head; who was despised and rejected of men; who made himself in the form of a servant and became obedient unto death, even the death of the cross. Yours may be a God of power, but ours is a God of love: of love than which none is greater, in that he has laid down his life for our sakes.

Such, as we learn it from nature and from the Bible, is the mystery of godliness: such are the purposes of God in the creation and government of this world. And now I ask you to tell me whether this is a scheme of things which a philosopher should view with horror and disgust: which he should regard (I am quoting from the Autobiography) "with the feelings due not to a mere mental delusion, but to a great moral evil." Is this a belief which is likely "radically to vitiate the standard of morals"? Do you recognise in the Being I have tried to describe, "the most perfect conception of wickedness which the human mind can devise"? If not, was not the abhorrence on which Mill dwells so forcibly directed not against the Deity whom we worship, but against a demon of his own imagining? But observe (and this brings me back to the direct line of my argument), that the truth and the beauty of such a system as I have tried to paint, depends entirely on our admitting that man's will is free. Deny that and the picture changes at once and returns to the hideous colours in which Mill has described it. The whole argument lies in the nutshell of this single unassailable truth: it is just and righteous that man should be rewarded for his good or punished for his bad actions, provided, and only provided, that he is free to act.

If then this doctrine of freedom was denied both by James Mill and his son (of which there is ample proof), then their rejection of religion followed in strict logical sequence. In the case of James Mill there is evidence enough that this denial was influenced by the religious school in which he had been brought up. He was educated we are told for the ministry of the Scottish church, and doubtless therefore in the strict doctrine of Calvinism. Now without wishing to pronounce any judgment on that doctrine, there can be no doubt that if it does not deny free will, at any rate it so obscures and disfigures it as to make it almost invisible. James Mill therefore had only to accept that doctrine and push it to its rigorous consequences. Man, according to Calvin, is not free to rise; therefore, Mill would argue, he is not free to fall. The injustice of what he had been taught to regard as the only true scheme of religion would then appear clear to his logical mind; and we can imagine how even his good qualities—courage, philanthropy, love of justice—helped his natural self-assertion and pugnacity to open revolt. With his son the work was easier, for the two reasons I have already given; first, that the training was begun and persevered in from earliest childhood; and secondly, that the same training, together with the tone of the society in which he moved, so inculcated the superior wisdom of unbelief, that to a much more humble man it might have seemed a truth beyond all possibility of question. Therefore I claim to have proved that the rejection of Christianity by these two men, and more especially by the son, is no evidence at all against its truth except in so far as it is an evidence against the truth of free will.

But I can do more than this: I can call these very men to give testimony on my side of the argument. For whilst rejecting with all possible emphasis the idea of freedom they yet, by an inconsistency of thought which they would have been the first to blame in others, retained a belief in morality—in those conceptions of right and duty which, as I have already shown, are absolutely meaningless, unless man is free. The doctrine I have insisted on, namely that the only thing worth living for is to uphold the right and strive against the wrong, had no firmer adherent than James Mill. Listen to the account which his son gives of his convictions on this head (p. 46). "My father's moral convictions, wholly dissevered from religion, were very much of the character of those of the Greek philosophers; and were delivered with the force and decision which characterised all that came from him." "His moral inculcations were justice, temperance (to which he gave a very extended application), veracity, perseverance, readiness to encounter pain, and especially labour; regard for the public good, estimation of persons according to their merits, and of things according to their intrinsic usefulness; a life of exertion in contradiction to one of self-indulgent ease and sloth. These and other moralities he conveyed in brief sentences, uttered as occasion arose, of grave exhortation, or stern reprobation and contempt." Reprobation and contempt! What can be more irrational than for Mr. Mill to cherish such feelings against persons who are only acting as he acted, that is in absolute harmony with the motives imposed on them by nature and circumstances? We should all think it absurd to be angry with a lunatic, and on this theory sane men and lunatics stand on exactly the same footing so far as praise and blame are concerned. They each of them act *just as their nature makes them act;* the nature of the one is rational and of the other not; but rationality and irrationality are not moral qualities, and have no praise or blame attaching to them. In short man is a machine: and it is no more reasonable to blame him for committing a crime, than to blame a steam engine for causing an accident. Therefore I say that these moral sentiments and inculcations of James Mill are a proof that his scheme, however complete in theory, broke down in practice; that in spite of himself he felt what all do feel —that human actions, according as they are good or evil, deserve praise or censure, reward or punishment. His theory ran altogether counter to those feelings, and the feelings got the better of it. There is a line of Horace which says forcibly that you may pitchfork Nature out of the cart, but she will always find her way back again; and that I hold to have been the case with James Mill. But further, his language goes to prove that true philosophers, whatever may be their speculative opinions, do unite in that practical conviction which the strong sense of honest men has in all ages approved;

the conviction that the life to which all men should and can aspire, the only life worth living, is (to use Mill's own words) a life of justice, temperance, veracity, perseverance: a life of exertion in contradiction to one of self-indulgent ease and sloth. Like the Christian he paid honour to that man, and that man only, who walks the straight path of duty proof against flattery, fear, or pain; and by so doing he bears unconscious witness to the truth of that great principle which I have been defending. For what is the true essence of this life of exertion, the inward principle to which honour is due? Why has England but lately leapt up to welcome those gallant men who have been fighting her battles in the deadly air of Africa? Why has she still more lately been earnest to offer all that remained to pay of honour to that great traveller who in a yet nobler spirit gave up everything, even to life itself, for the welfare of that same distant land? Why but because they did this when they might have done otherwise—because when they might have shrunk from the danger they pressed on to meet it; because they preferred the life of labour and suffering to that of luxury and ease which lay equally within their reach; because, in a word, they made a right and noble use of God's sovereign gift of will.

My task is well nigh over. I have tried to show you that no argument against the truth of Christianity can properly be drawn from the unbelief of James and John Mill. I have put before you the theory of life and being as it was held by them, and also the theory which underlies the faith of the Christian. I must leave you to choose between them. Only in choosing there is one point which I would ask you to weigh well and carefully, and that is, how far each theory suits itself to the great moral facts of our experience, and to those needs and yearnings and aspirations of which all enlightened souls are conscious. This moral evidence has no small weight in a question which concerns exclusively the moral and not the physical side of man's nature; and he is a fool who in making up his beliefs neglects to inquire how those beliefs square with his inmost needs, and how they will aid him through the troublesome voyage of life. Now the philosophy of the Secularists, as represented by James and John Mill, is utterly powerless as to any moral influence; it has no nourishment to strengthen the weak, no medicine to heal the afflicted. It asserts that concerning the origin and end of things nothing is or can be known; whence we come and whither we are going is alike behind a veil; of the existence and nature of God we are wholly ignorant, except that he cannot be, as Theists hold, infinite both in power and goodness. Placed as we are in this life we have only to do the best we can for our own happiness; and that is to be found in promoting the happiness of the world at large, in abjuring pleasure and excitement, and leading a life of philanthropic exertion. Now this view of life may suit men who have the cold unimpassioned temperament characteristic of sceptical philosophers. Thus of James Mill we read (p. 48): "He had scarcely any belief in pleasure, at least in his late years. He was not insensible to pleasures, but he deemed very few of them worth the price which, at least in the present state of society, must be paid for them. He never varied in rating intellectual enjoyments above all others even in value as pleasures, independently of their ulterior benefits. The pleasures of the benevolent affections he placed high in the scale. For passionate emotions of all sorts he professed the greatest contempt. He regarded them as a form of madness. The intense was with him a by-word of scornful disapprobation." Now we can imagine a man of this character being well contented with a life of self-denying labour and philanthropy. But a voluptuary may answer him: "I have no objection to your idea of life, so long as you carry it out yourself; but unfortunately it does not suit me. You may have no belief in pleasure, but I have a great deal. The satisfaction you find in working for your fellow men, I find in gratifying my senses; and so long as I do not interfere with others I claim the right to follow my own instincts as you do yours. You may perhaps urge that indulgence in pleasure will bring its own punishment; but I reply that this is by no means a certain and universal consequence—that what is certain is the immediate gratification: lastly, that if enjoyment should one day cease and life become a burden, there is still an unfailing resource—one can always die." To such an argument I do not see how this philosophy can possibly make any answer whatever. It fails therefore in finding means to enforce those rules of morality which it professes to uphold. But if it can offer no defence against vice, still less has it any supporting force against the pressure of care. A man may perhaps live well enough on such a creed while the world smiles on him and all things are prosperous. But let adversity come, as sooner or later it comes to all, and I know nothing more dreary, more utterly blank and hopeless than his view of life must be. For remember that this creed takes away all that to us Christians makes life bearable at its worst—the promises of Scripture and the hope full of immortality, the glory of patience, and the inseparable love of Christ—it takes away all these and it gives nothing whatever in their stead. All that it can tell of or point to is earthly happiness, and now earthly happiness is gone. I am here drawing no fancied picture. I need go no further for my authority than the book before us. Remember that these two men, James and John Mill, lived on the whole singularly prosperous and useful lives; they reached the highest eminence in the paths they had chosen, and might boast of having done much to advance the cause of humanity. Yet of the father we read as follows (p. 48) : " He thought human life a poor thing at the best, after the freshness of youth and of unsatisfied curiosity had gone by. This was a topic on which he did not often speak, especially it may be supposed in the presence of young persons ; but when he did it was with an air of settled and profound conviction. He would sometimes say that if life were made what it might be by good government and good education it would be worth having; but he never spoke with anything like enthusiasm even of that possibility." And the son, with his loftier mind and keener sensibilities, found even less refuge in the tenets of his philosophy against the storms of life. In that moral crisis of early manhood, of which he has left the record, we find his mind turning to suicide as its natural resource. " I frequently asked myself (p. 140) if I could, or if I was bound to go on living, if life was to be passed in this manner. I generally answered to myself that I did not think I could possibly bear it beyond a year." And in later days how sad and hopeless is his clinging to the image of her whose mind he had made his standard of intellect, and whose character he had worshipped with a devotion that was almost akin to idolatry. "Her memory is to me a religion, and her approbation the standard by which—summing up as it does all worthiness—I endeavour to regulate my life." "Because I know she would have wished it, I endeavour to make the best of what life I have left, and to work on for her purposes with such diminished strength as can be derived from thoughts of her, and communion with her memory."

To me, thinking over this the last utterance of scepticism's last apostle, there seems to come the voice of another teacher, speaking in words no less sweet because so familiar: "Come unto me, all ye that travail and are heavy laden, and I will give you rest. Take my yoke upon you and learn of me, for I am meek and lowly of heart, and ye shall find rest unto your souls." So to the weary and oppressed of that distant place and day spoke the man Jesus of Nazareth; so across the centuries he speaks to the heavy-hearted now, and they believe him.

www.ingramcontent.com/pod-product-compliance
Lightning Source LLC
Chambersburg PA
CBHW030818230426
43667CB00008B/1269